The Penguin Dictionary of Statistics

David Nelson, born in 1938, was educated at Calday Grange Grammar School, Cheshire, and Christ's College, Cambridge. After postgraduate studies in mathematical logic at Cambridge and Bristol universities, he entered the teaching profession. He has published papers in mathematical journals and is a Fellow of the Institute of Mathematics and its Applications.

He was a lecturer at the University of Manchester from 1981 to 2001, specializing in mathematical cognition and the history of mathematics. He is now an Honorary Fellow. His publications include *Extensions of Calculus, Multicultural Mathematics* and *The Penguin Dictionary of Mathematics*. He has lectured in Poland, Italy, France and the USA, and in 1995, at the invitation of the State Education Committee of the People's Republic of China, organized and led a three-week National Seminar on Mathematics Education to initiate reform of the Chinese national mathematics curriculum.

A former member of the National Youth Orchestra, his main recreations are playing the flute and piano. He also enjoys gardening and golf. His wife, Gillian, is a writer and they have three children.

The Penguin Dictionary of

Statistics

David Nelson

PENGUIN BOOKS

PENGUIN BOOKS

Published by the Penguin Group
Penguin Books Ltd, 80 Strand, London WC2R 0RL, England
Penguin Group (USA) Inc., 375 Hudson Street, New York, New York 10014, USA
Penguin Books Australia Ltd, 250 Camberwell Road, Camberwell, Victoria 3124, Australia
Penguin Books Canada Ltd, 10 Alcorn Avenue, Toronto, Ontario, Canada M4V 3B2
Penguin Books India (P) Ltd, 11 Community Centre, Panchsheel Park, New Delhi – 110 017, India
Penguin Group (NZ), cnr Airborne and Rosedale Roads, Albany, Auckland 1310, New Zealand
Penguin Books (South Africa) (Pty) Ltd, 24 Sturdee Avenue, Rosebank 2196, South Africa

Penguin Books Ltd, Registered Offices: 80 Strand, London WC2R 0RL, England

www.penguin.com

First published 2004

Set in Times New Roman
Typeset by Tradespools, Frome, Somerset
Printed in England by Clays Ltd, St Ives plc

Preface

The Penguin Dictionary of Statistics aims to provide school and university students with definitions and explanations of elementary statistical terms and tests. It tries to cover all the main branches of statistics and to include illustrative examples which will be helpful to those who use statistics in their work. It is hoped that it will be a useful reference source for non-specialists.

The illustrative examples are drawn from the wide range of fields to which statistics is applied, including agriculture, business studies, industry, medicine, physics and psychology. However, the inclusion of an example of the use of a term or statistical method in a particular context, e.g. market research, should not be taken to mean that this is the only area in which the term or method is used. It should also be stressed that the numerical illustrations of statistical methods are included primarily to assist understanding of the procedures involved. To this end, these illustrations deal with only small amounts of data – in most instances, smaller than would be desirable in practice.

Diagrams are provided where they help with the definition of a term. There is also a network of cross-references. Some entries merely refer the reader to another entry. This may indicate that the terms are synonyms, or that one term is more conveniently discussed within the entry for another, in which case the term is printed in italics in the other entry. An asterisk placed before a term indicates that this term has its own entry in the dictionary which will provide additional information. References are also made to the tables in the Appendix.

Some of the entries use mathematical terms and notation. To assist readers who are unfamiliar with such terminology, definitions are included of the mathematical terms which are relevant to the statistical entries. For example, explanations are given of terms such as *absolute value*, *factorial* and *modulus sign*. For more advanced terms, and for biographies of mathematicians such as Fisher, Laplace, Pascal and Pearson who have made important contributions to statistics, the reader is referred to the companion volume, *The Penguin Dictionary of Mathematics*.

The author is deeply indebted to Peter Sprent for his dedicated support throughout the project, and for his advice on the work at all stages. He is also extremely grateful to Colin Gray, Graham Hitch and Eos Kyprianou for helpful discussions and for their comments on the final draft. All these contributions have greatly improved the work; any faults that remain are the responsibility of the author.

R.D.N.
2004

absolute error The magnitude (ignoring sign) of the deviation of an observation or approximation from the true or predicted value. For example, if two thermometers read 31°C and 27°C when the true temperature is 30°C, then the absolute errors are 1°C and 3°C respectively.

In general, if b is an approximation to a, then, using the *modulus sign, the absolute error is $|b - a|$. With this notation, the absolute errors in our example are

$$|31 - 30| = |1| = 1 \quad \text{and}$$
$$|27 - 30| = |-3| = 3.$$

See error; relative error.

absolute frequency *See* frequency.

absolute value (modulus) The positive number that has the same magnitude (ignoring sign) as a given number. Thus, the absolute value of 6 is 6, and the absolute value of -6 is 6. The absolute value or modulus of a number a is written using the notation $|a|$. The symbol $| \, |$ is called the *modulus sign*. With this notation, $|6| = 6$ and $|-6| = 6$.

absorbing barrier *See* random walk.

acceptance region *See* hypothesis testing.

acceptance sampling A *quality-control method in which a sample is taken from a batch of items, and a decision whether or not to accept the batch is based on the proportion of defective items in the sample. For example, a sample of 100 might be taken from a batch of 10 000 items, and the decision rule might be to reject the batch if more than 1 item of the sample is defective.

In any particular situation, the choice of sample size and decision rule is usually made after the producer (or seller) and consumer (or buyer) have agreed on outcomes they wish to avoid. In practice, a producer will not want batches with a small percentage of defective items to be rejected, and the consumer will not want to accept batches with a large percentage of defective items. Statistical methods exist to calculate, for a given sample size and decision rule, the probabilities (called the producer's risk and consumer's risk) of outcomes each wishes to avoid. In the above example, the probability of the producer having batches with 0.5% or less defectives rejected can be shown to be 0.090, and the probability of the consumer having batches with 5% or more defectives accepted is 0.037. If these risks are unacceptable they can be adjusted by changing the sample size and/or the decision rule. For example, if the sample size were increased to 200 and the rule were to reject only for more than 3 defectives, the risks would be 0.019 and 0.009 respectively. Economic factors such as production costs, or the cost of rectifying defective items (where possible), or of scrapping or selling rejected batches at a lower price, play a key role in selecting sampling schemes with acceptable characteristics.

accuracy *See* precision.

addition law *See* probability.

adjusted standard deviation *See* sample standard deviation.

adjusted variance *See* sample variance.

AH *Abbreviation for* alternative hypothesis (*see* hypothesis testing).

algorithm A mechanical procedure for solving a problem in a finite number of steps. A simple statistical example is the following algorithm for recalculating the *mean of a set of n numbers when the set is enlarged to include an extra observation:

'Multiply the existing mean by n, add the extra number to the result and divide the sum by $n + 1$'.

Thus if a set of 15 numbers has a mean of 22, and an extra observation with a value of 30 is to be included in the set, then the mean of the enlarged set is

$$\frac{(22 \times 15) + 30}{16} = \frac{360}{16} = 22.5.$$

Another (example is the *bubble sort algorithm, which rearranges any set of numbers in order of magnitude.

alpha reliability coefficient (Cronbach's alpha) A measure of the *reliability of a psychological or educational test, based on the scores obtained by a sample of individuals. The test consists of a number of *items each designed to assess components of a particular characteristic or trait such as general intelligence, language skills or arithmetic ability. If scores across individuals show broadly similar orderings for all items the test is said to have high reliability for assessing the characteristic, whereas if these score orderings show marked differences between items, the reliability is poor. For a test containing n items, let the *variance of the total scores of the candidates be s^2 and the variances of the scores on the individual items be $s_1^2, s_2^2, \ldots, s_n^2$. Then the reliability

coefficient α of the test is given by:

$$\alpha = \frac{n}{n-1}\left(1 - \frac{1}{s^2}\sum_1^n s_i^2\right).$$

To illustrate the procedure, suppose a trial of a test with 7 items is given to 5 students and their scores on a scale of 0–5 for each item are as in the following table:

Student	Item							Total
	1	2	3	4	5	6	7	
a	5	4	3	4	5	4	5	30
b	4	4	5	3	4	2	3	25
c	5	3	2	1	4	3	2	20
d	2	1	4	2	3	3	4	19
e	3	0	1	3	2	4	1	14
Variance	1.36	2.64	2.00	1.04	1.04	0.56	2.00	29.84

Here, $n = 7$, $s^2 = 29.84$ and

$$\sum s_i^2 = 1.36 + 2.64 + \cdots + 2.00 = 10.64.$$

So, the formula gives

$$\alpha = \frac{7}{6}\left(1 - \frac{10.64}{29.84}\right) = 0.75.$$

Alpha generally takes a value between 0 and 1, but negative values can occur. For tests run with a large sample of participants, an alpha below 0.65 is regarded as unacceptable or undesirable, between 0.65 and 0.8 is acceptable and between 0.8 and 0.9 is very good. A test with an alpha of 0.9 to 1 is excellent and might be shortened.

The procedure can also be used to identify items that could be dropped from the test. In the above example, the students' scores on item 6 do not correlate well with their total scores. If item 6 is dropped the value of alpha rises to 0.82.

alternate forms reliability *See* reliability.

alternative hypothesis *See* hypothesis testing.

analysis of covariance (ANCOVA, ANOCOVA) An extension of the *analysis of variance where allowance is made for additional variables (called *concomitant variables*), especially when those variables are not influenced by the treatments under investigation but may affect individual responses to the treatments. For example, in an experiment to compare the effects of several methods of teaching a statistics course, an appropriate concomitant variable might be a measure of each student's statistical knowledge immediately before taking the course. The technique uses *regression methods to examine the effect of the different initial knowledge of students on their response to teaching.

analysis of variance (ANOVA) Analysis of the variation in a set of observations by separating it into two or more parts associated with independent sources of variation such as *treatments, design grouping and error. Thus, for example, in an experimental trial of four medicines on groups of male and female patients, analysis of variance examines the extent, if any, to which variation in patients' responses is attributable to differences in the effectiveness of the medicines, or to difference in gender, or is unattributable.

The total variation is expressed as the sum of squares of deviations of observations from the overall mean (sometimes called the *grand mean*). The sums of squares associated with the specified sources of variation are divided by their *degrees of freedom to give *mean squares*. These are estimates of the *variance of the observations. The extent to which these estimates differ is used to assess whether sources such as treatments are having significantly different effects.

The simplest ANOVA is that for a *one-way classification* in which treatments are allocated at random to experimental units. For example, the treatments might be 3 fertilizers A, B and C, and the units might be 12 similar potato plots, 4 chosen at ran-

dom receiving treatment A, 4 treatment B and 4 treatment C. ANOVA is used to assess whether the treatments differ in effect. First, the overall mean and the sum of squares of deviations from the mean are found. This sum is then separated into:

(i) a *between-treatments sum of squares*, which is what the sum of squares of deviations from the overall mean would have been if, instead of the observed response for each unit, each response had been equal to the mean for all units receiving that treatment; and

(ii) an *error (residual) sum of squares* equal to the remainder of the total sum of squares. (It also equals the sum of squares of deviations of individual responses from their treatment means.)

The *between-treatments mean square* and *error mean square* are obtained by dividing the respective sums of squares by their *degrees of freedom. The ratio of the between-treatments mean square to the error mean square is called the *variance ratio. Provided that errors are independently normally distributed with zero mean and equal variance, then under the *null hypothesis of no difference between treatments, the variance ratio has an *F-distribution. High values of this ratio indicate rejection of the null hypothesis. The variance ratio is sometimes called the F-ratio.

If, in our example, the potato yields are 39, 46, 45 and 38 (kg) for treatment A; 30, 40, 32 and 34 for B; and 39, 43, 47 and 47 for C; then the treatment means are 42, 34 and 44, respectively. The overall mean is 40, and the total sum of squares of deviations from this mean is 374. Replacing each yield by the mean yield for its treatment gives the between-treatments sum of squares as 150. The remaining error sum of squares is then $374 - 150 = 224$. The total, between-treatments and error degrees of freedom are 11, 2 and 9, respectively. These results, the two mean squares and their ratio are set out in an ANOVA table as shown overleaf.

Source	Degrees of freedom	Sum of squares	Mean square	Variance ratio
Treatments	2	224	112	6.72
Error	9	150	16.7	—
Total	11	374	—	—

The variance ratio of 6.72 is assessed using the F-distribution with 2 and 9 degrees of freedom. It has *p-value 0.016, and the minimum values for significance at the 5% and 1% levels are 4.26 and 8.02 respectively, so the hypothesis that there is no difference in effect between the three fertilizers can be rejected at the 5% level.

Experiments using a *randomized blocks design involve a *two-way classification* of observations: by treatment and by block. There are three component sums of squares associated with treatments, blocks and error, and these add to the total sum of squares of deviations from the mean. The associated degrees of freedom are also additive. In an experimental trial of 4 different growth hormones (treatments), one to each pig in 6 litters (blocks) of 4 pigs, the degrees of freedom for treatment, block and error would be 3, 5 and 15, respectively.

The method extends to more complicated designs such as *Latin squares and *factorial experiments. *See also* Graeco-Latin square.

ANCOVA *See* analysis of covariance.

angular data Information given in terms of angles. *See* data; circular histogram; rose diagram.

anonymous marking *See* blinding.

ANOCOVA *See* analysis of covariance.

ANOVA *See* analysis of variance.

approximation A result that is not exact but is sufficiently close to be of practical value.

arbitrary origin *See* assumed mean.

arc *See* graph.

area sampling A sampling method in which a geographical area is divided into small sub-areas by a grid of squares or rectangles, or by some other means. Sub-areas are selected at random, and all units in them are included in the sample. For example, in a study of farming in a small country, a grid of 10×10 km squares might be used. Squares are selected at random, and every farm in the selected squares is included in the sample. *See also* cluster sample; multi-stage sampling; quadrat; sample survey.

arithmetic–geometric mean inequality The arithmetic *mean of any number of non-negative numbers is always greater than or equal to their geometric mean. For example, the numbers 4 and 16 have an arithmetic mean of $\frac{1}{2}(4 + 16) = 10$. Their geometric mean is $\sqrt{4 \times 16} = 8$. The two means are equal only when all the numbers are equal.

arithmetic mean *See* mean.

arithmetic progression (arithmetic sequence) A *sequence in which each term (except the first) differs from the previous one by a constant amount, the *common difference*. For example, the arithmetic progression whose first 5 terms are

$$2, \quad 5, \quad 8, \quad 11, \quad 14$$

has common difference equal to 3. In general, if the first term is a and the common difference is d, then the progression takes the form

$$a, a + d, a + 2d, a + 3d, \ldots$$

and the nth term is

$$a + (n - 1)d.$$

A sum of the terms of such a progression is an *arithmetic series*:

$$a + (a + d) + (a + 2d) + \cdots$$

The sum of the first n terms is given by

$$\tfrac{1}{2}n[2a + (n - 1)d].$$

In our example $a = 2$, and $d = 3$. The sum of

the first 10 terms of the progression will be

$$\tfrac{1}{2} \times 10[(2 \times 2) + (9 \times 3)] = 155.$$

Similarly, if 15 holiday resorts are *ranked 1 to 15 in popularity then the sum of the ranks is an arithmetic series with $a = 1$, $d = 1$ and $n = 15$. The sum is

$$\tfrac{1}{2} \times 15[(2 \times 1) + (14 \times 1)]$$
$$= \tfrac{1}{2} \times 15 \times 16 = 120$$

In general, the sum of the integers from 1 to n is $\tfrac{1}{2} n(n + 1)$.

Compare geometric progression.

arithmetic series *See* arithmetic progression.

array 1. An ordered collection of elements of the same type. A one-dimensional array (or *vector) is a list of elements a_i, where i is the *index value* (an integer). A two-dimensional array (or *matrix) has elements a_{ij}, where i is the number of the row and j the number of the column. Three- and higher-dimensional arrays are similarly defined. An array is sometimes called a *subscripted variable*.
2. A display of a set of observations, usually in some explicit order such as increasing or decreasing order of magnitude. Thus the observations 4, 22, 18, 1, 13, 7, 13 arranged in increasing order of magnitude form the array

$$\{1, 4, 7, 13, 13, 18, 22\}.$$

See also order statistics.

association In general, the degree of dependence between two variable quantities. *See* chi-squared test; contingency table; correlation.

association, coefficient of *See* phi coefficient.

assumed mean (working mean, arbitrary origin) A convenient value to which a set of observations may be referred when calculating their *mean. For example, referred

to 1990, the observations 1996, 1991, 1999 and 1994 are 6, 1, 9 and 4 respectively, and the mean of these numbers is $20/4 = 5$. The mean of the original observations is then $5 + 1990 = 1995$.

In general, if the observations are $x_1, x_2, \ldots, x_n$ and the assumed mean is a, then the mean $\bar{x}$ of the observations is given by the formula

$$\bar{x} = \frac{1}{n} \sum_{1}^{n} (x_i - a) + a.$$

The method can also be used to find the *standard deviation s_x or *variance s_x^2 of the observations by means of the formula

$$s_x^2 = \frac{1}{n} \sum_{1}^{n} (x_i - a)^2 - (\bar{x} - a)^2.$$

In our example, $a = 1990$, $\bar{x} = 1995$, $n = 4$ and the formula gives

$$s_x^2 = \tfrac{1}{4}(36 + 1 + 81 + 16) - (1995 - 1990)^2$$
$$= 33.5 - 25 = 8.5.$$

Thus the variance is 8.5, and the standard deviation equals $\sqrt{8.5}$, i.e. 2.9.

The availability of statistical packages and calculator routines has reduced the need for the use of an assumed mean.

See also data coding.

asymmetry *See* skewness.

asymptote A line related to a curve such that the distance from the line to a point on the curve approaches zero as the distance of

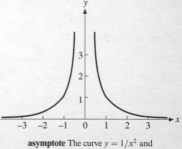

asymptote The curve $y = 1/x^2$ and its asymptotes $y = 0$ and $x = 0$.

the point from an origin increases without bound. In other words, the line gets closer and closer to the curve but does not touch it. For example, the line $y = 0$ is one of the asymptotes of the curve $y = 1/x^2$ (*see* diagram). A *normal curve has one asymptote, the line $y = 0$. *See* sigmoid curve.

asymptotic Describing a curve that has one or more lines as *asymptotes. For example, the curve $y = 1 + (1/x^2)$ is asymptotic. It has the lines $y = 1$ and $x = 0$ as asymptotes.

average *See* mean.

axis (*plural* **axes**) In general, a reference line associated with a geometric figure or object such as a *graph or *bar chart.

1. (reference axis) A line from which distances or angles are measured in a *coordinate system.

2. (axis of symmetry) A line associated with a geometric figure such that every point on one side of the line has a corresponding point on the other side. The axis bisects the line segment joining any such pair of points. For example, any diameter of a circle is an axis of symmetry.

balanced block design *See* randomized blocks.

balanced incomplete block design *See* randomized blocks.

Banach's matchboxes, problem of A certain mathematician carries one matchbox in his right-hand pocket and one in his left. Whenever he wants a match, he is equally likely to take it from either box. Suppose that initially each box is full and contains n matches. At the first moment when he opens a box and discovers that it is empty, find the probability that the other box contains r matches. The solution is

$$\frac{1}{2^{2n-r}}\binom{2n-r}{n}, \quad \text{where } r = 0, 1, 2, \ldots, n$$

and $\binom{2n-r}{n}$ is a *binomial coefficient.

The problem originated in an address by H. Steinhaus in honour of the Polish mathematician S.M. Banach, and has become popular.

See also birthday problem; de Méré's problem; problem of coincidences; problem of points.

bar chart (bar diagram, bar graph) A graph consisting of bars of equal widths and with lengths proportional to the frequencies of some event for each of several categories (*see* e.g. diagram (a)), or to magnitudes

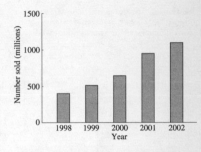

bar chart (a) The number of pirate sales of CDs worldwide annually from 1998 to 2002.

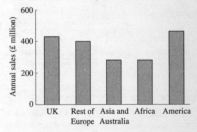

bar chart (b) The value of the sales made by a company in different parts of the world in a year.

associated with the categories (*see* e.g. diagram (b)).

The idea can be extended in several ways. For instance, each bar can be subdivided to show the component parts of the frequency or magnitude it represents. This is a *sectional* (or *component*) *bar chart* (*see* diagram (c)). Two charts can be combined and compared visually by placing corresponding bars side by side or by drawing them either

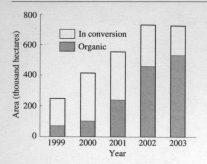

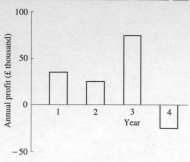

bar chart (c) The area of land in the UK which was organically farmed or in conversion to organic farming each year from 1999 to 2003.

bar chart (e) The annual profit made by a new company in its first four years.

has a different variance. *See also* Hartley's test; Levene's test.

Bayesian inference A method of *statistical inference based on *Bayes' theorem. It is central to the solution of inference problems where the question of interest is of the form 'What can be said about a *parameter given the observed data?' The parameter in question might be a population mean or the probability of an event. The approach used in Bayesian inference is that the parameter is assumed to have a *prior probability distribution* (or *prior distribution*) reflecting the current state of knowledge. An experiment is performed to provide the observed data, and the information from it is combined with the prior distribution to give a *posterior probability distribution* (or *posterior distribution*) for the parameter. A *confidence interval may be based on this distribution. If there is general agreement on the prior distribution, then consistent inferences may be made, but difficulties arise if there is disagreement about an appropriate prior distribution, the choice of this distribution often being subjective. A posterior distribution derived from one experiment may be used as a prior distribution for a subsequent experiment.

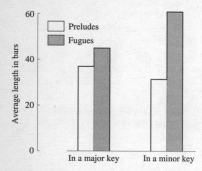

bar chart (d) The average length of the preludes and fugues in major and minor keys in Book 1 of J.S. Bach's *Well-tempered Clavier*.

side of the base line. This is a *double bar chart* or *dual chart* (*see* diagram (d)). Finally, positive and negative magnitudes, e.g. profits and losses, can be shown by bars which rise or fall from the base line (*see* diagram (e)).

See also histogram.

bar diagram *See* bar chart.

bar graph *See* bar chart.

Bartlett's test A test of the *null hypothesis that m ($\geqslant 2$) samples are from *normal populations having equal variances, against the alternative that at least one population

Bayesian inference is often thought of as an alternative to *frequential inference*, but it is more appropriate to regard it as complementary since the frequentialist approach makes statements about the probability of obtaining the observed data, given a fixed value of the parameter. This approach avoids the subjective choice of a prior distribution, but may not answer the question of interest. In many cases both approaches lead to similar inferences, but not invariably so. Besides tests about parameters, either method of inference can be applied to tests of other hypotheses and to the fitting of statistical *models.

Bayes' theorem A theorem on *conditional probability that evaluates the probability of an event (a cause) conditional on another event (a consequence) having taken place. Suppose that $B_1, B_2, \ldots, B_n$ are a mutually exclusive and exhaustive set of events (e.g. causes or hypotheses) and that some further event A is observed. The probability that B_j was the causal event leading to A, i.e. the conditional probability of B_j upon A, is given by the formula

$$\Pr(B_j|A) = \frac{\Pr(B_j)\Pr(A|B_j)}{\sum_i \Pr(B_i)\Pr(A|B_i)}.$$

For example, consider two boxes of eggs with box 1 containing 4 eggs of which 1 is bad, and box 2 containing 8 eggs of which 3 are bad (*see* diagram). A box is selected by the toss of a coin, and an egg chosen from it. The egg is found to be bad. What is the probability that it came from box 1?

To apply the theorem, we make A the event 'bad egg chosen', and B_1 and B_2 the mutually exclusive events 'egg chosen from box 1' and 'egg chosen from box 2',

respectively. We know that

$$\Pr(A|B_1) = \tfrac{1}{4}, \Pr(A|B_2) = \tfrac{3}{8},$$

and also that

$$\Pr(B_1) = \Pr(B_2) = \tfrac{1}{2}.$$

We seek $\Pr(B_1|A)$, and Bayes' theorem gives

$$\Pr(B_1|A) =$$
$$\frac{\Pr(B_1)\Pr(A|B_1)}{(\Pr(B_1)\Pr(A|B_1) + \Pr(B_2)\Pr(A|B_2))}$$
$$= \frac{\tfrac{1}{2} \times \tfrac{1}{4}}{\tfrac{1}{2} \times \tfrac{1}{4} + \tfrac{1}{2} \times \tfrac{3}{8}} = \tfrac{2}{5}.$$

Similarly, $\Pr(B_2|A) = \tfrac{3}{5}$.

An important application of Bayes' theorem is to the interpretation of the results of medical tests for diseases. Suppose, for example, that 1 in 100 people have disease or condition X. Suppose also that there is a 95% chance that a person with X will test positive for X, and a small, 3% chance that a person without X will test positive. An individual chosen at random tests positive for X. What is the probability that the individual actually has X?

To apply the theorem, let A be the event 'tests positive for X', and B_1 and B_2 the events 'has X' and 'does not have X'. We seek $\Pr(B_1|A)$. From the data, $\Pr(B_1) = 0.01, \Pr(B_2) = 0.99, \Pr(X|B_1) = 0.95$ and $\Pr(X|B_2) = 0.03$. Substituting in the formula given earlier,

$$\Pr(B_1|A) = \frac{0.01 \times 0.95}{0.01 \times 0.95 + 0.99 \times 0.03}$$
$$= 0.24.$$

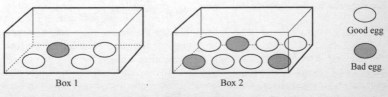

Box 1   Box 2   ◯ Good egg   ⬤ Bad egg

Bayes' theorem

So before the test, the individual's probability of having X was 0.01. After the test, the individual's probability of having X is 0.24, i.e. an approximately 1 in 4 chance.

See also Bayesian inference.

bell-shaped curve *See* Cauchy distribution; normal distribution.

Bernoulli distribution *See* Bernoulli trial.

Bernoulli trial One of a sequence of independent *trials or experiments, each of which has just two possible outcomes, which are sometimes called 'success' and 'failure', with constant probabilities p and q $(= 1 - p)$, respectively. For example, throwing a fair die and regarding a six as a 'success' is a Bernoulli trial with $p = \frac{1}{6}$ and $q = \frac{5}{6}$. Another example is tossing a fair coin and regarding 'heads' as a success; here $p = q = \frac{1}{2}$.

A *Bernoulli variable* is a *random variable X taking one of just two values, 1 and 0, with probabilities p and q $(= 1 - p)$, respectively. Its *distribution is a *Bernoulli distribution* having *mean p and *variance pq.

The number of successes in a fixed number of Bernoulli trials is a random variable with a *binomial distribution. The number of failures before the first success in an unlimited sequence of Bernoulli trials is a random variable with a *geometric distribution.

See binary variable; binomial variable.

Bernoulli variable *See* Bernoulli trial.

Bessel's correction *See* unbiased estimator.

beta distribution A continuous *distribution on the interval [0,1] with frequency function

$$f(x) = \frac{1}{B(m, n)} x^{m-1}(1 - x)^{n-1},$$

where $m, n > 0$, and $B(m, n)$ is the *beta function. The frequency function takes a wide variety of shapes for varying values

of the *parameters m and n, including *U-shaped distributions, heavily skewed distributions (*see* skewness) and the *uniform distribution on (0,1).

beta function The *function denoted by $B(p, q)$ and defined by

$$B(p, q) = \int_0^1 x^{p-1}(1 - x)^{q-1}\,dx.$$

See beta distribution.

between-groups design *See* experimental design.

between-subjects design *See* experimental design.

between-treatments mean square *See* analysis of variance.

bias **1.** In general, an effect that prevents a statistical result from being representative by systematically distorting it. For instance, a survey of opinion which states that it is based on telephone calls to a random sample of the population will only represent the opinions of those who have telephones, answer the calls and are willing to cooperate in the survey. Thus it will suffer from bias. *See* blinding; experimenter bias; placebo.
2. (of an estimator) *See* unbiased estimator.

biased estimator *See* unbiased estimator.

billion One thousand million (10^9). The term has always been used in this sense in the USA. In the UK the term originally meant one million million (10^{12}), but increasingly it is now being used to mean one thousand million.

bimodal Having two *modes. For example, the following set of observations, arranged in ascending order, is bimodal:

1 1 2 3 3 4 5 5 5 6 7 8 9 9 9.

Its two modes are 5 and 9.

binary notation The method of positional notation using the digits 1 and 0 in the *binary system.

binary number The representation of a number in the *binary system.

binary system A system of numeration using the base 2 and just two characters (0 and 1). Decimal $1, 2, 3, 4, 5, \ldots$ are $1, 10, 11, 100, 101, \ldots$. Whereas the positions in the decimal system correspond to powers of 10, those in the binary system correspond to powers of 2. Thus the binary number 1101 is equal to $(1 \times 2^3) + (1 \times 2^2) + (0 \times 2) + 1 = 13$ in decimal.

binary tree *See* tree.

binary variable A random variable that can take only two possible values. For example, the result of a driving test is a pass or a fail, and the outcome of a toss of a coin may be 'heads' or 'tails'. Such binary variables can be represented by a variable X that takes only the values 0 and 1. Thus, in a study of test results, we might assign $X = 0$ to a failure and $X = 1$ to a pass.

binomial A *polynomial consisting of two terms added or subtracted, for example $1 - 2x$ or $p + q$.

binomial coefficients $\binom{n}{r}$, the coefficients of x^r in the expansion of $(1 + x)^n$. Thus, for $n = 3$, the expansion of $(1 + x)^3$ is $1 + 3x + 3x^2 + x^3$, and the coefficients 1, 3, 3, 1 of $1, x, x^2, x^3$ are $\binom{3}{0}, \binom{3}{1}, \binom{3}{2}, \binom{3}{3}$, respectively.

In general, $\binom{n}{0} = 1$, and

$$\binom{n}{r} = \frac{n(n-1)\ldots(n-r+1)}{r!}$$

for each positive integer r, where $r!$ denotes *factorial r. For instance,

$$\binom{10}{3} = \frac{10.9.8}{3!} = \frac{10.9.8}{3.2.1} = 120.$$

When n is a positive integer, the binomial coefficients form a row of *Pascal's triangle. In this case the coefficients $\binom{n}{r}$ and $\binom{n}{n-r}$ are always equal. Thus

$$\binom{10}{3} = \binom{10}{7} = 120.$$

See binomial theorem.

binomial distribution The *distribution of the number of successes obtained in a series of n independent trials, at each of which the probability of success is p. It is often denoted by B(n, p). Letting $q = 1 - p$, the probabilities of $0, 1, 2, \ldots, n$ successes are

$$q^n, \binom{n}{1}pq^{n-1}, \binom{n}{2}p^2q^{n-2}, \ldots, p^n,$$

respectively. These are the terms of the binomial expansion of $(p + q)^n$, and $\binom{n}{1}, \binom{n}{2}, \ldots$ are *binomial coefficients.

In general, the probability of r successes, where $0 \leqslant r \leqslant n$, is $\binom{n}{r}p^rq^{n-r}$. The mean equals np and the variance is equal to npq.

For example, if a fair coin is tossed 6 times and 'heads' is a success, then $n = 6$ and $p = \frac{1}{2}$, and the probability of four successes is $\binom{6}{2}\left(\frac{1}{2}\right)^2\left(\frac{1}{2}\right)^4 = \frac{15}{64} = 0.23$. Here the distribution is B($6, \frac{1}{2}$), the mean equals 3 and the variance equals 1.5. The complete distribution is given in the table, and its graph is shown in diagram (a).

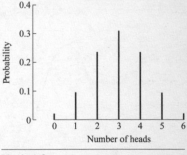

Number of successes	0	1	2	3	4	5	6
Probability	$\frac{1}{64}$	$\frac{6}{64}$	$\frac{15}{64}$	$\frac{20}{64}$	$\frac{15}{64}$	$\frac{6}{64}$	$\frac{1}{64}$

binomial distribution (a) The distribution B($6, \frac{1}{2}$).

Similarly, when 80 flower seeds are sown in a row and each seed has a 75% chance of germinating, then the number of germinations in the row follows the binomial distribution B(80, 0.75). Another example is when students attempt a multiple-choice test in which there are 20 questions, each with 4 answers to choose from, only one of which is correct. If the answers to each question are chosen completely at random, then the total number of correct choices will have the binomial distribution B(20, 0.25), the mean being 5.

When n is large enough for both np and nq to be 5 or more, the binomial distribution can be approximated by the *normal distribution with the same mean np and variance npq. Diagrams (b) and (c) show respectively the binomial distribution B(25, $\frac{1}{5}$) and the normal distribution N(5, 4) with the same mean and variance.

See normal approximation; Poisson distribution; continuity correction; negative binomial distribution; sign test.

binomial expansion The expansion given by the *binomial theorem.

binomial series An infinite *series that is the expansion of $(1 + x)^n$ or $(x + y)^n$ when n is not a positive integer or zero, for example

$$(1 + x)^{-2} = 1 - 2x + 3x^2 - 4x^3 + \cdots,$$

provided that $|x| < 1$. *See* binomial theorem.

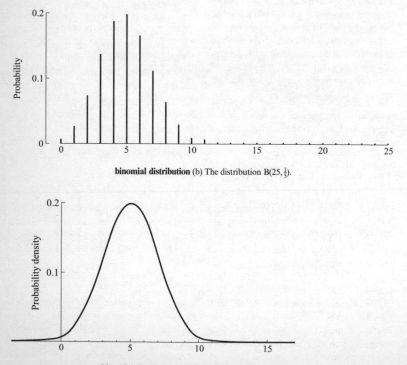

binomial distribution (b) The distribution B(25, $\frac{1}{5}$).

binomial distribution (c) The normal distribution N(5, 4).

binomial theorem A theorem that gives the expansion of $(1 + x)^n$ as

$$1 + nx + \frac{n(n-1)}{2!}x^2$$
$$+ \frac{n(n-1)(n-2)}{3!}x^3 + \cdots.$$

This is known as the *binomial expansion*.

When n is a positive integer, the expansion is a finite series with $n + 1$ terms, the last term equalling x^n. For instance, when $n = 3$, the theorem gives

$$(1 + x)^3 = 1 + 3x + \frac{3 \times 2}{2 \times 1}x^2 + \frac{3 \times 2 \times 1}{3 \times 2 \times 1}x^3$$
$$= 1 + 3x + 3x^2 + x^3.$$

When n is not a positive integer or zero, the expansion is an infinite series as the coefficients are never zero; it is known as the *binomial series*. It is a *convergent series when $|x| < 1$.

For example, when $n = -1$, the theorem gives

$$(1 + x)^{-1} = 1 - x + x^2 - x^3 + \cdots.$$

When $n = \frac{1}{2}$, the theorem gives

$$(1 + x)^{1/2} = 1 + \frac{1}{2}x - \frac{1}{8}x^2 + \frac{1}{16}x^3 - \cdots.$$

More generally, an expansion for $(x + y)^n$ is

$$x^n + nx^{n-1}y + \frac{n(n-1)}{2!}x^{n-2}y^2 + \cdots.$$

When n is a positive integer, the expansion is a finite series with $n + 1$ terms; the last term equalling y^n. When n is not a positive integer or zero, the expansion is an infinite series and is convergent when $|y| < |x|$.

binomial variable A *random variable having a *binomial distribution. The binomial variable with distribution $B(n, p)$ is equivalent to the sum of n independent *Bernoulli variables, each of which takes the values 1 and 0 with probabilities p and q $(= 1 - p)$, respectively. If X and Y are independent binomial variables with distributions $B(m, p)$ and $B(n, p)$, respectively, then their sum $X + Y$ is a binomial variable with distribution $B(m + n, p)$.

birthday problem A popular problem of probability. Given a group of n people, find the probability that at least two of them have the same birthday – the same day of the same month. An approximate solution is obtained by ignoring leap years and assuming that each person has an equal chance of being born on any one of the 365 days in the year. Then the required probability is

$$1 - \frac{364}{365} \times \frac{363}{365} \times \cdots \times \frac{366 - n}{365}.$$

For example, when there are 10 people the probability is 0.117. As the number in the group increases this probability of a shared birthday increases rapidly. It begins to exceed 0.5 when there are 23 people and exceeds 0.75 once there are 32. *See also* Banach's matchboxes; de Méré's problem; problem of coincidences; problem of points.

birth rate The number of births per unit of population in a particular time period, for example 13 births per 1000 of population in a year. *Compare* death rate.

biserial correlation coefficient *See* correlation coefficient.

bit A unit of information consisting of one binary digit; i.e. the amount of information required to specify one of two alternatives, such as the 0 and 1 in the binary system. *See* byte.

bivariate data *See* data.

bivariate distribution The *joint distribution of two *random variables, usually denoted by X and Y, which may be either discrete or continuous. If both are discrete then the joint distribution can be completely specified by giving the probabilities associated with every pair of values the variables may take. For example, an investigation into the relationship between numerical and linguistic skills might score each member of a large population on a scale of 1 to 3 in tests of each skill. By denoting numerical and linguistic test scores by the variables X and Y, the probabilities for each of the 9 possible pairs of scores by individuals are given by their relative frequencies and can be set out in a *bivariate table* as follows:

X (numerical skills)	Y (linguistic skills)			Row total
	1	2	3	
1	0.13	0.05	0.07	0.25
2	0.10	0.20	0.12	0.42
3	0.08	0.10	0.15	0.33
Column total	0.31	0.35	0.34	

The sum of the 9 probabilities in the table is 1, since all possible pairs are covered, and a visual inspection shows that the highest probability value in each row or column corresponds to the case of identical scores for each skill. This suggests that scores in numerical and linguistic skills are not *independent. If we sum the probabilities in a row we obtain the probability associated with that level of numerical skill irrespective of performance in linguistic skills. These totals (often called *marginal totals*) give the *marginal distribution* of X. Similarly, the column totals specify the marginal distribution of Y. We may be interested in the distribution of X for some value of Y, or vice versa. Such distributions are called *conditional distributions*. For example, the conditional distribution of Y when $X = 1$ will have probabilities proportional to those in row 1 of the table, i.e. 0.13, 0.05, 0.07. Dividing these by their sum, 0.25, we obtain the conditional probabilities 0.52, 0.20, 0.28. These are the probabilities of Y taking the values 1, 2, 3 when $X = 1$.

These ideas generalize to discrete distributions that take any number of discrete values, to bivariate continuous distributions, or to a mix of a discrete and a continuous distribution.

Formally, for bivariate discrete distributions we may denote the probability that X takes the value x_i and Y takes the value y_j by p_{ij}, i.e.

$$p_{ij} = \Pr(X = x_i, Y = y_j).$$

If these probabilities are known for all i, j, then this specifies the *bivariate frequency* (or *probability*) *function* $f(x, y)$, which is such that $f(x_i, y_j) = p_{ij}$. In our example, $f(1, 2) = p_{12} = 0.05$.

The cumulative distribution function is

$$F(x, y) = \Pr(X \leqslant x, Y \leqslant y) = \sum \sum p_{ij},$$

where the double summation is over all i and j such that $x_i \leqslant x$ and $y_j \leqslant y$. In the example above,

$$F(1, 2) = 0.13 + 0.05 = 0.18,$$

and this would also be the value of, say, $F(1.5, 2.5)$.

The marginal distribution of X is given by

$$\Pr(X = x_i) = \sum_j p_{ij}.$$

The conditional distribution of X, given $Y = y_j$, is given by

$$\Pr(X = x_i | Y = y_j) = \frac{p_{ij}}{\Pr(Y = y_j)}.$$

The definitions for marginal and conditional distributions of Y take a similar form, with X and Y interchanged.

If X and Y are *independent, then

$$p_{ij} = \Pr(X = x_i)\Pr(Y = y_j)$$

for all i, j. It is easily verified that this is not the case in the above example, for considering $X = 1$ and $Y = 2$, 0.05 is not equal to $0.25 \times 0.35 = 0.0875$.

When X and Y are both continuous, representing for example the heights in centimetres and weights in kilograms of adult males in a population, the definitions of the frequency function and cumulative distribution function take basically similar forms to those in the discrete case but with p_{ij} replaced by an appropriate continuous *bivariate frequency* (or *probability density*) *function* $f(x, y)$ and summations replaced by integrals. The cumulative distribution function is

$$F(x, y) = \int_{-\infty}^{x} \int_{-\infty}^{y} f(s, t) \, dt \, ds.$$

Thus, in the above example $F(170, 70)$ is the probability that an adult male has height and weight less than or equal to 170 cm and 70 kg.

The marginal distribution of X has *marginal frequency function* defined as

$$f_1(x) = \int_{-\infty}^{\infty} f(x, t) \, dt,$$

with a similar definition for $f_2(y)$, the marginal frequency function of Y. The marginal cumulative distribution functions of X and Y are written as $F_1(x)$ and $F_2(y)$. So, in our example $F_1(170)$ is the probability that an adult male is less than or equal to 170 cm in height.

The conditional distribution of X, given $Y = y$, has conditional frequency function

$$g_1(x | Y = y) = \frac{f(x, y)}{f_2(y)},$$

with a similar definition for $g_2(y | X = x)$.

If X and Y are independent variables, then $f(x, y) = f_1(x) f_2(y)$ for all x, y.

A *bivariate normal distribution* is a continuous bivariate distribution in which, for any fixed value of one random variable, the other random variable has a *normal distribution. In other words, all conditional distributions are normal.

See also multivariate distribution.

bivariate frequency function *See* bivariate distribution.

bivariate normal distribution *See* bivariate distribution.

bivariate probability density function *See* bivariate distribution.

bivariate probability function *See* bivariate distribution.

blind *See* blinding.

blinding A procedure in *experimental design that makes either the participants or the experimenter (or both) unaware of, or *blind* to, aspects of the experiment which could lead to bias in the results. A *single-blind* procedure withholds relevant information from either the participants or the experimenter. For example, participants rating two brands of tea for taste could be kept ignorant of the brands they were tasting. Similarly, in the *anonymous marking* of test papers, the experimenter does not know the identity of participants and consequently cannot be influenced by any expectations or previous results. With a *double-blind* procedure both the subjects and the experimenter are blind to the allocation of treatments; a third party has this information. Drug trials in which drugs are compared or a drug is tested against a *placebo often use this procedure. The patients do not know which drug they are receiving, or whether they are receiving the drug or the placebo. When measuring and assessing each patient's response to treatment, the experimenter is also unaware of which treatment the patient has received. This removes a possible source of *experimenter bias*.

block *See* randomized blocks.

block design *See* randomized blocks.

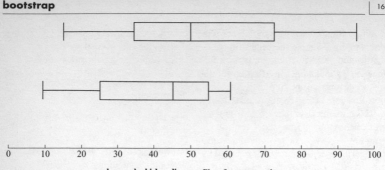

box-and-whisker diagram Plots for two samples.

bootstrap A method for obtaining information about population parameters or characteristics by first taking a *random sample of *n* observations from a population, and then forming from this initial sample further random samples, called *bootstrap samples*. These are also of size *n*, and are obtained by sampling with replacement.

box-and-whisker diagram (box plot) A graphical representation of the information contained in a *five-number summary of a set of observations, i.e. the least value, the lower *quartile, the *median, the upper quartile and the greatest value. The box is a rectangle, the length of which indicates the *interquartile range and arbitrary breadth, divided at the *median. The whiskers are lines extending beyond the rectangle to indicate the *range. Adjacent plots for data for two or more samples make it easy to see major differences between their characteristics. Box-and-whisker plots are shown in the diagram for two samples with the following five-number summaries:

Sample 1	15	34	50	72	95
Sample 2	9	25	45	54	61

bubble sort An *algorithm for putting in order an *array of objects such as numbers or names. For example, to rearrange the array of numbers

$$61 \quad 54 \quad 25 \quad 45 \quad 9$$

in ascending order, the sort begins by comparing the second number from the left with the first, and interchanging them if necessary. The array then becomes

$$54 \quad 61 \quad 25 \quad 45 \quad 9.$$

Next, the third number is compared with the second number of the new array, and they are interchanged if necessary. The array then becomes

$$54 \quad 25 \quad 61 \quad 45 \quad 9.$$

The process continues until the last pair of numbers has been compared and the array has become

$$54 \quad 25 \quad 45 \quad 9 \quad 61.$$

The largest number in the array, 61, is now in its correct position.

Starting from the left, the process of comparing and interchanging pairs is applied to the first four numbers, then to the first three, and finally to the first two. At the end of these stages the array is

$$25 \quad 45 \quad 9 \quad 54 \quad 61$$
$$25 \quad 9 \quad 45 \quad 54 \quad 61$$

and finally

$$9 \quad 25 \quad 45 \quad 54 \quad 61.$$

The term 'bubble' arises from the fact that a number, such as 61 in our example, which is too low in the order rises like a bubble. This is one of the simplest and slowest sorting algorithms.

See complexity.

Buffon's needle problem A needle of length l is dropped at random onto a level plane surface ruled with parallel lines a distance d apart, where $d > l$ (*see* diagram). What is the probability that the needle lands across one of the lines? Comte de Buffon proposed and solved this problem in 1777, the answer being $2l/\pi d$. For a needle of length 2 cm and lines 4 cm apart, the probability is thus $1/\pi$.

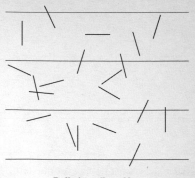

Buffon's needle problem

byte A unit of information equal to eight *bits.

C

cap The symbol $\cap$, used to denote the *intersection of two sets A and B, as in $A \cap B$. *Compare* cup; *see* probability.

capture–recapture sampling A statistical procedure for estimating the size of an animal population. A sample of n_1 animals is captured, each is tagged, and all are released. A second sample of n_2 animals from the same population is captured at a later date, and the number m of tagged animals in the sample is recorded. If it can be assumed that both the samples were *random samples then the unknown size N of the total population is estimated to be $N* = n_1 n_2 / m$, provided that $m \neq 0$ (since $m = 0$ implies an infinite population). This quantity is sometimes called the *Lincoln index* or *Petersen estimator*.

The *standard error of $N*$ is estimated by

$$\sqrt{\frac{n_1 n_2 (n_1 - m)(n_2 - m)}{m^3}}.$$

For example, suppose that a sample of 80 animals in a region is tagged, and a later sample of 75 animals contains 10 tagged animals. Here $n_1 - 80$, $n_2 - 75$ and $m = 10$, and $N*$, the estimate of the size of the population in the region, is $(80 \times 75)/10 = 600$. The estimated standard error is 165.2, and an approximate 95% *confidence interval for N, the actual size of the population, has end points $600 \pm 1.96 \times 165.2$. So the interval is $277 \leqslant N \leqslant 923$.

The method tends to overestimate the true population size, especially when m, the number of tagged animals in the second sample, is small. It is also dependent on the assumptions that both the size of the population and the probability of capture are the same when the two samples are taken. The first assumption ignores births, deaths and migrations in the period between the two samples. The second assumption may not be justifiable if tagging the animals in the first sample decreases or increases their probability of recapture. Adjustments can be made to take these factors into account.

carry-over effect *See* cross-over design.

Cartesian coordinate system A coordinate system in which the position of a point is determined by its relation to reference lines (*axes*). In two dimensions, two lines are used; usually the lines are at right angles, forming a *rectangular coordinate system* (*see* diagram (a)). The horizontal axis is the *x-axis* and the vertical axis is the *y-axis*. Their point of intersection O is the *origin* of the coordinate system. Distances along the *x-*axis to the right of the origin are usually taken as positive, and distances to the left as negative. Distances along the *y-*axis above the origin are positive; distances below are negative. The position of a point anywhere on the plane can then be specified by two numbers, the *coordinates* of the point, written as (x, y). The *x-coordinate* is the distance of the point from the y-axis in a direction parallel to the x-axis (i.e. horizontally). The *y-coordinate* (or *ordinate*) is the distance from the x-axis in a direction parallel to the y-axis (vertically). For example, the point $(3, 2)$ is 3 units from the y-axis and 2 units from the x-axis. The origin is the point $(0, 0)$. The two axes divide the plane into four *quadrants*, numbered anticlockwise starting from the top right (positive) quadrant: the *first quadrant*. Diagram (a) shows a general point $P(a, b)$ in the first quadrant.

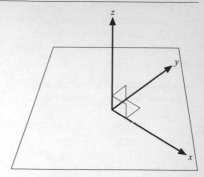

Cartesian coordinate system (b) in three dimensions.

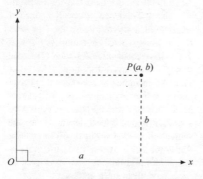

Cartesian coordinate system (a) in two dimensions.

While points in Cartesian coordinates are represented by coordinates (x, y), lines and curves may be represented by equations. Thus, $y = x$ represents a set of points for which the x-coordinate equals the y-coordinate; i.e. a straight line through the origin, and $y = x^2$ represents a parabola touching the x-axis at the origin. A curve drawn in a Cartesian coordinate system for a particular equation is said to be the *graph* of the equation.

Cartesian coordinate systems can also be used for three dimensions by including a third axis – the z-axis – through the origin at right angles to the other two (*see* diagram (b)). The position of a point is then given by three coordinates, (x, y, z).

categorical data The *data obtained when the subject of measurement is merely placed in one of several categories. For example, records of the gender (male, female), favourite colour (red, blue, green, etc.) or most feared animal (mouse, lion, snake, etc.) constitute categorical data for a group of individuals. If individual subjects can be allocated only to one of two categories, as with data about gender, then the data are said to be *dichotomous data*.

By extension, the term is also used for counts of the numbers of subjects or objects falling into each of several categories.

See contingency table; scale of measurement.

categorical variable A *random variable whose values are categories. For example, the state of a traffic light at any time (red, red and amber, green, amber) and the gender of members of a population (male, female) are categorical variables. A categorical variable, such as gender, that can only take one of two values is called a *dichotomous variable*.

A categorical variable such as marital status (single, married, divorced, widowed), whose values have no natural ordering, is often referred to as a *nominal variable*. A categorical variable such as a quality rating (very poor, poor, moderate, good, very good), whose values have a natural ordering, is referred to as an *ordinal variable*.

See categorical data; scale of measurement.

Cauchy distribution The *distribution of a continuous random variable X with *frequency function

$$f(x) = \frac{1}{\pi} \frac{\lambda}{\lambda^2 + (x - \theta)^2},$$

which has two parameters, θ and λ. It is a *symmetrical distribution about $x = \theta$. The case where $\lambda = 1$ and $\theta = 0$ is called the *standard Cauchy distribution*. The curve of the frequency function is bell-shaped and broadly similar to that of the *normal distribution; that for the standard Cauchy distribution is less peaked and has longer tails than that for the standard normal distribution (*see* diagram).

The Cauchy distribution is sometimes described as a 'pathological case' since none of its *moments exist. They cannot be calculated because the defining integrals are all *divergent integrals. One consequence is that the *central limit theorem does not hold and, in fact, the mean of a sample of n independent observations from a Cauchy distribution has the Cauchy distribution with the same parameters as the parent distribution. The parameter θ may, however, be estimated by the sample *median or by a *trimmed mean, although substantial trimming is needed to obtain a reliable estimate.

Despite the lack of moments the distribution has many important theoretical and practical properties. For example, the *t-distribution with one degree of freedom is the same as the standard Cauchy distribution; also, if X and Y are independent normal variables each with mean zero, then the ratio $U = X/Y$ has a Cauchy distribution. If X and Y also have equal variances, then U has the standard Cauchy distribution. If a point source emits radioactive particles that travel in straight lines and emission is equally likely in any direction, then the points of impact on a straight line at a fixed distance from the source will have a Cauchy distribution. The distribution also arises in fields as diverse as geophysics and finance (as a descriptor of the behaviour of stock markets).

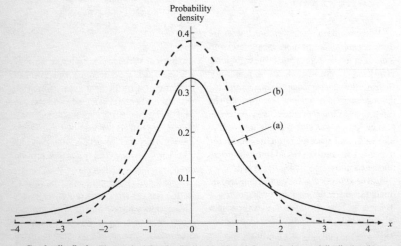

Cauchy distribution The standard Cauchy distribution (a), and the standard normal distribution (b).

cause variable (causal variable) An alternative name for an explanatory variable (*see* regression).

c.d.f. *See* d.f.

cell When data are classified into categories, as in for example *grouped data for one variable or in a *contingency table, the subcategories are sometimes called cells. The frequency with which data fall into a particular cell is the *cell frequency*.

For example, the following *frequency table for the ages of the estimated population of the UK in 1988 has five cells:

Age (years)	0–19	20–39	40–59	60–79	80 and over
Frequency (millions)	15.0	17.0	13.3	9.8	2.0

The following contingency table, giving information on the germination of seed samples of two plant varieties, has four cells:

	Seeds germinating	Seeds not germinating
Old variety	350	50
New variety	427	73

censored data Data that are incomplete in the sense that the true values for some units are not known or are unavailable. For example, in a 6-year study of the survival times of a sample of 8 patients with a rare fatal disease, some may survive beyond the end of the study. Thus, if one patient is still alive 312 weeks after contracting the disease, the observation for that patient is said to be censored, and the survival times (in weeks) for the sample might be recorded as

49   59   115   143   189   228   251   *312.

The asterisk indicates the censored observation. More precisely, this observation is *right censored* in that the true survival time for that patient will be larger than, i.e. to the right of, the one recorded. Right-censored data are also encountered in studies involving times to failure or breakdown, e.g. of machines or machine components.

A similar difficulty is found in recording the time of onset of a disease, for this may not be known if the disease is detected only when the patient is clinically examined. In these cases the observations are described as *left censored*, in the sense that the true times are earlier than the recorded values.

Censoring also arises when sample units withdraw from the study before the response of interest occurs. For example, severe side-effects may cause some patients to withdraw from a trial of a new treatment; or, in a study of the time taken to solve a problem, some subjects may fail to solve the problem and give up.

census A complete survey of an entire population or group as distinct from a *sample survey, for example a census of the population of a country at a point in time, or a census of all traffic using a particular road on one day.

centile *See* percentile.

centrality (central tendency) The tendency of data to cluster around some central value. This value is usually one of the measures of *location such as the *mean, *median or *mode. The closeness with which data cluster round the central value is measured by one of the measures of *dispersion such as the *standard deviation, *variance, *mean deviation or *semi-interquartile range.

central limit theorem A fundamental theorem of statistics which states that, under very general conditions, the distribution of the *mean of n *random variables tends to a *normal distribution as n tends to infinity. The main condition is that the *variances of the variables are such that no single variance is large in comparison with the total.

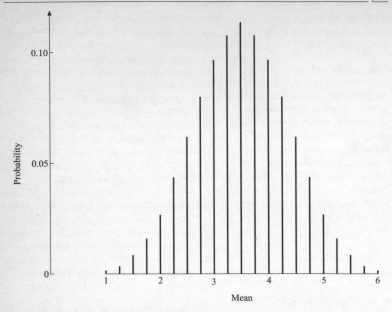

central limit theorem (a) The distribution of the mean score when 4 dice are rolled together.

To illustrate this, consider the mean score when *n* dice are rolled together. The theorem implies that the distribution of this mean will resemble a normal distribution more and more closely as *n* increases. Even when *n* is only 4 the resemblance is becoming evident (*see* diagram (a)).

The theorem does not require the variables to have the same distribution. However, an important application is to the case

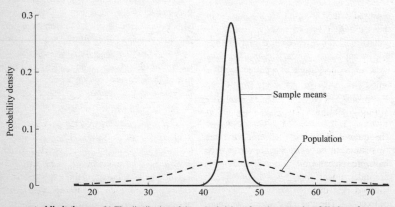

central limit theorem (b) The distribution of the mean heights of random samples of 50 plants from a population whose heights are normally distributed with mean 45 cm and variance 100 cm^2.

when all the variables do have the same mean and variance. In particular, this occurs when taking a random sample of n observations from a population with mean μ and variance σ^2. For large n, the theorem implies that the mean of this sample will be approximately normally distributed with mean μ and variance σ^2/n, i.e. will be $N(\mu, \sigma^2/n)$. Thus random samples of 50 plants from a large population with mean height 45 cm and variance 100 cm^2 will have mean heights approximately normally distributed with mean 45 cm and variance 2 cm^2.

Of course, in the special case when all the variables have normal distributions, the distribution of their mean is normal for all values of n. It follows that means of samples of size n taken from a normal population will always be normally distributed (*see* diagram (b)).

See confidence interval; standard error.

central measures *See* location.

central tendency *See* centrality.

certain *See* event.

Champernowne's number The number

$$0.123\,456\,789\,101\,112\,131\,415\ldots,$$

whose digits are those of all the numbers 1, 2, 3, 4, 5, 6, 7, 8, 9, 10, 11, 12, ... in succession. It is an example of a *normal number*, which is one whose decimal expansion is such that all possible blocks of digits of equal length occur and are equally likely. For instance, a block of three digits chosen at random is just as likely to be 216 as 729.

chi-squared distribution If X and Y are two standard *normal variables (i.e. each has zero *mean and unit *variance) and are independent, then $X^2 + Y^2$ has a chi-squared (χ^2) distribution with 2 *degrees of freedom. The mean is 2 and the variance is 4.

In general, the sum of the squares of v independent standard normal variables has a chi-squared distribution with v degrees of freedom (*see* diagram (a)). The distribution has mean v and variance $2v$. It is commonly denoted by $\chi^2_{(v)}$.

Tables of the distribution usually give upper *percentage points for various values of v. These are particular values exceeded by some percentage of the distribution and are useful in the *chi-squared test. For example, for $v = 5$, Table 5 in the Appendix states that the upper 5% and 99% points are 11.07 and 0.55 respectively. Thus 5% of the $\chi^2_{(5)}$ distribution exceeds 11.07, and 1% is less than 0.55 (*see* diagram (b)).

Statistical packages will give *p-values associated with calculated chi-squared values. For example, when $v = 5$, a chi-squared value of 12.05 has $p = 0.0341$, so that 3.41% of the distribution exceeds 12.05.

chi-squared test 1. A test of *goodness of fit of a set of observations to a theoretical discrete *distribution. For example, the test can assess whether the scores obtained when throwing a die fit the theory that all scores are equally likely, and thus indicate whether the die is biased or not. A second example has to do with plant breeding. The geneticist Mendel crossed 556 plants with round yellow seeds with plants with wrinkled green seeds. This yielded 315 plants with round yellow seeds, 108 with round green seeds, 101 with wrinkled yellow seeds and 32 with wrinkled green seeds. In theory these numbers should be in the ratio $9:3:3:1$. The test can assess whether the results fit the theory.

The test begins by making a *frequency table of the observations. For each value or category x_i $(i = 1, 2, \ldots, n)$ this gives the observed frequency O_i. The table is extended by calculating the expected frequency E_i of each x_i, according to the proposed theoretical distribution. Modifications may be needed if some of the

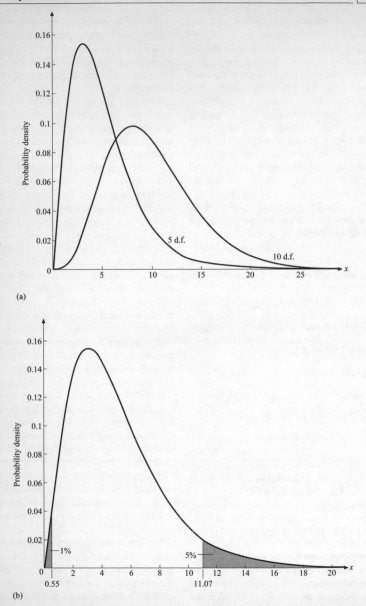

(a)

(b)

chi-squared distribution (a) The chi-squared distributions with 5 and 10 degrees of freedom (d.f.). (b) Percentage points of the chi-squared distribution with 5 degrees of freedom.

expected frequencies are small, e.g. less than 5.

The next stage is to calculate the statistic

$$\chi^2 = \sum_i \frac{(O_i - E_i)^2}{E_i}.$$

This has a *chi-squared distribution with $n - r$ *degrees of freedom, where r is the number of restrictions observed in the calculation of the expected frequencies, e.g. the restriction that they must have a certain total.

The final stage is to use tables or a statistical package to assess the value of χ^2. Significantly high values lead to rejection of the hypothetical distribution.

In the case of Mendel's experiment, the expected frequencies of each of the four types of seed are found by dividing 556 in the ratio $9:3:3:1$. The observed and expected frequencies are as follows:

Seed type	Round yellow	Round green	Wrinkled yellow	Wrinkled green
Observed frequency	315	108	101	32
Expected frequency	312.75	104.25	104.25	34.75

The value of χ^2 is

$$\chi^2 = \frac{(315 - 312.75)^2}{312.75} + \frac{(108 - 104.25)^2}{104.25}$$
$$+ \frac{(101 - 104.25)^2}{104.25} + \frac{(32 - 34.75)^2}{34.75}$$
$$= 0.4700.$$

The only restriction on the expected frequencies is that their total is 556, so the number of degrees of freedom is $4 - 1 = 3$.

Finally, by consulting tables, we see that the value of χ^2 needs to exceed 7.81 to be significant at the 5% level. The calculated value of 0.47 is a great deal less than this, so the hypothesis that the ratio is $9 : 3 : 3 : 1$ is not rejected. The *p-value of 0.47 is 0.9254.

The test is commonly used to examine the goodness of fit of observations with discrete distributions such as the *uniform, *binomial and *Poisson distributions. It can be adapted and applied to grouped data from a continuous distribution, when data are available only in grouped form, to see whether they are consistent with some specified distribution (e.g. a *normal distribution). Thus data of the blood pressures of adults in a country might be tested for goodness of fit to a normal distribution with the same mean and variance as the data. However, the outcome of the test is not independent of the choice of class intervals for grouping the data, so some groupings may lead to a significant value of the chi-squared statistic, while others may not.

See also Kolmogorov–Smirnov test.

2. A test for lack of association (independence) between two characteristics observed on each member of a sample. Pairs of characteristics investigated could be, for example, colour of hair and colour of eyes; blood group and ethnicity; or voting intention in an election and sex of voter. Each characteristic is classified into types, and the data are displayed in a *contingency table. Each *cell of the table records the number of members having some combination of the two characteristics; e.g., in the first example above, one cell will give the observed frequency of the combination 'black hair and blue eyes'.

The test begins by calculating the expected frequency for each cell, based on the assumption that the two characteristics are independent. This is done using the *marginal totals* of the rows and columns of the table of observed frequencies. Modifications may be needed if some of the expected frequencies are small, e.g. less than 5.

The next stage is to calculate χ^2 by applying the formula given in **1** above to the observed and expected frequencies in each cell, and summing over all cells. If the table has r rows and c columns, then this statistic has the chi-squared distribution with $(r-1)(c-1)$ degrees of freedom.

The final stage is to use tables or a statistical package to assess the value of χ^2. Significantly high values lead to rejection of the hypothesis that there is no association between the two characteristics.

Suppose, for example, that a *random sample of 120 girls and 80 boys were asked to express a preference for the colour red, green or blue. The results can be given in a 2×3 table of observed frequencies with, in addition, the marginal totals for the rows and columns of the table as follows:

Gender	Preferred colour			Row total
	Red	Green	Blue	
Boys	46	13	21	80
Girls	44	22	54	120
Column total	90	35	75	Grand total 200

If there is no association between sex and preferred colour, then, since 90 out 200 children preferred red, the expected frequencies of this preference for the 80 boys and 120 girls are

$$\frac{90}{200} \times 80 = 36 \quad \text{and} \quad \frac{90}{200} \times 120 = 54,$$

respectively. The complete table of expected frequencies is:

Gender	Preferred colour		
	Red	Green	Blue
Boys	36	14	30
Girls	54	21	45

The value of χ^2 is

$$\chi^2 = \frac{(46-36)^2}{36} + \frac{(13-14)^2}{14} + \frac{(21-30)^2}{30}$$
$$+ \frac{(44-54)^2}{54} + \frac{(22-21)^2}{21} + \frac{(54-45)^2}{45}$$
$$= 9.25.$$

The table has 2 rows and 3 columns, so the number of degrees of freedom is $(2-1)(3-1) = 2$.

Finally, by consulting tables, we see that the value of χ^2 needs to exceed 9.21 to be significant at the 1% level. The calculated value of 9.25 is greater than this, so the hypothesis that colour preference is independent of gender is rejected. In fact, the *p-value of 9.25 is 0.0098.

In the special case of 2×2 tables, *Yates's correction* should be made when calculating χ^2. This is done by subtracting 0.5 from the magnitude of each difference between the observed and expected frequencies before squaring. For example, if the observed and expected frequencies for a cell were 41 and 56, respectively, then the contribution of this cell to χ^2 would be $(15-0.5)^2/56$.

See also Fisher's exact test.

circular chart *See* pie chart.

circular histogram A form of representation of grouped *angular data. Whereas a standard *histogram has rectangular blocks standing on a line, the circular histogram has blocks attached to the appropriate sections of the circumference of a circle. This is a convenient way to represent data such as the direction of the prevailing wind at a weather station each day of a year.

A common approach is to have blocks tapering towards the centre of the circle with their lengths proportional to the associated frequencies (*see* diagram). A drawback is that the areas of the blocks are not proportional to the frequencies. A simple but less compact alternative is to have rectangular blocks drawn outwardly, each based on a chord, whose areas are proportional to the frequencies they represent.

Using the 24-hour divisions of a clock, a circular histogram can also be made to represent the frequencies for each hour of the day of events such as admissions to the accident and emergency unit of a hospital,

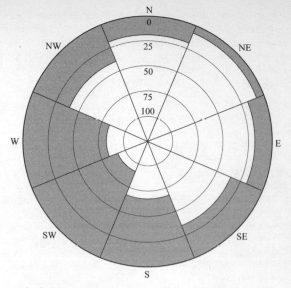

circular histogram showing the number of days in one year on which the prevailing wind at a location was from a certain direction.

vehicles passing a point on a motorway, or calls to a regional or national fire service. *See also* rose diagram.

circular permutation *See* cyclic permutation.

class *See* class intervals; set.

class frequency The number of observations in a given *class interval.

class intervals The intervals in which data are grouped. The group of observations falling in a particular interval is sometimes called a *class*. For example, if the ages of all inhabitants of a village are known, we can count how many are under 20 years of age, aged 20 to 39, aged 40 to 59, etc. The class intervals are 0–19, 20–39, 40–59, etc. The number of inhabitants in each class interval is the *class frequency* for that interval. The mid-point of a class interval is the *mid-interval value*. Class intervals often are, but need not necessarily be, of the same length. *See also* grouped data; histogram.

class mark The mid-point of a *class interval; the term is almost obsolete. *See also* grouped data.

closed interval *See* interval.

closed question *See* open-ended question.

cluster A group of elements of a statistical population that are, in some sense, close together, for example the people in a household, or a set of locations of outbreaks of a disease.

cluster analysis Statistical techniques that are used to help decide, on the basis of data on a set of items or individuals, whether the items or individuals fall into recognizable groups, called *clusters*. Items in one cluster will be closer to one another than to items in another cluster. Criteria are needed in order to put items into clusters, so all methods rely on some choice of *metric in order to define how 'close' one item or individual is to another. For example, 'closeness' might be based on the physical distance between items, or on differences in age between the individuals being studied, or on some measure of socio-economic status of individuals. Data on the geographical incidence of certain diseases sometimes show evidence of several distinct clusters.

cluster sample A sample in which groups of units (each called a *cluster*), rather than individual units, are selected from a population. The population is first divided into clusters, and then a *random sample of clusters is taken. Observations are then made on all the units in the selected clusters. Cluster sampling is useful when the units of a population occur naturally in clusters. For example, a household may be regarded as a cluster in the population of a region, and a survey conducted by making a random selection of households and then interviewing each person in each household.

The clusters from which the random selection is made are sometimes called the *primary sampling units*. In the above example, the primary sampling units are all the households in the region.

The method is particularly useful when the population is large and widely dispersed, for it will be less time-consuming and involve less administration to make observations on a cluster sample than on a simple random sample.

See also multistage sampling.

coded data *See* data coding.

coding *See* data coding.

coefficient 1. A number that provides a measure of some statistical property or characteristic. Thus a *correlation coefficient measures the extent to which two variables are related. Similarly, a coefficient of *skewness indicates the lack of symmetry in a distribution. A coefficient is sometimes called an *index*. Thus the FTSE 100 (*see* FTSE share index) is a measure of the level of leading share prices on the London Stock Exchange.

2. The multiplier of a specified factor in an algebraic term. Thus the coefficients of x in the terms $4x$, x, ax and $-5x$ are 4, 1, a and -5, respectively. Similarly, the coefficients of the terms in x^2 in the expressions $1 + 2x + 3x^2 + 4x^3$ and $ax^2 + bx + c$ are 3 and a respectively.

*Pascal's triangle is an *array of coefficients. A row such as

$$1 \quad 4 \quad 6 \quad 4 \quad 1$$

provides the coefficients, and the constant term, in the expansion of $(1 + x)^4$, which is

$$1 + 4x + 6x^2 + 4x^3 + x^4.$$

See polynomial.

coefficient of association *See* phi coefficient.

coefficient of concordance A statistic measuring the amount of agreement between several sets of *rank of a group of objects, such as the ranks given by several judges to the competitors for a literary prize. It is sometimes referred to as *Kendall's coefficient of concordance*.

If there are m judges and n competitors, then each judge awards the ranks 1 to n to the contestants. The average rank is $\frac{1}{2}(n + 1)$ per judge, so the average sum of the ranks received by a competitor from all the m judges is $\frac{1}{2}m(n + 1)$. Letting the actual sum of the ranks awarded to the ith competitor be s_i, the sum of the squares of the deviations of the s_i from their mean is

$$S = \sum_i \left[s_i - \tfrac{1}{2}m(n + 1) \right]^2.$$

The coefficient of concordance is then

$$W = \frac{12S}{m^2 n(n^2 - 1)}.$$

This lies between 0 and 1. If the judges are in complete agreement and give identical ranks, then $W = 1$. The minimum value, $W = 0$, indicates complete disagreement and values near to zero imply little agreement.

Suppose, for example, that 4 judges give the ranks shown in the following table to 5 competitors:

Competitor	Judge				s_i
	A	B	C	D	
a	4	4	5	5	18
b	1	1	2	1	5
c	2	3	1	2	8
d	3	2	4	3	12
e	5	5	3	4	17

Using the above formula with $m = 4$ and $n = 5$, the average sum of ranks for a competitor is found to be $\frac{1}{2} \times 4(5 + 1) = 12$. Then

$$S = (18 - 12)^2 + (5 - 12)^2 + (8 - 12)^2$$
$$+ (12 - 12)^2 + (17 - 12)^2$$
$$= 126.$$

Finally,

$$W = \frac{12 \times 126}{16 \times 5 \times (25 - 1)} = 0.7875.$$

This is near to 1, and reflects the fact that the judges are generally but not entirely in agreement.

A value of W can be assessed by means of tables or statistical packages. Thus, for this example, if judges were awarding ranks at random, tables state that the probability of W exceeding 0.66 is 0.01, i.e. a 1% chance. Our value of 0.7875 is greater than 0.66 and is significant at the 1% level (its *p-value is 0.0022), so a hypothesis that there is no communal agreement among the judges can be rejected.

coefficient of correlation See correlation coefficient.

coefficient of determination (index of determination) The square of the product moment *correlation coefficient between two variables, r^2. This is a number between 0 and 1. If the variables are x and y, and the *regression line of y on x has been found, then r^2 expresses the proportion of the *variance of y which comes from its dependence on x. Thus when all pairs of values (x, y) lie on the line and $r = \pm 1$, the dependence is total and $r^2 = 1$. On the other hand, when there is no correlation and the regression line completely fails to account for the variance of y, then $r^2 = 0$. See also multiple correlation coefficient.

coefficient of equivalence See reliability coefficient.

coefficient of internal consistency See reliability coefficient.

coefficient of kurtosis See kurtosis.

coefficient of multiple determination See multiple correlation coefficient.

coefficient of skewness See skewness.

coefficient of stability See reliability coefficient.

coefficient of variation See variation, coefficient of.

cohort See longitudinal study.

cohort study See longitudinal study.

collinear Having a common line. Thus a set of points is said to be collinear if all the points lie on a straight line.

column A vertical line of elements in an array, as in a *vector, *contingency table or *matrix.

column vector (column matrix) A *vector (or *matrix) having a single column of elements, for example the vector

$$\begin{pmatrix} 4 \\ 2 \\ -3 \end{pmatrix}.$$

Compare row vector.

combination If two letters are chosen from the five letters A, E, I, O, U and the order of selection is ignored, then there are ten possible selections or *combinations*: AE, AI, AO, AU, EI, EO, EU, IO, IU and OU.

In general, if r items are selected from n different items, and the order of selection is ignored, then the number of possible selections or *combinations* is denoted by $\binom{n}{r}$ or by ^nC_r, often spoken as 'n choose r'. Its value is given by

$$\binom{n}{r} = \frac{n!}{r!(n-r)!} = \frac{n(n-1)\dots(n-r+1)}{r!}$$

where, for example, $r!$ denotes *factorial r.

Thus, when choosing 2 letters from 5, the number of combinations is $\binom{5}{2}$, and the formula gives

$$\binom{5}{2} = \frac{5 \times 4}{2 \times 1} = 10.$$

Similarly, the number of possible selections of 6 lottery numbers from 49 is equal to

$$\binom{49}{6} = \frac{49 \times 48 \times 47 \times 46 \times 45 \times 44}{6 \times 5 \times 4 \times 3 \times 2 \times 1}$$
$$= 13\ 983\ 816.$$

For any particular value of n, the numbers $\binom{n}{r}$ form a row in *Pascal's triangle and are coefficients in the *binomial expansion of $(1 + x)^n$. They have the property that

$$\binom{n}{r} = \binom{n}{n-r},$$

so, for example, $\binom{5}{3}$ and $\binom{5}{2}$ are both equal to 10. These numbers also have the property that

$$\binom{n}{r} + \binom{n}{r-1} = \binom{n+1}{r}.$$

For instance, setting $n = 5$ and $r = 3$, we have

$$\binom{5}{3} + \binom{5}{2} = 10 + 10 = \binom{6}{3} = 20.$$

See binomial distribution; *compare* permutation.

combinatorial theory (combinatorial analysis) *See* combinatorics.

combinatorics The branch of mathematics that is concerned with the enumeration of arrangements, *combinations and *permutations of discrete objects to meet certain conditions. It has important applications in statistics, providing, for example, an enumeration of *Latin squares which is useful in *experimental design.

common difference *See* arithmetic progression.

common ratio *See* geometric progression.

comparative experiments Experiments that aim to compare two or more treatments. *See* experimental design.

complement The complement of a *set A is the set of all elements that are not in A. It is denoted by A', or sometimes by $\bar{A}$ or $C(A)$. For example, within the integers, if A is the set of even numbers then its complement A' is the set of odd numbers. Similarly, among all births in a maternity hospital, if M is the set of all multiple births, then M' is the set of all single births. *See* event.

complementary event *See* event.

completely balanced block design *See* randomized blocks.

completely randomized design A very simple form of *experimental design in which the *treatments are allocated at random to the experimental units.

complexity (of an algorithm) The number of steps, such as addition and multiplication, needed to complete the execution of an *algorithm. It is expressed in terms of the size of the input. For example, if the basic computational step is to add or multiply a pair of digits, then the number of steps needed to square an n-digit number by the standard method is fewer than $4n^2$. The complexity of the method is thus proportional to n^2.

component bar chart *See* bar chart.

composite hypothesis *See* simple hypothesis.

compound distribution (mixed distribution)
A* distribution formed by combining several distributions to form a single one. This single distribution is said to be *compounded* of the separate distributions. For example, the distribution of the weights of adults is compounded of the distributions of the weights of adult females and adult males. The term is also used to describe a distribution that results when a *parameter of a given distribution is allowed to vary, i.e. is itself a *random variable.

concomitant variable *See* analysis of covariance.

concordance *See* coefficient of concordance.

condition *See* experimental design.

conditional distribution *See* bivariate distribution.

conditional probability *See* probability.

confidence interval An *interval, derived from a sample, which has some stated probability of containing the value of some unknown *population parameter (often the mean). The end points of the interval are called the *confidence limits*, and the stated probability is called the *confidence level* of the interval. For example, if, having taken a sample of 20 components, a manufacturer gives a 95% confidence interval for the average length of all such components to be '59.8 mm to 60.6 mm', then there is a 95% chance that the interval contains the true mean length of the component. Here the confidence limits are 59.8 and 60.6, and the confidence level is 95%. Another way

of interpreting this interval is to say that there is a 5% (1 in 20) chance that it fails to include the true mean, i.e. that in the long run only 5% of such samples will produce intervals that do not contain the mean. Common confidence levels are 90%, 95%, 99% and 99.9%. These correspond to 10%, 5%, 1% and 0.1% chances of failure.

An important application is when a random sample of n observations is taken from a population which has a *normal distribution with a known standard deviation σ. If m is the mean of the sample, then a 95% confidence interval for the unknown population mean μ is

$$\left[m - 1.96 \frac{\sigma}{\sqrt{n}}, \ m + 1.96 \frac{\sigma}{\sqrt{n}} \right].$$

The number 1.96 is the $2\frac{1}{2}$% upper *percentage point of the standard normal distribution. Thus, in the example above, if the lengths of components were known to be normally distributed with a standard deviation of 0.5 mm, and a random sample of 25 components had a mean length of 60.1 mm, then the 95% confidence limits for the population mean μ would be

$$60.1 \pm 1.96 \times \frac{0.5}{\sqrt{25}}.$$

The 95% confidence interval is then $59.9 \leqslant \mu \leqslant 60.3$ (to 3 significant figures).

If the population is normal but the standard deviation is unknown, then the 95% confidence interval takes the same form except that σ is replaced by s, the *unbiased estimate of σ made from the sample, and 1.96 is replaced by the $2\frac{1}{2}$% upper percentage point of the *t-distribution having $n-1$ degrees of freedom, often denoted by $t_{n-1, \, 0.025}$. Thus the 95% confidence interval for the population mean has limits

$$m \pm t_{n-1, \, 0.025} \frac{s}{\sqrt{n}}.$$

For example, suppose that a random sample of 10 observations from a normal population has mean 24.5 and that the sample estimate of the standard deviation of the population is 1.7. Here $n = 10$ and the t-distribution with $10 - 1 = 9$ degrees of freedom has a $2\frac{1}{2}\%$ upper percentage point of 2.306. Then the 95% confidence limits for the population mean are

$$24.5 \pm 2.306 \times \frac{1.7}{\sqrt{10}},$$

i.e. 23.26 and 25.74.

Another important application is when a random sample is taken from a population which cannot be assumed to be normal and whose standard deviation is unknown. Then, provided that the sample size, n, is *large* (e.g. $n > 30$), an approximate 95% confidence interval for the population mean μ is

$$\left[m - 1.96 \frac{s}{\sqrt{n}}, \ m + 1.96 \frac{s}{\sqrt{n}} \right],$$

where m is the mean of the sample and s is the sample estimate of the standard deviation of the population.

See also proportion.

confidence level *See* confidence interval.

confidence limit *See* confidence interval.

connected graph *See* graph.

constant A fixed quantity or numerical value. Thus, under standard conditions, the temperature at which water boils is a constant, and in mathematics the value of π is a constant.

constant of integration *See* integration.

constant term The term in a *polynomial that does not involve any power of the variable. For example, in the polynomials

$$2x + 5, \ 3x^2 - 2x - 1$$

and

$$x + x^2 + 4x^3,$$

the constant terms are 5, -1 and 0, respectively.

constraint *See* degrees of freedom.

Consumer Prices Index (CPI) *See* Retail Prices Index.

contingency table When each member of a sample is examined for two characteristics and each characteristic has been divided into several categories, then the numbers having particular combinations of the sub-categories can be displayed in a contingency table. Each *cell* of the table gives the frequency with which members of the sample have the corresponding form of the two characteristics. Such a table is sometimes called a *two-way* table, and provides a method for displaying *bivariate data*.

For example, a sample of 700 individuals might be classified according to ethnic type (I, II or III) and blood group (O, A, B or AB). The following 3×4 table, with 3 rows and 4 columns, gives the frequencies of the 12 possible combinations of ethnic type and blood group.

Ethnic type	Blood group			
	O	A	B	AB
I	75	43	47	14
II	87	66	49	25
III	105	71	63	55

Usually, in practice, *marginal totals* are added, i.e. an extra column is added giving the total frequency for each row, and an extra row is added giving the total frequency for each column. Both the sum of the extra column and the sum of the extra row will equal the total number of individuals observed. In our example, inclusion of marginal totals gives the table below.

A *chi-squared test may be carried out to see whether there is some degree of association between the two characteristics. In our example, it would test whether the propor-

| Ethnic | Blood group | | | | Total |
type	O	A	B	AB	
I	75	43	47	14	179
II	87	66	49	25	227
III	105	71	63	55	294
Total	267	180	159	94	(Grand total 700)

tions in each blood group differed significantly between the ethnic groups.

For *multivariate data*, involving three or more characteristics, a different method of display is needed. A common way of presenting data from a three-way classification is to present two-way tables for each of the sub-categories of one of the characteristics. For example, in a study of heart disease, patients were classified on three characteristics: having chronic heart disease (with/ without), blood cholesterol level (A, B, C) and blood pressure group (1, 2, 3, 4, 5). The information in this $2 \times 3 \times 5$ data set can be presented as two 3×5 tables, one for those with chronic heart disease and one for those without. This approach presents the data by means of *cross-sectional tables*, and is sometimes called a *multiway table*.

See also Simpson's paradox.

continuity correction The addition or subtraction of 0.5 to integer values of a *discrete random variable when approximating to its distribution by means of a *continuous distribution.

For example, when a fair coin is tossed 100 times, H, the number of 'heads' obtained has a *binomial distribution with mean 50 and standard deviation 5. This distribution can be approximated by the *normal distribution with the same mean and standard deviation. So the discrete variable H is linked to a continuous normal variable X. Then probabilities such as

$$\Pr(H < 40), \ \Pr(H \geqslant 70) \text{ and } \Pr(H > 70)$$

are approximated by

$$\Pr(X < 39.5), \ \Pr(X \geqslant 69.5) \text{ and } \Pr(X > 70.5)$$

See normal approximation. *See also* Yates's correction.

continuous variable *See* variable.

continuous distribution *See* distribution.

continuous function A *function such as $y = x^2$ for which a small change in x causes only a small change, and not a sudden jump, in the value of y. The *graph of a continuous function has no breaks in it.

More formally, a function $f(x)$ is said to be *continuous at a point* $x = a$ if (i) it has a value $f(a)$ when $x = a$, and (ii) the value of $f(x)$ approaches $f(a)$ as x approaches a in any manner, i.e. $f(x) \to f(a)$ as $x \to a$. Otherwise, it is *discontinuous* at $x = a$.

A function is continuous if and only if it is continuous at all points. If it fails to be continuous anywhere then it is a *discontinuous function*. For example, the function $y = 1/x^2$ fails to be continuous at one point, $x = 0$, and is thus a discontinuous function: there is a break in its graph at $x = 0$.

continuous random variable *See* random variable.

control In an experiment to compare the effectiveness of a new treatment (or treatments) with some standard treatment (or no treatment, or a *placebo), the subjects or units receiving the new treatment form the *experimental group* and those receiving the standard treatment (or no treatment) form the *control* or *control group*. For example, in testing a new remedy for migraine, the experimental group of patients would receive the remedy while the control would be given a standard treatment. Similarly, in an investigation of whether a vaccine gives protection from a disease, the experimental group of subjects would receive the vaccine and the control would not be vaccinated.

control chart A graph used in *quality control to monitor some feature of mass-produced items. For example, it may be used to see whether the weights of individual items are falling within acceptable limits, or whether the mean length or variability of lengths of items in batches are satisfying certain criteria. It can thus give a warning of possible faults in the production process.

A common procedure for checking weights of items is to take a fixed number of items (e.g. four) from the production line at regular intervals (every hour, say) and record their total weight. This is plotted on a graph on which there is a *target line* representing the ideal total weight. Upper and lower *control lines* are drawn above and below this line at a calculated distance from it (e.g. three *standard deviations). If the total weight falls outside the control lines, then it is necessary to check whether the production process is faulty. There may be additional warning lines indicating the need for action if a specified number of consecutive samples give results that fall outside them. Charts are also constructed to detect other faults in production, such as excessive variability of some features of the items produced.

See also cusum chart.

control condition (control experiment) The part of an experiment that involves the *control. *Compare* experimental condition.

control group *See* control.

controlled variable (controllable variable) *See* regression.

control line *See* control chart.

convenience sample (opportunity sample) A *sample obtained by choosing units to which access is easy or convenient. Typical examples of convenience samples include those obtained by a market researcher who interviews cooperative passers-by in a shopping mall, and those composed of vol-unteers or drawn from a captive audience. Such samples are unlikely to be representative or provide a sound basis for generalizations. *Compare* representative sample.

convergent integral *See* infinite integral.

convergent sequence An infinite *sequence that has a *limit. For example, the sequence of terms of the form $1/2^n$, where $n = 1, 2, 3, 4, \ldots$, i.e.

$$\frac{1}{2}, \frac{1}{4}, \frac{1}{8}, \frac{1}{16}, \cdots$$

is convergent and has a limit of zero.

The sequence of terms of the form $n/(n + 1)$, where $n = 1, 2, 3, 4$ etc., i.e.

$$\frac{1}{2}, \frac{2}{3}, \frac{3}{4}, \frac{4}{5}, \cdots$$

is also convergent. Its limit is equal to 1. An infinite sequence that does not have a limit is a *divergent sequence*.

convergent series An infinite *series which is such that the sum of its first n terms approaches a *limit S as the number of terms, n, approaches infinity. The series is said to have the *sum S*, or to converge to S.

For example, the infinite series whose nth term is $1/2^n$ is convergent and has sum equal to 1. This is written as

$$\frac{1}{2} + \frac{1}{4} + \frac{1}{8} + \frac{1}{16} + \cdots = 1.$$

The terms of the above series are equal to the *probability of a fair coin first turning up 'heads' on the first, second, third, fourth, … toss of an unlimited sequence of tosses. An infinite series that is not convergent is called a *divergent series*.

See also exponential series; geometric series; St Petersburg paradox.

converse The statement or theorem obtained by interchanging the premise and conclusion of a given statement or theorem.

For example, the converse of the statement

'if a triangle is isosceles then two angles are equal'

is the statement

'if two angles are equal then a triangle is isosceles'.

The converse of a true statement or theorem is not necessarily true. For instance, the statement

'if $x = 2$ or -2 then $x^2 = 4$'

is true, and its converse

'if $x^2 = 4$ then $x = 2$ or -2'

is also true. However, though the statement

'if $x = 2$ then $x^2 = 4$'

is true, its converse

'if $x^2 = 4$ then $x = 2$'

is not true, since, if $x^2 = 4$, x might possibly equal -2.

convex hull *See* convex set.

convex hull trimming A method applied to the *scatter diagram of a sample of bivariate data in order to reduce the effect of *outliers on the estimate of the population *product moment correlation coefficient. The vertices of the convex hull (*see* convex set) of the set of points in the diagram are identified, and

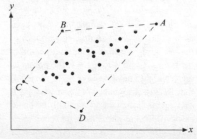

convex hull trimming The observations corresponding to the points A, B, C and D are removed.

the data corresponding to these points are removed before the correlation coefficient is calculated. The method removes extreme observations while leaving the main body of data unaltered.

convex set A set of points which, if it contains two points A and B, also contains the line segment AB. The *convex hull* of a set of points is the intersection of all convex sets containing it, i.e. the smallest convex set containing it. *See* convex hull trimming.

coordinate One of a set of numbers (coordinates) giving the position of a point relative to certain other lines or points. *See* coordinate system.

coordinate system A system for locating points in space by using reference lines or points. The position of a point is given by a set of numbers (*coordinates*) that are distances or angles from the reference frame. *See* Cartesian coordinate system; polar coordinate system; geographical coordinates.

corrected moment *See* moment.

correlation In a general sense, correlation indicates the association or dependence between two variables. There is *positive correlation* if the variables tend to increase or decrease together, and *negative correlation* if one variable tends to increase as the other decreases. Thus, for example, height and weight in humans show positive correlation, while there is generally a negative correlation between consumer demand for a product and the price at which it is sold.

However, the term is often restricted to describing the extent to which the variables have a *linear* relationship. Thus, if corresponding pairs of values are plotted as points on a graph, to give a *scatter diagram, the correlation between the variables is indicated by how close the points are to lying in a straight line. If the points are close to some line, the variables are said to be *highly correlated* (*see* diagrams (a) and (c)).

Correlation between two variables is measured by a *correlation coefficient. This is a number between -1 and $+1$. The

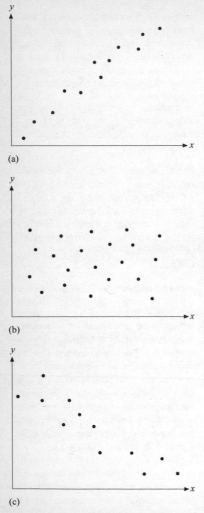

(a)

(b)

(c)

correlation Scatter diagrams showing (a) high positive correlation, (b) approximately zero correlation and (c) high negative correlation.

value is close to $+1$ if the variables are highly positively correlated, and close to -1 if they are highly negatively correlated. High correlation need not imply a direct causal relationship. For example, data for the number of car owners and the average daily sales of milk in each of a number of towns are likely to show high correlation, but this simply reflects the influence of population size on each variable. This is an example of an *illusory* or *nonsense correlation*, i.e. a case where a significant correlation exists but does not imply causal connection between the variables. Similarly, low correlation, indicated by a coefficient close to zero, only shows a lack of *linear* association; the variables may have some other kind of relationship.

See correlation coefficient.

correlation coefficient 1. For a *sample of n paired observations (x_i, y_i), the *product moment correlation coefficient r* (sometimes called *Pearson's correlation coefficient* or *Pearson's r*) is most easily calculated from the formula

$$r = \frac{n \sum_i x_i y_i - \sum_i x_i \sum_i y_i}{\sqrt{\left(n \sum_i x_i^2 - \left(\sum_i x_i\right)^2\right)\left(n \sum_i y_i^2 - \left(\sum_i y_i\right)^2\right)}}.$$

This is equivalent to

$$r = \frac{s_{xy}}{s_x s_y},$$

where s_x, s_y are the sample *standard deviations and s_{xy} is the sample *covariance of the x- and y-values. This is a number between -1 and $+1$. If $r = 1$, the points lie on a straight line of positive slope; if $r = -1$, they lie on a straight line of negative slope. If r is near zero, then there is virtually no linear association, but there may be some other form of association, e.g. the points may be scattered around the circumference of a circle (*see* diagram).

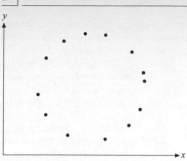

correlation coefficient 1 A situation where r is approximately zero but there is a clear nonlinear association.

As an example, the following table gives the ages at the time of marriage of a random sample of 8 couples:

Husband's age (x_i)	22	27	37	34	25	26	40	53
Wife's age (y_i)	18	22	26	27	28	30	32	41

Here $\sum_i x_i = 264, \sum_i y_i = 224, \sum_i x_i^2 = 9448, \sum_i y_i^2 = 6602$ and $\sum_i x_i y_i = 7803$. Using the above formula,

$$r = \frac{8 \times 7803 - 264 \times 224}{\sqrt{(8 \times 9448 - 264^2)(8 \times 6602 - 224^2)}}$$

$$= \frac{3288}{\sqrt{5888 \times 2640}} = 0.83.$$

For a *population* of pairs of values (x, y) of two random variables X and Y, the product moment correlation coefficient is defined as

$$\rho = \frac{\text{Cov}(X, Y)}{\sqrt{\text{Var}(X)\text{Var}(Y)}}$$

(*see* covariance, variance). For a linear relationship between X and Y, $\rho = \pm 1$. If the variables are independent then $\rho = 0$, but the *converse is not necessarily true.

If X and Y have a *bivariate normal distribution, then the coefficient r of a random sample is an estimate of the population coefficient ρ. In these circumstances tables and statistical packages are available to test the *null hypothesis that $\rho = 0$. Table 3 in the Appendix gives critical values of r for significance at certain levels and for a range of values of n. In this example, $n = 8$ and the test is one-tailed (*see* hypothesis testing) since we expect correlation to be positive if it is not zero. The minimum value for significance at the 1% level is 0.7887. The calculated value of 0.83 is greater than this, so the hypothesis that there is no association between the ages is rejected. The alternative, that there is some positive correlation between the ages of couples when they marry, is accepted. A *confidence interval for ρ can be constructed using *Fisher's z-transformation.

2. *Spearman's rank correlation coefficient* (*Spearman's rho*) can be used if the data consist of pairs of *ranks rather than pairs of values. Thus the data might be the ranks in order of merit for exams in Mathematics and English for a set of students, rather than their actual marks. Spearman's coefficient, commonly denoted by ρ (rho), is the product moment correlation coefficient between the sets of ranks. If no students are ranked equally in any one subject (i.e. if there are no *tied ranks*) it is usually calculated from the formula

$$\rho = 1 - \frac{6T}{n(n^2 - 1)},$$

where T is the sum of the squares of the difference between the ranks for each of the n pairs.

For example, six students might be ranked as follows in Mathematics and English:

	Student					
	a	b	c	d	e	f
Mathematics rank (M)	5	4	3	1	6	2
English rank (E)	1	5	3	2	6	4
Difference ($M - E$)	4	−1	0	−1	0	−2

Here $T = 16 + 1 + 0 + 1 + 0 + 4 = 22$, and

$$\rho = 1 - \frac{6 \times 22}{6 \times 35} = 0.37.$$

correlation coefficient 2 Scatter diagram of the ranks of six students in Mathematics and English.

If each student had been like students c and e and achieved the same rank in each subject, the coefficient would be equal to $+1$. There is complete agreement between the two sets of rankings. If there had been complete disagreement, with one set of rankings the reverse of the other, then the coefficient would be equal to -1.

If measurements x and y have been replaced by ranks, a value of $\rho = +1$ (or -1) merely implies that y always increases (or always decreases) as x increases. But x and y are not necessarily *linearly* related.

3. *Kendall's rank correlation coefficient (Kendall's tau)* is a measure of the agreement between two sets of rankings of the same objects. Thus it might be applied to the rankings given by two judges to six entries for a prize, or to the rankings in two subjects based on the examination marks of eight candidates. The coefficient depends on a statistic S which is calculated by considering every pair of objects being ranked. The work is eased if the data are tabulated so that the first set of ranks is in ascending order, as in the following example:

	Prize entry					
	d	f	c	b	a	e
Rank from Judge 1	1	2	3	4	5	6
Rank from Judge 2	2	4	3	5	1	6

The value of S is found from the second set of ranks by starting with the first rank on the left (2) and counting the number of ranks to the right which are larger than it, i.e. 4. We then subtract from this the number of ranks to the right which are smaller, i.e. 1. This rank contributes $4 - 1 = 3$ to S. The same procedure is applied to the second rank on the left (4) and it is found to contribute $2 - 2 = 0$. Continuing the process and adding up the contributions,

$$S = (4 - 1) + (2 - 2) + (2 - 1) + (1 - 1)$$
$$+ (1 - 0)$$
$$= 3 + 0 + 1 + 0 + 1 = 5.$$

Kendall's coefficient, denoted by τ(tau), is defined by

$$\tau = \frac{S}{\frac{1}{2}n(n - 1)},$$

where n is the number of objects being ranked. In our example, $n = 6$ and $S = 5$, so

$$\tau = \frac{5}{\frac{1}{2} \times 6 \times 5} = 0.33.$$

In effect, using this method on the second set of ranks,

S = (number of pairs in natural order)

    − (number of pairs not in order).

The coefficient takes a value between $+1$ (complete agreement) and -1 (complete disagreement). Complete disagreement occurs when one set of rankings is the reverse of the other.

4. The *point biserial correlation coefficient* is a measure of the dependence between a *continuous variable X and a discontinuous *binary variable Y that only takes two values. It is assumed that for each value of Y, the distributions of X are *normal distributions and have equal *variances. Thus X might be a measure of the general intelligence of a candidate and Y the score on a question in a test (correct = 1, incorrect = 0). For a sample, the coefficient, r_{pb}, can be calculated from the formula for the product moment correlation coefficient (*see* 1 above) or from the formula

$$r_{pb} = \frac{(\bar{x}_1 - \bar{x}_0)\sqrt{pq}}{s_x},$$

where $\bar{x}_1$ and $\bar{x}_0$ are the means of the X-values when $Y = 1$ and 0 respectively, s_x is the *standard deviation of the X-values, p is the proportion of Y-values equal to 1, and $q = 1 - p$.

To illustrate the procedure, suppose that eight individuals attempt an item in an intelligence test, scoring 1 if correct and 0 otherwise, and that the following table gives the general intelligence x and score y for each individual:

Intelligence (x)	110	95	101	128	89	98	116	106
Score on item (y)	1	1	0	1	0	0	1	1

Here, $\bar{x}_1 = 111$, $\bar{x}_0 = 96$ and $s_x = 11.7$. The proportion of Y-values equal to 1 is 0.625, so $p = 0.625$ and $q = 0.375$. The formula gives

$$r_{pb} = \frac{(111 - 96)\sqrt{(0.625 \times 0.375)}}{11.7} = 0.62.$$

If the variable Y is obtained from an underlying continuous normal variable by a *dichotomy, as for example when adults are categorized as 'tall' or 'not tall' according as their heights are greater or less than 1.82 metres, then an appropriate measure of correlation with a continuous variable X is the *biserial correlation coefficient*, usually denoted by r_{bis} or r_b. With the above nota-

tion, the formula is

$$r_{bis} = \frac{(\bar{x}_1 - \bar{x}_0)}{s_x} \frac{pq}{u}, \quad \text{where}$$

$$u = \frac{1}{\sqrt{2\pi}} e^{-h^2/2},$$

and h is such that $\Pr(Z \leqslant h) = p$ for a standard normal variable Z (*see* normal distribution). Thus if $p = 0.625$, then $h = 0.319$ and $u = 0.379$.

5. The *tetrachoric correlation coefficient* is an estimate of the product moment correlation coefficient between two variables (assumed to be *normal) based on *binary variables obtained from them by *dichotomies. For example, the scores of a sample of 100 students in Mathematics might be classified as 'adequate' or 'weak', and in Computing as 'satisfactory' or 'unsatisfactory', and the following 2×2 table of frequencies obtained:

Maths	Computing	
	Satisfactory	Unsatisfactory
Adequate	40	9
Weak	21	30

When the cell frequencies are $\begin{matrix} a & b \\ c & d \end{matrix}$, the tetrachoric correlation coefficient, r_t, is given by

$$r_t = \cos\left(\frac{180°}{1 + \sqrt{(ad/bc)}}\right).$$

In the above example, $a = 40$, $b = 9$, $c = 21$ and $d = 30$. Using these values,

$$r_t = \cos 51.14° = 0.64.$$

See also multiple correlation coefficient; partial correlation coefficient; phi coefficient.

correlation matrix A *matrix representation of the *correlation coefficients between all pairs of variables or sets of observations when there are two or more variables or sets. The entry in the ith row and jth column is the correlation coefficient between the ith and jth variables. The matrix is symmetric since the correlation coefficient between two different variables X and Y is the same as that between Y and X. All the elements on the leading diagonal are equal to 1 since the correlation coefficient between a variable X and itself is the correlation between pairs of values (x, x) and is thus 1.

For example, if the correlation coefficients between the pairs of variables (X, Y), (X, Z) and (Y, Z) are 0.83, 0.79 and 0.61, respectively, the correlation matrix is

$$\begin{array}{c} \\ X \\ Y \\ Z \end{array} \begin{array}{ccc} X & Y & Z \\ \left(\begin{array}{ccc} 1 & 0.83 & 0.79 \\ 0.83 & 1 & 0.61 \\ 0.79 & 0.61 & 1 \end{array} \right) \end{array}$$

See also covariance matrix.

covariance For a *bivariate distribution of random variables X and Y, the covariance is the expected value of the product of deviations from their means μ_x and μ_y, i.e.

$$\begin{aligned} \text{Cov}(X, Y) &= \text{E}((X - \mu_x)(Y - \mu_y)) \\ &= \text{E}(XY) - \mu_x\mu_y \\ &= \text{E}(XY) - \text{E}(X)\text{E}(Y). \end{aligned}$$

If X and Y are *independent, then $\text{Cov}(X, Y) = 0$. The *converse, that if $\text{Cov}(X, Y) = 0$ then X and Y are independent, is not necessarily true.

For a *sample of n paired observations (x_i, y_i), the sample covariance is

$$\begin{aligned} s_{xy} &= \frac{1}{n} \sum_i (x_i - \bar{x})(y_i - \bar{y}) \\ &= \frac{1}{n} \sum_i (x_i y_i) - \bar{x}\bar{y}, \end{aligned}$$

where

$$\bar{x} = \frac{1}{n} \sum_i x_i \quad \text{and} \quad \bar{y} = \frac{1}{n} \sum_i y_i$$

are the means of the samples of x- and y-values.

The covariance of X and Y divided by the product of their *standard deviations is the product moment *correlation coefficient. Similarly, for a sample, the product moment correlation coefficient is the sample covariance divided by the product of the sample standard deviations.

covariance matrix The analogue of the *correlation matrix, with *covariances between variables instead of *correlations, and with variances instead of unit elements on the leading diagonal.

CPI *Abbreviation for* Consumer Prices Index. *See* Retail Prices Index.

critical region *See* hypothesis testing.

critical value *See* hypothesis testing.

criterion variable *See* regression.

cross-over design (cross-over trial) A form of *experimental design in which each experimental unit is arranged to receive each treatment. For example, in a trial of two drugs A and B designed to relieve arthritic pain, patients could be divided into two equal groups. One group is first given a course of drug A and then, after an appropriate interval, a course of drug B. The other group is given the drugs in the reverse order. This procedure yields a set of *matched pairs of results for the two drugs, one pair for each patient. The interval between the administration of the treatments is called the *wash-out period*, and it should be longer than the time it takes for the effect of the first treatment (the *carry-over effect*) to wear off.

cross-over trial *See* cross-over design.

cross-sectional study A survey of a *representative sample of a population at a particular point in time. *Compare* longitudinal study.

cross-sectional table *See* contingency table.

cross-validation A procedure whereby a large data sample is divided into two sub-samples, often, but not necessarily, by a random method of allocation. The first sub-sample is used to fit some *model. The second sub-sample is then used as what is effectively a new data set to assess the predictive value of the fitted model and thus to attempt to validate it. An example where a non-random allocation to sub-samples may be appropriate arises if it is suspected that the relationship between two variables is represented by a *linear (straight line) regression, but there is a possibility that the slope of the relationship changes, or the linear model breaks down altogether at some fixed time. If pairs of observations of the two variables are available before and after that fixed time, then a regression line might be calculated using all observations before that fixed time, and the remaining set of observations used to see whether this line continued to fit the data, i.e. to validate the model.

cumulative frequency The sum of the *frequencies of all values less than or equal to a given value of a variable. For example, if a die is thrown 50 times and scores of 1, 2, 3, 4, 5 and 6 are obtained with frequencies 5, 9, 8, 9, 11 and 8, respectively, then the cumulative frequency associated with the score of 3 is $5 + 9 + 8 = 22$. Values and their cumulative frequencies can be conveniently displayed in a *cumulative frequency table*. Thus, our example leads to the following table:

	Score					
	1	2	3	4	5	6
Frequency	5	9	8	9	11	8
Cumulative frequency	5	14	22	31	42	50

The sums 5, 14, 22, 31, 42 and 50 are sometimes called the *absolute cumulative frequencies*. If each is divided by the total number of observations, 50, we obtain the *cumulative relative frequencies* or *cumulative proportions* 0.1, 0.28, 0.44, 0.62, 0.84 and 1. These are the proportions of values less than or

equal to the values 1, 2, 3, 4, 5 and 6. Cumulative relative frequencies are sometimes given as percentages and are then called *cumulative percentages*. In our example, the cumulative percentages for the values 1, 2, 3, 4, 5 and 6 are 10, 28, 44, 62, 84 and 100, respectively.

See grouped data.

cumulative frequency function An alternative name for a (cumulative) *distribution function. For each value of a variable it gives the probability or *frequency of the variable being less than or equal to it. A *graph of the cumulative frequency function is called a *cumulative frequency diagram, cumulative frequency curve* or *cumulative frequency graph*.

cumulative frequency graph *See* cumulative frequency function.

cumulative frequency polygon *See* grouped data.

cumulative frequency table *See* cumulative frequency.

cumulative percentage *See* cumulative frequency.

cumulative proportion *See* cumulative frequency.

cumulative relative frequency *See* cumulative frequency.

cup The symbol ∪, used to denote the *union of two sets A and B, as in $A \cup B$. *Compare* cap; *see* probability.

curvilinear regression *See* regression.

cusum chart A *control chart designed to detect the failure of a process to meet operating standards. It is constructed by recording the sum of deviations from an ideal or target value for each of a succession of samples taken at intervals. If the process is under control, the cumulative sum (abbreviated to *cusum*) of these deviations should remain small, positive and negative deviations almost cancelling out. A run of samples in which either positive or negative deviations dominate indicates that the process may be out of control. Cusum charts are designed in a way that makes it easy for operatives to decide whether the cumulative data indicate that the process is out of control.

cyclic permutation (circular permutation) A *permutation in which each member of a set replaces a successive member or in which each member is replaced by a successive member. Thus DABC, CDAB and BCDA are cyclic permutations of ABCD, but BACD is not.

D

DAFOR A *rating scale used in assessing the abundance of a species of plant, insect, etc., in a plot or sub-area of a grid. The letters stand for 'dominant', 'abundant', 'frequent', 'occasional' and 'rare'. *See* area sampling.

data (*singular* **datum**) In statistics, information of a quantitative or qualitative nature. Data obtained from records, *sample surveys or designed experiments (*see* experimental design), or in observational studies, are called *primary* or *raw data*. They may consist of measurements, counts, *ranks or preferences expressed by means of a *rating scale. Summary *statistics such as a *mean, *standard deviation or *range derived from primary data are sometimes called *secondary data*.

Bivariate data consist of pairs of measurements or observations of two variables, for example measurements of the height and weight of each of 50 children, or records of the eye colour and sex of each of 50 children. This concept extends to *multivariate data*, which consist of measurements or observations of more than two variables taken for each individual or item. For example, the amount in parts per million of four trace elements might be recorded for a chemical analysis of each of 20 elm leaves.

See also categorical data; grouped data; contingency table; measurement; scale of measurement.

data coding A way of simplifying calcula-

tions or reducing *rounding errors when using pocket calculators or computers. In statistics, when calculating the *mean or *standard deviation of a set of data, coding is based on two rules:

(i) If a constant a is added to (or subtracted from) each observation, then the mean is increased (or decreased) by a and the standard deviation is unaltered.

(ii) If each observation is multiplied (or divided) by a constant b, then the mean and standard deviation are each multiplied (or divided) by b.

For example, to calculate the mean and standard deviation of 988, 991 and 997, we could subtract 990 to give the *coded data* -2, 1 and 7. The mean and standard deviation of these numbers are easily found to be 2 and $\sqrt{42/3} = 3.74$. So the mean and standard deviation of the original data are $990 + 2 = 992$ and 3.74, respectively.

Similarly, if the data are 10.137, 10.130 and 10.141, subtraction of 10.135 and then multiplication by 1000 gives the coded data 2, -5 and 6, whose mean and standard deviation are 1 and $\sqrt{62/3} = 4.55$, respectively. Reversing the coding, the mean of the original data is

$$\frac{1}{1000} \times 1 + 10.135 = 10.136$$

and the standard deviation is

$$\frac{1}{1000} \times 4.55 = 0.00455.$$

data mining The exploration of large data sets with the aim of detecting evidence of relationships that may have been hypothesized or thought likely, or to detect patterns in the data that might suggest plausible *models that could account for the data. Modern computer-based data sets have made data mining easy to carry out on an informal basis, but statistical safeguards such as *cross-validation are needed to ensure that spurious random patterns in a small portion of the data are not confused with true relationships between the variables. *See also* meta-analysis.

death rate The number of deaths per unit of population in a particular time period. In practice the period is often a specified 12-month interval, often a calendar year, and the rate is expressed for a unit of 1000 members of the group or population at risk. Death rates are often compiled separately for sub-groups of a general population, and sometimes also for specific causes of death. Typical sub-groups might be males and females, or an age-specific division such as those aged 75 or more and those under 75. Rates may also be calculated for different causes of death, e.g. cancer, cardiac failure or road accidents. For example, if in a calendar year in a city of 250 000 inhabitants 82 people die from alcohol-induced disorders, then the death rate from that cause is $(82/250\,000) \times 1000 = 0.0328$ per thousand. Death rate is also called *mortality rate*. *Compare* birth rate; *see also* life tables.

decile The deciles of a *distribution are the nine values that divide the range of values of the variable into ten intervals having equal frequencies. For $r = 1, 2, \ldots, 9$, the rth decile is the value of the variable such that r-tenths of the distribution is less than or equal to it. Thus 3/10 of the distribution is less than or equal to the third decile. The fifth decile is the *median.

For *grouped data, estimates of deciles can be found by *interpolation in the *cumulative frequency table or from the *cumulative frequency polygon; the rth decile being the value with a cumulative frequency of $r/10$ (or $10r\%$).

For a continuous *random variable X with (cumulative) *distribution function $F(x)$, the rth decile is the value x such that $\Pr(X \leqslant x) = F(x) = r/10$. Deciles for a discrete random variable can also be defined in terms of its distribution function, using a procedure similar to that used in the definition of its *median.

The deciles define ten intervals. Sometimes these intervals are referred to as 'deciles'.

See also percentile; quartile; quantile.

definite integral An expression for the difference between the values of an *integral when evaluated for two values of the independent variable (*see* function), written as

$$\int_a^b f(x)\mathrm{d}x.$$

The values $x = b$ and $x = a$ are called the *upper* and *lower limits* of the definite integral. If $F(x)$ is an integral of $f(x)$, then the value of the above definite integral is $F(b) - F(a)$. This is also written as

$$[F(x)]_a^b.$$

The following example illustrates the evaluation of a definite integral:

$$\int_2^3 2x\,\mathrm{d}x = [x^2]_2^3 = 3^2 - 2^2 = 9 - 4 = 5.$$

Compare indefinite integral.

degree 1. The *exponent of a variable in an algebraic term. For example, in the term $5x^2$, the variable x has degree 2. If a term involves several variables, the degree of the term is the sum of the degrees of the variables. Thus in the term $3xy^3$, the variable x

has degree 1, y has degree 3 and the degree of the term is $1 + 3 = 4$.

The degree of a *polynomial or equation is the degree of the term with the highest degree. For instance, in the equation $x^2 - 2x + 1 = 0$ the term with the highest degree is x^2. So the degree of the equation is 2.

2. *See* graph.

degrees of freedom (d.f.) For a set of observations in a given context, the number of values that can be assigned freely, without restriction. Thus, when finding the *mean of a sample of n observations there are no restrictions (or *constraints*) on the sample values, and there are n degrees of freedom. However, if the observations are to have a fixed total then there are only $n - 1$ degrees of freedom, for once $n - 1$ values are assigned the final one is fixed in order to ensure that the total is correct. Similarly, if the n values are to have a certain mean then there are $n - 1$ degrees of freedom. In calculating the *variance or *standard deviation of a set of n observations the mean must be found and known, so in these contexts there are $n - 1$ degrees of freedom.

The term is also used in connection with *contingency tables. For example, in a 2×2 table with fixed marginal (i.e. row and column) totals there is only one degree of freedom, for once a value has been assigned to one of the four cells the remaining values are determined by the totals. For example, in the table below, with the given row and column totals, if we choose to make $a = 14$ then it follows that $b = 36$, $c = 26$ and $d = 24$:

	Column 1	Column 2	Row totals
Row 1	a	b	50
Row 2	c	d	50
Column totals	40	60	

Similarly, if we put $a = 1$, then immediately $b = 49$, $c = 39$ and $d = 11$.

In general, in an $r \times c$ contingency table (with r rows and c columns) with fixed marginal totals, there are $(r - 1)(c - 1)$ degrees of freedom. Thus, in a 3×4 table there are six degrees of freedom.

See also analysis of variance; residual variation; t-test.

de Méré's problem One of several questions put to Blaise Pascal by Antoine Gombaud, Chevalier de Méré in 1654: Explain why there is a better chance of throwing a six with four throws of a die, than of obtaining a double six with 24 throws of two dice. The respective probabilities are $1 - \left(\frac{5}{6}\right)^4 = 0.52$ and $1 - \left(\frac{35}{36}\right)^{24} = 0.49$. Pascal communicated his solutions to Pierre de Fermat, beginning their historic correspondence about problems in probability. *See also* Banach's matchboxes; birthday problem; problem of coincidences; problem of points.

demography The statistical study of human populations, in particular *vital statistics* (*birth rates and *death rates), but also with reference to their structure and distribution, and changes in them due to such factors as births, deaths, emigration and immigration. The aim is often to predict patterns of change in structure or distribution by analysing both current and historic information on the factors that induce change. The subject extends to include the interrelationship between characteristics such as social class distribution and economic factors such as agricultural and manufacturing output, and also the impact on population movement of factors such as urban congestion.

density function *See* probability density function.

dependent variable *See* function; regression.

derivative The rate of change of a *function with respect to the independent variable. It is also called the *differential coefficient* or the *derived function*. For a function $y = f(x)$, the derivative can be written as

$$\frac{dy}{dx}, \quad y' \quad \text{or} \quad f'(x).$$

An important feature of the derivative is that it gives the *gradient of the tangent to the curve with equation $y = f(x)$ at any point on the curve. For example, the function $y = x^2$ has derivative $dy/dx = 2x$, and the slope of the tangent at the point where $x = 3$ (i.e. the point $(3, 9)$) is $2 \times 3 = 6$.

Taking derivatives of derivatives gives derivatives of higher *order*. For instance, the function $y = x^4$ has first derivative $dy/dx = 4x^3$. The second derivative, written as d^2y/dx^2, is obtained by differentiating this to give $12x^2$; the third derivative, d^3y/dx^3, is $24x$. For $n > 1$, the nth derivative is denoted by $d^n y/dx^n$; alternative notations are $y^{(n)}$ and $f^{(n)}(x)$.

Some common derivatives are given in Table 8 of the Appendix. *See also* differentiation.

derived function *See* derivative.

descriptive statistics *See* statistics.

designed experiment *See* experimental design.

determination *See* coefficient of determination.

deviation *See* mean absolute deviation; standard deviation.

d.f. *Abbreviation for* *degrees of freedom; less frequently for *distribution function. A preferred abbreviation for the latter is *c.d.f.* (cumulative distribution function).

diagonal matrix *See* matrix.

dichotomous data *See* categorical data.

dichotomous question A question which asks the respondent to choose one of two responses, e.g. the question

Have you ever had influenza?

with responses

Yes/No.

The term is also used for questions seeking information about dichotomous variables (i.e. *categorical variables that can take only one of two values), such as gender, where the response is 'female' or 'male'.

Compare multiple-choice question; *see* rating scale.

dichotomous responses A trial, experiment or question which can have only one of two possible outcomes or responses is said to have dichotomous responses.

dichotomous variable *See* categorical variable.

dichotomy Division of a population or sample into two groups based either on a measurable variable (e.g. age under 65, age 65 or over) or on a characteristic or attribute (e.g. colour-blind, not colour-blind).

die *Singular of* dice.

differential coefficient *See* derivative.

differentiation The process of obtaining the *derivative of a *function. For example, if the function is $y = x^2$, differentiation gives the derivative $dy/dx = 2x$. More generally, if $y = x^n$ then $dy/dx = nx^{n-1}$.

Some common derivatives are given in Table 8 of the Appendix.

digraph *See* graph.

directed graph *See* graph.

directly proportional *See* variation.

direct probability *See* inverse probability.

discontinuous function *See* continuous function.

discrete *See* variable.

discrete distribution *See* distribution.

discrete random variable *See* random variable.

disjoint Describing sets that have no common members. Two sets are disjoint if their *intersection is empty. For example, the sets $A = \{1, 5\}$ and $B = \{2, 3\}$ are disjoint sets.

When a die is cast the possible scores are 1, 2, 3, 4, 5, 6. If A is the set of odd scores and B is the set of even scores, then A and B are disjoint since $A = \{1, 3, 5\}$ and $B = \{2, 4, 6\}$. If C is the set of scores divisible by 3, then $C = \{3, 6\}$, and neither A and C nor B and C are disjoint sets since A and C have the element 3 in common, and B and C have the element 6 in common.

dispersion The spread of a set of observations or of a *random variable. It is usually measured by some appropriate function of the deviations from some central value, as in the *standard deviation or the *mean absolute deviation. The *variance gives the average square deviation from the *mean. Other *measures of dispersion* include the *interquartile range, the semi-interquartile range and the *range. *See also* centrality.

distance function *See* metric.

distractor *See* multiple-choice question.

distribution Any description or presentation of the values taken by a *variable which gives the *frequency or *probability with which values or sets of values occur. The term is applied to presentations that are empirical and simply report observed data, and also to descriptions that are theoretical and expressed in mathematical terms. Specifications that give frequencies are often called *frequency distributions*, and those that give probabilities are often called *probability distributions*.

If the variable can only take discrete, isolated values then it is *discrete* and said to have a *discrete distribution*. For example, the score on a die can take only the (discrete) values 1, 2, 3, 4, 5, 6. If it is thrown 50 times, the empirical distribution of scores might be as follows:

Score	1	2	3	4	5	6
Frequency	9	8	8	6	10	9

If the die is believed to be fair, then the theoretical distribution of scores is as follows:

Score	1	2	3	4	5	6
Probability	$\frac{1}{6}$	$\frac{1}{6}$	$\frac{1}{6}$	$\frac{1}{6}$	$\frac{1}{6}$	$\frac{1}{6}$

This is an example of a *uniform distribution. Other important discrete distributions are the *binomial distribution, the *Poisson distribution and the *geometric distribution.

If the variable can take any value in a given range, then it is *continuous* and said to have a *continuous distribution*. For example, heights and weights of individuals are continuous variables. For observed data it is possible to form an empirical frequency distribution by finding the numbers of values falling in a set of non-overlapping sub-intervals that cover the range of observed values (*see* grouped data). Well-known theoretical continuous distributions include the *normal distribution and the rectangular distribution (*see* uniform distribution).

See also bivariate distribution; chisquared distribution; F-distribution; multivariate distribution; negative binomial distribution; t-distribution.

distribution curve *See* distribution function.

distribution-free method A method for making *statistical inferences from samples that does not assume the sample to come from any specific underlying family of distributions such as the *normal and *exponential distributions. There may, however, be weaker requirements such as the assumption that the distribution is a *symmetrical distribution.

A simple example of a distribution-free method is the *sign test for a single sample. In essence, this tests the hypothesis that a sample comes from a population with a *median M, by comparing the number of observations in the sample that are greater than M with the number less than M. The test makes no assumption about the type of population distribution and is thus distribution-free.

Distribution-free methods include *nonparametric methods in which no assumptions are made about population *parameters for any specific family. They are usually taken to also include tests such as the *Kolmogorov–Smirnov test, which tests whether a sample may reasonably be supposed to come from some completely specified population. This is because the nature of this test is completely independent of what population is specified, and it can therefore be applied to *any* hypothesized, fully specified distribution.

See coefficient of concordance; correlation coefficient; Friedman's test; Jonckheere–Terpstra test; Kruskal–Wallis test; McNemar's test; median test; Page test; permutation test; runs test; Tukey's quick test; Wilcoxon rank sum test; Wilcoxon signed rank test.

distribution function (c.d.f.) The (cumulative) distribution function of a *random variable gives, for each value of the variable, the probability of the variable taking values less than or equal to it. More formally, for a random variable X the distribution function $F(x)$ is defined for all values of x by

$$F(x) = \Pr(X \leqslant x).$$

For example, taking X to be the score when a fair die is thrown, $F(3)$ is the probability of the score X being less than or equal to 3 i.e. being 1, 2 or 3. Thus,

$$F(3) = \tfrac{1}{6} + \tfrac{1}{6} + \tfrac{1}{6} = \tfrac{3}{6} = \tfrac{1}{2}.$$

Similarly, $F(6) = 1$, $F(1) = \tfrac{1}{6}$ and $F(0) = 0$ (*see* diagram (a)).

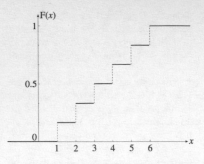

distribution function (a) The distribution function of the score on a fair die.

In general, for a discrete variable taking values $x_1, x_2, x_3, \ldots,$

$$F(x) = \sum_{x_i \leqslant x} \Pr(X = x_i),$$

and for a continuous variable, with *frequency function $f(x)$,

$$F(x) = \int_{-\infty}^{x} f(t)\,dt.$$

As x increases, the value of $F(x)$ increases from 0 to 1. The graph of the distribution function is sometimes called the *distribution curve*.

For example, suppose the continuous variable X has frequency function $f(x)$ defined by

$$f(x) = \begin{cases} 0 & \text{for } x < 0, \\ 2 - 2x & \text{for } 0 \leqslant x \leqslant 1, \\ 0 & \text{for } x > 1. \end{cases}$$

Then, for $x < 0, F(x) = 0$. For $0 \leqslant x \leqslant 1$,

$$F(x) = \int_{0}^{x} (2 - 2t)\,dt = 2x - x^2.$$

Finally, for $x > 1, F(x) = 1$. The graphs of $F(x)$ and $f(x)$ are shown in diagram (b). As a further example, diagram (c) shows the graphs of the frequency function and the distribution function of a variable with

distribution function (b) A frequency function $f(x)$ and the corresponding distribution function $F(x)$.

a *normal distribution. It illustrates that $F(x)$ is equal to the *ordinate of the distribution curve and also equal to a certain area under the frequency curve. Table 1 in the Appendix gives the distribution function of the standard normal distribution. Some statistical tables also give the distribution functions of the *Poisson distribution and

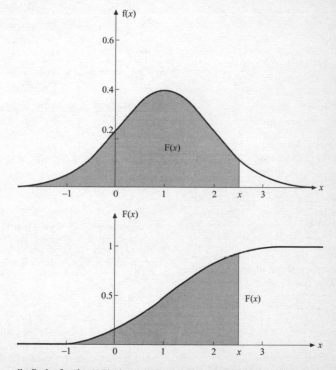

distribution function (c) The frequency function $f(x)$ and the distribution function $F(x)$ of a variable with the normal distribution $N(1, 1)$.

*binomial distribution for certain values of their parameters.

The definition extends to *multivariate distributions. For a *bivariate distribution,

$$F(x, y) = \Pr(X \leqslant x, Y \leqslant y)$$

divergent integral *See* infinite integral.

divergent sequence *See* convergent sequence.

divergent series *See* convergent series.

division problem *See* problem of points.

d.o.f. *Abbreviation for* *degrees of freedom.

double bar chart *See* bar chart.

double-blind *See* blinding.

double log paper *See* logarithmic paper.

down run *See* run.

dual chart *See* bar chart.

e The number that is the base of natural *logarithms. It has the value 2.718 281 828..., the *limit of $(1 + (1/n))^n$ as $n \to \infty$. It is the sum of the *infinite series

$$1 + \frac{1}{1!} + \frac{1}{2!} + \frac{1}{3!} + \cdots.$$

See also exponential distribution; exponential function; exponential series.

EDA *Abbreviation for* *exploratory data analysis.

effect variable An alternative name for the response variable (*see* regression).

efficiency **1.** One *unbiased estimator of a population parameter is more efficient than another unbiased estimator of the parameter if it has the smaller variance. The *relative efficiency* of the first estimator to the second can be measured by the ratio of the second variance to the first. For example, if two estimators T_1 and T_2 have variances of 8 and 16 respectively, then T_1 is the more efficient estimator, and the relative efficiency of T_1 to T_2 is $16/8 = 2$. Thus, T_1 is twice as efficient as T_2.
2. One *experimental design is more efficient than another if it achieves the same *precision in a shorter time or at a lower cost, or achieves greater precision in the same time or at the same cost. However, one of two designs may be more efficient when comparing some treatments yet less efficient when comparing others.

element *See* matrix; set.

empirical Based on observation or experiment rather than deduction from basic laws or axioms. An *empirical formula* is a formula devised to fit known data. An *empirical curve* is a curve drawn as the best approximation to fit a set of points.

empty set *See* null set.

endogenous variable A term used largely in economics to describe variables in a *model that are inherent parts of the system. In a model of sales, for example, price, demand, supply and storage might appear as endogenous variables, but factors such as adverse weather conditions or a national emergency that may impinge on the system from outside by affecting demand and hence sales are called *exogenous variables*.

end point One of the numbers defining an *interval.

entry *See* matrix.

equiprobable Having equal probability. For example, the toss of a fair coin has two equiprobable outcomes: 'heads' and 'tails'.

equivalence, coefficient of *See* reliability coefficient.

equivalent forms reliability *See* reliability.

error The difference between an observation or approximation and the true or predicted value. If two thermometers read 31°C and 27°C when the true temperature is 30°C, then the errors are 1°C and −3°C, respectively. If the number 23.6 is rounded to the nearest whole number, 24, the *rounding error* is 0.4. In general, if b is an approximation to a, then the error is $b - a$.

In statistics a *random error* is the difference between an observed value and the value predicted by some *model, and represents uncontrolled *variation. In many practical situations errors are assumed to be independent and to have a *normal distribution with zero mean.

See absolute error; relative error; residuals; rounding; sampling error.

error mean square *See* analysis of variance.

error of the first kind *See* Type I error.

error of the second kind *See* Type II error.

estimate *See* estimation; estimator; extrapolation; interpolation.

estimation The use of evidence such as the data in a sample to make a prediction about an unknown population *parameter, e.g. the *mean. If the prediction consists of a single value, then it is called a *point estimate*. If the prediction consists of an interval which, in some way, is predicted to contain the parameter, then it is an *interval estimate*. A *confidence interval is an interval estimate.

For example, a manufacturer who uses a sample of 20 components with mean length 31 cm to estimate the mean length of all such components to be 31 cm is making a point estimate of the required mean. Another possible point estimate would be to use the sample *median as an estimate of the median length of all components. If the manufacturer calculated the 95% confidence interval for the mean and found this to be 29.8–32.2 cm, this would be an interval estimate. Similarly, a 99% confidence interval would be another interval estimate.

See also extrapolation; interpolation; least squares; maximum likelihood estimation.

estimator A *statistic (i.e. some function of the observations in a sample) used to estimate a population *parameter. A particular value of an estimator is an *estimate*. For example, the *mean of a sample, $\bar{x}$, is an estimator of the population mean. Here, the estimator is the statistic $\bar{x}$; its value in a particular case, 98.4 say, is an estimate. *See* unbiased estimator.

even permutation A *permutation that is equivalent to an even number of *transpositions. For example, 312 is an even permutation of 123 since it is equivalent to two transpositions, e.g. (32) then (31). *Compare* odd permutation.

event A *subset, E say, of the set of all possible outcomes (i.e. the *sample space*) of an experiment. If the outcome of an experiment belongs to E, then event E has occurred. If the outcome does not belong to E, then the *complementary event* 'E has not occurred' has taken place; the outcome belongs to the *complement of E, denoted by E'.

For example, if a letter is chosen from the English alphabet, so that the sample space S of outcomes is the set {a, b, c, ..., z}, and E is the event 'the letter is a vowel', then E is represented by the subset {a, e, i, o, u}. If the letter e is selected, then event E has occurred; but if the letter f is chosen, then E has not occurred and the complementary event 'the letter is not a vowel' or, alternatively, 'the letter is a consonant' has occurred.

The complete space S represents a *certain* event.

If E and F are two subsets of S, then their *union*, $E \cup F$, is the event 'E or F or both occur'. Their *intersection*, $E \cap F$, is the event 'both E and F occur'. Thus if, in our example, F is the event 'the letter is a, b or c', then $E \cup F$ is the event 'the letter is a vowel, or a, b or c' represented by the subset {a, e, i, o, u, b, c}. Similarly, $E \cap F$ is the

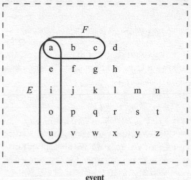

event

event 'the letter is both a vowel and one of a, b or c' represented by the subset {a} (*see* diagram).

Events that cannot both occur are said to be *mutually exclusive*, for example the events E: 'the letter is a vowel' and G: 'the letter is x, y, or z'. Their intersection, 'the letter is both a vowel and one of x, y or z', is an *impossible* event.

See also probability.

exogenous variable *See* endogenous variable.

exp *See* exponential function.

expansion A mathematical expression that is written as a sum of a number of terms. Expansion is also the process of putting an expression into this form; for example, the expansion of $(1 + x)(2 + 3x)$ to give $2 + 5x + 3x^2$. The method of expanding such an expression is as follows:

$$(1 + x)(2 + 3x) = 1(2 + 3x) + x(2 + 3x)$$
$$= 2 + 3x + 2x + 3x^2$$
$$= 2 + 5x + 3x^2.$$

The expansion of a function is the form of the function when it is represented as a *series of terms, i.e. as a finite series, or as an infinite series that converges to the function for certain values of the variable. The expansion as an infinite series is called the *series expansion* of the function.

For example,

$$\frac{1}{1 + x} = 1 - x + x^2 - x^3 + \cdots,$$

for $-1 < x < 1$, is the series expansion of $1/(1 + x)$.

The binomial expansion is the expansion given by the *binomial theorem.

expectation (expected value) The *mean value of a *random variable. The expectation of a variable X is denoted by $\mathrm{E}(X)$.

If X is a *discrete* variable, taking values $x_1, x_2, x_3, \ldots$ with probabilities $p_1, p_2, p_3, \ldots$, then the expectation of X is given by

$$\mathrm{E}(X) = p_1 x_1 + p_2 x_2 + p_3 x_3 + \cdots$$
$$= \sum_i p_i x_i.$$

For instance, if X is the points obtained when a football team plays a match, and X equals 0, 1 or 3 for a loss, draw or win, with probabilities $\frac{1}{4}, \frac{1}{2}$ and $\frac{1}{4}$, respectively, then

$$\mathrm{E}(X) = \frac{1}{4} \times 0 + \frac{1}{2} \times 1 + \frac{1}{4} \times 3$$
$$= 1\frac{1}{4}.$$

Thus the expectation is an average of $1\frac{1}{4}$ points per match.

If X is a *continuous* variable with *frequency function $\mathrm{f}(x)$, then the expectation of X is given by

$$\mathrm{E}(X) = \int_{-\infty}^{\infty} x\mathrm{f}(x)\mathrm{d}x.$$

For instance, if $\mathrm{f}(x)$ is defined as

$$\mathrm{f}(x) = \begin{cases} 2 - 2x & \text{for } 0 \leqslant x \leqslant 1, \\ 0 & \text{otherwise,} \end{cases}$$

then the expectation of X is calculated as

$$E(X) = \int_0^1 x(2 - 2x)dx = \int_0^1 (2x - 2x^2)dx$$

$$= \left[x^2 - \frac{2}{3}x^3 \right]_0^1 = \left(1 - \frac{2}{3} \right) - (0) = \frac{1}{3}.$$

The expected value of a function $g(X)$ of a *discrete* variable X is defined by

$$E(g(X)) = \sum_i p_i g(x_i).$$

Thus in our first example above, where X took values 0, 1, 3 with probabilities $\frac{1}{4}, \frac{1}{2}, \frac{1}{4}$, respectively, the expectation of X^2 is given by

$$E(X^2) = \frac{1}{4} \times 0^2 + \frac{1}{2} \times 1^2 + \frac{1}{4} \times 3^2 = 2\frac{3}{4}.$$

When X is a *continuous* variable, the expected value of $g(X)$ is defined by

$$E(g(X)) = \int_{-\infty}^{\infty} g(x)f(x)dx.$$

Thus in our second example above, where $f(x) = 2 - 2x$ for $0 \leqslant x \leqslant 1$ and $f(x) = 0$ otherwise, the expectation of X^2 is given by

$$E(X^2) = \int_0^1 x^2(2 - 2x)dx = \left[\frac{2}{3}x^3 - \frac{1}{2}x^4 \right]_0^1$$

$$= \frac{1}{6}.$$

In both the above examples, the expectation of X^2 is not equal to the square of $E(X)$. In fact,

$$E(X^2) = (E(X))^2 + Var(X),$$

where $Var(X)$ is the *variance of X. This is often presented in the form

$$Var(X) = E(X^2) - (E(X))^2$$

and used to calculate variances. Thus in the

second example above,

$$Var(X) = \frac{1}{6} - \left(\frac{1}{3} \right)^2 = \frac{1}{18}.$$

When g is a *linear function of X, i.e. $g(X) = aX + b$, where a and b are constants, then

$$E(g(X)) = E(aX + b) = aE(X) + b.$$

For two random variables X and Y, the following laws hold for some simple functions of X and Y:

(i) $E(X + Y) = E(X) + E(Y)$;
(ii) $E(X - Y) = E(X) - E(Y)$;
(iii) $E(aX + bY) = aE(X) + bE(Y)$, where a and b are constants;
(iv) $E(XY) = E(X)E(Y) + Cov(X, Y)$, where $Cov(X, Y)$ is the *covariance of X and Y; and
(v) $E(XY) = E(X)E(Y)$ if X and Y are *independent*.

See moment.

experiment *See* trial.

experimental condition The part of an experiment that involves the experimental group (*see* control).

experimental design Many experiments aim to assess the effect of *treatments* such as medicines, fertilizers or written tests on *units* such as patients, plots of land or students. Treatments are sometimes called *conditions* or *factors*. A unit is sometimes called an *experimental unit*, *plot*, *subject* or *participant*. A plan for applying treatments is an experimental design, and an experiment with such a plan is a *designed experiment*.

To allow for variations in response, any treatment will need to be applied to a number of different units under identical experimental conditions. This use of two or more units for each treatment is called *replication*. It is often desirable, though not essential, to have equal numbers of units receiving each treatment, i.e. to aim for *equal replication* of treatments. However, there are situations where it might be desirable to have twice the replication for one or two treatments than for others of lesser interest. Also, economic factors such as the cost or availability of a scarce commodity may also make unequal replication necessary if the experiment is to be done at all.

It is also important that treatments are allocated to units by a random process of some kind, so that the units receiving each treatment are a random selection from the available units.

In a *completely randomized design*, treatments are allocated to units completely at random. For example, suppose that a sample of 16 patients, numbered 1 to 16, is available for testing two new drugs, A and B, against the standard drug C for treating a heart condition. Using *random numbers, and aiming for equal replication, drug A might be allocated to the patients with numbers 1, 3, 4, 5, 10 and 16; drug B to those numbered 2, 6, 8, 13 and 14; and drug C to those numbered 7, 9, 11, 12 and 15. Designs which use groups of unrelated units are sometimes called *independent samples designs*, *unrelated designs*, *between-groups designs* or *between-subjects designs*.

However, the *precision of an experiment can usually be increased by working with groups (or *blocks*) of related units. The groups are formed so that the units in any one group share certain characteristics thought likely to affect response to treatment. The units are said to be *matched* or *related*. Treatments are then allocated randomly to units within a group. Designs that use groups of matched or related units are sometimes called *matched samples designs*, *related designs* or *within-groups designs*.

The simplest such design is *randomized blocks. Thus, in the above trial of drugs A, B and C, a larger sample of patients could be grouped according to their cholesterol level giving three groups, 'low', 'medium' and 'high'. Drugs A, B and C are then allocated randomly within each group. With these designs an *analysis of variance can be used to remove the effect of differences in response between units in different groups and to focus more precisely on differences due to the treatments.

See blinding; control; cross-over design; efficiency; factorial experiment; Latin square; matched pairs; repeated measures.

experimental group *See* control.

experimental variable *See* regression.

experimenter bias A bias introduced into the conduct of an experiment by the experimenter. Possible sources of bias include the influence of the experimenter's expectations of the outcomes, for these can subtly affect the way the experiment is carried out. *See* blinding.

explanatory variable *See* regression.

exploratory data analysis (EDA) A term used to describe the examination of *data by operations such as grouping, graphing, tabulating and presenting the data in such a way that will highlight its characteristics. This may include the calculation of such characteristics as the *mean, *median, *quartiles and *range, and also the use of *stem-and-leaf diagrams, *five-number summaries, *box-and-whisker diagrams, *histograms, *scatter diagrams and similar devices that are often helpful in deciding what formal statistical analyses may be appropriate.

exponent (index) A number placed in a superscript position to the right of another number or variable to indicate repeated multiplication: 4^2 indicates 4×4, 4^3 indicates $4 \times 4 \times 4$, etc. Sometimes *power* is used instead of 'exponent'; more strictly, *power* is the result of the multiplication – e.g. 16 is the second power of 4 (i.e. 4^2). If the exponent is negative, then the expression is the reciprocal of the number with the positive value of the exponent – e.g. $4^{-2} = 1/4^2 = 1/16$.

Any number with an exponent of zero is equal to 1, e.g. $4^0 = 1$.

Certain *laws of exponents* (*laws of indices*) apply:

(i) *multiplication*: $a^m a^n = a^{m+n}$;

(ii) *division*: $a^m/a^n = a^{m-n}$;

(iii) *raising to a power*: $(a^m)^n = a^{mn}$.

Fractional exponents are defined by $a^{m/n} = \sqrt[n]{a^m}$. For example, $8^{2/3} = \sqrt[3]{8^2} = \sqrt[3]{64} = 4$.

exponential curve A curve with an equation of the form $y = a^x$, for example the curve with equation $y = 2^x$ (*see* diagram).

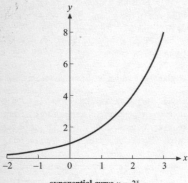

exponential curve $y = 2^x$.

exponential distribution The distribution of a continuous random variable X with *frequency function $f(x) = \lambda e^{-\lambda x}$, where λ is a positive parameter and $x \geqslant 0$. The *mean is $1/\lambda$ and the *variance is $1/\lambda^2$.

If a certain type of event occurs randomly but at an average rate of λ times in some unit of time, then the time interval between successive events has an exponential distribution with parameter λ. This interval between events is sometimes called the *waiting time* or *wait time*.

For example, during a period when a radioactive substance is emitting particles at an average rate of 0.5 per second, the time interval X between successive emissions has an exponential distribution with

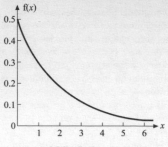

exponential distribution with $\lambda = 0.5$.

$\lambda = 0.5$. The mean is $1/0.5 = 2$ seconds, and the variance is $1/(0.5)^2 = 4$. The frequency function is $0.5\,e^{-0.5x}$ (*see* diagram). Similarly, if, during some period, a website (or call-centre) is receiving hits (or calls) at an average rate of 10 per minute, then the interval between hits (or calls) is exponentially distributed with a mean of $1/10$ minute, i.e. 6 seconds.

The exponential distribution is related to the *Poisson distribution. If an event occurs randomly at an average rate of λ times in some unit of time, then the number of events occurring in the time unit has a Poisson distribution with mean λ. Thus in the above examples, the number of emissions observed per second has a Poisson distribution with mean 0.5, and the number of website hits per minute has a Poisson distribution with mean 10.

See Poisson process.

exponential function The function exp x or e^x (*see* e). The term is also used for functions of the type a^x, where a is a positive constant, or more generally ka^x, where k is constant.

exponential growth *or* decay A growth pattern in which some quantity y (e.g. size of a population, incidence of a disease, value of an investment, sales of a product) is an *exponential function of time. Thus at time t, the value of y is given by a relation such as $y = ae^{bt}$, where a and b are constants and $a > 0$ (or, more generally, $y = ac^{bt}$, where c

is a positive constant). The rate of growth or decay is given by $dy/dt = abe^{bt} = by$ and is thus proportional to y. For growth $b > 0$; for decay $b < 0$.

For example, when a sum P is invested at 5% compound interest per annum, its value grows exponentially since its value V after t years is given by

$$V = P \times 1.05^t.$$

exponential notation (standard form, index notation, scientific notation) A method of writing numbers as a product of a number between 1 and 10 and a power of 10. For example, 2 500 000 in exponential notation is 2.5×10^6, and 0.007 is 7×10^{-3}.

exponential series The *series

$$\sum \frac{x^n}{n!} = 1 + x + \frac{x^2}{2} + \frac{x^3}{6} + \cdots,$$

where $n!$ denotes *factorial n. The series is a *convergent series for all values of x, and its sum is the exponential function e^x.

extrapolation If the values of a function $f(x)$ are known for certain values of x, extrapolation is the process of estimating from these data the value of the function for a value of x outside the range of x-values for which f is known. Thus, if the value of the function is known to be 12, 18 and 21 when x is 1, 2 and 3, respectively, then estimating the function's value when x equals 3.5 is a process of extrapolation.

In general, extrapolation is based on the assumption that trends in the observations will continue outside the range for which data are known. Although they are sometimes useful, estimates obtained by extrapolation can be unreliable.

Compare interpolation; *see* line of best fit.

extreme value distribution The *distribution of the largest (or smallest) observation in a sample. These distributions are relevant to predicting the probability of, for example, future floods exceeding a certain magnitude on the basis of records for past floods, or for estimating the earliest likely failure time of a specified machine component. There are several extreme value distributions; the choice of which to use will depend on the type of population from which the samples are drawn. One such is the *Weibull distribution; two others are the *Frechet distribution* and the *Gumbel distribution*.

F

facility *See* item analysis.

factor *See* experimental design; factor analysis.

factor analysis A set of methods that attempts to find, from a large quantity and variety of measurements in some field, a small number of underlying dimensions or *factors* which to a large extent can account for the data. For example, a study of the job satisfaction of schoolteachers might analyse their responses on a five-point *rating scale to 32 relevant questionnaire items and propose five factors, calling them 'supervision', 'income', 'external pressures', 'advancement' and 'school culture'. Similarly, a study of performance on a range of tests of mental ability might yield seven underlying factors, described as 'spatial ability', 'numerical ability', 'memory', 'verbal fluency', 'perceptual speed', 'inductive reasoning' and 'verbal meaning'.

More formally, factor analysis is a form of multivariate analysis in which observations of the n variables $x_1, x_2, x_3, \ldots, x_n$ are available for each individual or unit in the study and an attempt is made to express each variable as a *linear function of a small set of m ($< n$) factors plus a term representing error variation. These factors are linear functions of the observed variables and act as a set of key variables underlying the data, for they are formed in such a way that scores on these factors, when appropriately weighted by coefficients (called *factor load-*

ings), predict or account for an individual's score on any particular variable. These coefficients range from -1 to $+1$ and are analogous to correlation coefficients. Factors are interpreted and named by examining the characteristics of the variables on which they have high loadings. This may involve examining tasks, activities or processes associated with the variables.

The first stage in the analysis is to calculate the *correlation matrix of the observed data. The second stage is to identify clusters of variables which correlate closely with one another and to associate a factor with each cluster; any variable that does not correlate with others is also associated with a factor. Having obtained a set of factors, the final stage is to adjust it by a process known as *rotation* so as to achieve as simple and meaningful a relation to the data as possible. If the factors are uncorrelated, they are said to be *orthogonal*. If they are correlated, then they are called *oblique*.

factorial A number obtained by multiplying together all the positive integers less than or equal to a given positive integer. Thus the factorial of 3 is $3 \times 2 \times 1 = 6$.

The factorial of a given positive integer n is usually written as $n!$, i.e.

$$n! = n \times (n-1) \times (n-2) \times \cdots \times 3 \times 2 \times 1.$$

It is spoken as 'factorial n' or 'n factorial'. By convention, zero factorial, $0!$, is defined to be equal to 1. The value of $n!$ increases rap-

factorial

n	0	1	2	3	4	5	6	7	8	9	10
$n!$	1	1	2	6	24	120	720	5040	40 320	362 880	3 628 800

idly as n increases; the table gives an indication of this.

The number of different ways of arranging n unlike objects in a row is $n!$. For example, the number of different ways of writing the 4 letters a, b, c and d in some order (e.g. abcd, dacb, ...) is $4! = 24$.

The number of different ways of arranging n unlike objects round a circle is $(n - 1)!$ if clockwise and anticlockwise arrangements are regarded as being different. Thus 6 persons can be seated round a circular table in $5! = 120$ essentially different ways. If clockwise and anticlockwise arrangements are not distinguished, then the number is $\frac{1}{2}(n - 1)!$. So if 4 beads of different colours are threaded on a ring, then $\frac{1}{2} \times 3! = 3$ different arrangements are possible (*see* diagram).

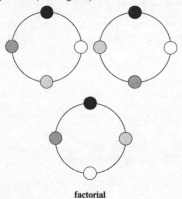

factorial

See also combination; permutation; binomial coefficients.

factorial experiment An *experimental design used to assess the effect of one or more treatments (or *factors*) occurring at two or more levels. The level of a factor may be measured quantitatively, as when the effect of operating temperature on an industrial process is tested by running the process at, say, 60, 70 and 80°C. Factors can also have qualitative levels, as when a study of children's memory for TV adverts tests the effect of two factors, the type of advert and the type of TV programme containing it, each at two levels: cartoon and non-cartoon.

When two or more factors are involved, the design enables the experimenter to assess whether the factors are independent of one another in their effects, or whether they are interdependent and there is some *interaction* between them. For example, a study of success in problem-solving could consider the effect of two factors: the degree of arousal of the participant (at a low, normal or high level) and problem difficulty (at an easy, average or hard level). If the factors are independent of one another in their effects, then the effect on performance of raising the participant's level of arousal would be the same whatever the level of problem difficulty. However, such studies tend to show that raising the level of arousal improves performance on easy problems but decreases it on hard problems. Thus there is an interaction between these two factors.

Designs can involve any number of factors and any number of levels for each factor. If all factor–level combinations are present, then a *randomized block design can be used. In an *analysis of variance of the results, the between-treatments sum of squares is separated into components associated with *main effects* (the effect of each factor independently of the others) and *interactions* (the effect of each factor dependent on the levels of one or more other factors). For example, suppose that there are two factors, A and B, each at two levels, present/absent; then there are four factor-levels, A_p, A_a, B_p, B_a, and four factor–level combinations, $A_p B_p$, $A_p B_a$, $A_a B_p$, $A_a B_a$. The main effect of A is measured by the difference between the average response when A is present and when it is absent, irrespective of the presence of B. Thus it equals the average response for combinations $A_p B_p$ and $A_p B_a$ minus the average for $A_a B_p$ and $A_a B_a$. The interaction of A and B, usually denoted by AB, is obtained by comparing the differences in response to the presence and absence of A at each of the levels of B. Thus it equals the average difference in response between combination $A_p B_p$ and combination $A_a B_p$ minus the average difference between combinations $A_p B_a$ and $A_a B_a$.

It is common, particularly in exploratory studies, for factors to be included at only two levels, e.g. present and absent or high and low. A standard notation in such situations denotes the factors by capital letters A, B, C,... and uses lower-case letters a, b, c,... to indicate the presence of the corresponding factors or their occurrence at the high level. Thus, when there are three factors A, B and C, the symbol ac, for example, denotes the combination with A and C present but B absent (or A and C high but B low). The symbol (1) is used to indicate that no factor is present (or that all are low). So the eight factor–level combinations for the three factors are denoted by (1), a, b, c, ab, ac, bc and abc. An experiment with k such two-level factors is called a 2^k-*factorial*.

family 1. A set of curves that are related by a common equation, so that all the curves can be generated by varying one or more *parameters in the equation. For example, the equation

$$y = mx$$

represents the family of straight lines passing through the origin that have finite gradients. Here the parameter m is the gradient of the line, and varying m produces the family of lines. The equation

$$y = a^x,$$

where the parameter a is positive, represents a family of *exponential curves.

The above cases are examples of *one-parameter families*. Families of curves can also be generated by varying two or more parameters. For example, in the equation

$$y = mx + c,$$

the parameters m (the gradient) and c (the y-intercept) can be varied to produce the two-parameter family of all straight lines that have finite gradients.

2. In statistics, a set of *distributions that are related by having a *frequency function that is completely specified apart from one or more *parameters which may be varied to designate all individual members of the set. For example, the general frequency function for the *Poisson distribution involves a positive parameter λ, the *mean of the distribution, and varying λ generates the family of all Poisson distributions. This is a one-parameter family and often denoted by Po(λ).

The frequency function of the *binomial distribution involves two parameters: n, the number of trials, and p, the probability of a 'success'. Varying n and p produces the family of all binomial distributions. This is a two-parameter family and is denoted by B(n, p). Similarly, the *normal distribution has a frequency function involving two parameters: μ, the mean, and σ^2, the *variance. The family of normal distributions is denoted by N(μ, σ^2).

See also chi-squared distribution; exponential distribution; F-distribution; geometric distribution; t-distribution.

F-distribution The *distribution of the ratio of two independent chi-squared variables (*see* chi-squared distribution), each divided by its *degrees of freedom. Thus, if X_1 and X_2 have independent chi-squared distributions with v_1 and v_2 degrees of freedom, respectively, then the variable X defined by

$$X = \frac{X_1/v_1}{X_2/v_2}$$

is said to have the F-distribution with v_1 and v_2 degrees of freedom. This distribution is denoted by $F(v_1, v_2)$ or F_{v_1, v_2}.

The distribution has *mean equal to

$$\frac{v_2}{v_2 - 2}, \text{ if } v_2 > 2,$$

and is approximately equal to 1 unless v_2 is small.

It is also the distribution of the ratio of two independent *unbiased estimates of the *variance of a *normal population. Thus, if the sample estimates s_1^2 and s_2^2 have v_1 and v_2 degrees of freedom, respectively, then the ratio s_1^2/s_2^2 has the F-distribution with v_1 and v_2 degrees of freedom. Because of this, the distribution has an important application in the *F-test* or *variance ratio test*.

In an *analysis of variance, the distribution is used to test the *null hypothesis that two components estimate the same variance by calculating the ratio of the larger estimate to the smaller one. A significantly high F-value leads to acceptance of the alternative hypothesis that the numerator component estimates a greater variance.

It is also used to test the hypothesis that two random samples are from normal distributions with equal variances (*see* variance ratio test).

Tables of the distribution give upper *percentage points for a comprehensive range of pairs of values of v_1 and v_2, usually at the 5%, $2\frac{1}{2}$% and 1% levels. The Appendix contains a set of such tables. Statistical packages will give *p-values associated with F-values. For example, when $v_1 = 4$ and $v_2 = 8$, an F-value of 2.70 has $p = 0.108$, so that 10.8% of the $F(4, 8)$ distribution exceeds 2.70. Table 6(a) in the Appendix

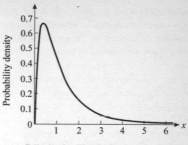

F-distribution The distribution $F(4, 8)$.

gives a 5% upper percentage point of 3.84, so 5% of this distribution exceeds 3.84.

The *t-distribution is closely related to a particular F-distribution. For if a random variable X has the t-distribution with v degrees of freedom, then the distribution of X^2 is identical to $F(1, v)$, i.e. the F-distribution with $v_1 = 1$ and $v_2 = v$.

The distribution was first tabulated and used by G.W. Snedecor, who named it the F-distribution in honour of the statistician R.A. Fisher. It is sometimes referred to as *Snedecor's F-distribution*.

Fisher–Freeman–Halton test *See* Fisher's exact test.

Fisher–Pitman test *See* permutation test.

Fisher's exact test A test for lack of association (independence) in a 2×2 *contingency table. It is available in most statistical software packages. It is sometimes called the *Fisher–Yates test* or the *Fisher–Irwin test*.

To illustrate its principles, consider the following table which gives the results of alternative medical treatments A and B on a small sample of 20 patients, and the marginal totals:

	Successful	Unsuccessful	Total
Treatment A	9	1	10
Treatment B	5	5	10
Total	14	6	

Under the *null hypothesis that the outcomes were independent of which treatment was given, then, with the above marginal totals, the table would be expected to be:

	Successful	Unsuccessful	Total
Treatment A	7	3	10
Treatment B	7	3	10
Total	14	6	

Fisher's test calculates the probability that, under the null hypothesis, a table of results is obtained which differs from the expected as much as or even more than the observed table. If the alternative hypothesis is that treatments A and B differ in effectiveness, then it calculates the probability of obtaining one of the following tables:

9	1		10	0		5	5		4	6
5	5		4	6		9	1		10	0

These correspond to treatment A achieving 2 or 3 more cures than the 7 expected, or 2 or 3 less than expected. This probability equals $0.0650 + 0.0054 + 0.0054 + 0.0650 = 0.142$. This is greater than 0.05, so the hypothesis that the treatments do not differ in effectiveness is retained.

However, if the alternative hypothesis is that treatment A is more effective than B, then the test calculates only the probability of obtaining one of these two tables:

9	1		10	0
5	5		4	6

This probability equals $0.0650 + 0.0054 = 0.0704$. This too is greater than 0.05, so the hypothesis that treatments do not differ in effectiveness is retained.

The calculations of probabilities are based on the fact that the probability of obtaining a table

a	b
c	d

when the marginal totals are fixed at $a + b$ and $c + d$ for the rows, and $a + c$ and $b + d$ for the columns, is

$$\frac{(a+b)!(c+d)!(a+c)!(b+d)!}{n!a!b!c!d!},$$

where $n = a + b + c + d$, and $n!$ etc. denotes *factorial n.

If the numbers in the cells are large, then the test can involve the calculation and summation of a considerable number of probabilities. The availability of statistical packages has removed the necessity for such tedious calculations. If the numbers in the cells are not too low, the *chi-squared test is a good approximation to this test.

The *Fisher–Freeman–Halton test* is an extension of this exact test to larger $r \times c$ tables, and is available in some software packages.

Fisher's z-transformation The transformation of the product moment *correlation coefficient r given by

$$z = \frac{1}{2} \ln\left(\frac{1+r}{1-r}\right).$$

When samples of n pairs of values are taken from a *bivariate normal distribution whose correlation coefficient is ρ, and n is large enough (e.g. 20 or more), z has an approximately *normal distribution with *mean

$$\frac{1}{2} \ln\left(\frac{1+\rho}{1-\rho}\right)$$

and *variance $1/(n-3)$. The transformation then enables a *confidence interval for ρ to be estimated from a sample coefficient r, or a significance test to be carried out (*see* hypothesis testing).

The function

$$\frac{1}{2} \ln\left(\frac{1+r}{1-r}\right)$$

is identical to the inverse hyperbolic function $\tanh^{-1} r$.

five-number summary Five numbers in ascending order giving a summary of a set of data. They are the least value, the lower *quartile, the *median, the upper quartile and the greatest value. They provide information about the location, dispersion and symmetry (if any) of the observations. For example, the five-number summary 21, 44, 50, 57, 75 indicates a set of observations ranging from 21 to 75, with half of them between 44 and 57, while the summary 5, 15, 22, 46, 95 indicates an asymmetric set with a greater range and a lower median.

The information in a five-number summary can be given a graphical representation in the form of a *box-and-whisker diagram or box plot. This is a useful aid when comparing two or more summaries.

Footsie 100 *See* FTSE share index.

fourfold point correlation *See* phi coefficient.

frame (sampling frame) A listing, map or other form of specification of all units in a *population in sufficient detail for the selection of samples. If *stratified samples are required, the frame will need to contain appropriate information on each unit. The UK Register of Electors provides a frame of all people in each district eligible to vote in parliamentary elections. The Driver and Vehicle Licensing Agency has a frame of all persons in the UK licensed to drive a road vehicle. A database kept by a mail-order firm and containing details of all its customers and their purchases could serve as a frame for a survey of customer opinion and satisfaction. A reasonably accurate frame is a prerequisite for a reliable survey. However, frames may be incomplete, inaccurate, or out of date to some degree.

Frechet distribution *See* extreme value distribution.

frequency The number of times a particular value or event occurs in a set of observations. It is sometimes called the *absolute frequency*. For example, the number of words in each title in a sample of 20 books were found to be

1,   1,   2,   2,   2,   2,   2,   2,   2,   3,
3,   3,   4,   4,   4,   4,   4,   5,   5,   6.

The frequency of 4 is 5, and that of 6 is 1. The data can be presented as follows:

Number of words in title	1	2	3	4	5	6
Frequency		2	7	3	5	2	1

This is called a *frequency table*. The sum of the frequencies is 20, the number of books in the sample. Similarly, if the results (win, draw, loss) of the last 10 matches played by a team were

W,   D,   W,   L,   D,   D,   W,   L,   W,   W,

then the event 'win' has frequency 5 in this set of matches.

The *relative frequency* of an observation is found by dividing its frequency by the total number of observations. In the examples above, the relative frequency of a book title with 4 words is $5/20 = 0.25$, and the relative frequency of a win is $5/10 = 0.5$. A relative frequency gives the *proportion* of the observations taking a particular form. Thus, a quarter of the sample of books had titles with 4 words, and half the matches were wins.

A *class frequency* is the number of observations falling in a particular *class interval*. In the first of the above examples, the class frequency for the interval '4 words or more' is 8.

The *cumulative frequency* associated with a particular value is the number of values less than or equal to this value. It is equal to the sum of the frequencies of all values less than or equal to the stated value. Thus in our first example, the cumulative frequency for 2 is 9, and this is equal to the sum of 2 and 7, the frequencies of 1 and 2, respectively. Cumulative frequencies are sometimes called *absolute cumulative frequencies*.

The *cumulative relative frequency* or *cumulative proportion* for a particular value is found by dividing its cumulative frequency by the total number of observations. This gives the proportion of the observations less than or equal to this value. When it is expressed as a percentage, it is called a *cumulative percentage*. In our first example, the cumulative relative frequency for 2 is $9/20 = 0.45$, the cumulative percentage being 45%. This indicates that almost half the sample of books had titles with 2 words or less.

See grouped data; probability.

frequency curve A smooth curve approximating a *frequency polygon for a large set of observations which have been grouped using small *class intervals. The term is also used for the graph of the *frequency function of a continuous variable. *See also* distribution curve.

frequency distribution A specification in some form of the frequencies or relative frequencies with which values of a variable occur.

For observed data, the distribution will usually be given in a *frequency table of some form. It can be represented graphically by means of a *bar chart, *histogram or *stem-and-leaf diagram.

A theoretical frequency distribution is specified by giving either its *frequency function or its *distribution function.

frequency function For a discrete *distribution, the frequency function gives the probability with which the random variable takes individual values. Common alternative names for the frequency function of a

discrete distribution are *probability function* and *probability mass function*.

More formally, the frequency function $f(x)$ gives the probability that the random variable X takes the value x, i.e.

$$f(x) = \Pr(X = x).$$

For example, a single decimal digit chosen at random is a discrete random variable X taking each one of the values 0, 1, 2, 3, ..., 9 with a probability of $\frac{1}{10}$. The frequency function is given as

$$f(x) = \tfrac{1}{10} \quad \text{for } x = 0, 1, 2, 3, \ldots, 9.$$

Similarly, if a fair coin is tossed repeatedly until a 'head' is obtained, the number of tosses needed to obtain the first 'head' is a discrete random variable X taking the values $1, 2, 3, 4, \ldots$ with probabilities of $\frac{1}{2}, \frac{1}{4}, \frac{1}{8}, \frac{1}{16}, \ldots$, respectively. So in this case, the frequency function is given as

$$f(x) = \left(\tfrac{1}{2}\right)^x \quad \text{for } x = 1, 2, 3, 4, \ldots.$$

Both the above frequency functions are shown graphically in diagram (a). In all cases the sum of the frequencies is equal to 1.

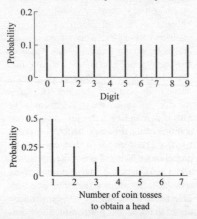

frequency function (a) for a decimal digit chosen at random and the number of coin tosses needed to first obtain a 'head'.

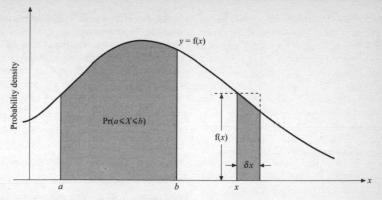

frequency function (b) for a continuous distribution.

For a set of discrete data, the frequency function (sometimes called the *relative frequency function*) gives the relative frequency of each x-value. For example, if for a group of 100 households the numbers having 0, 1, 2, 3 and 4 television sets are 1, 42, 37, 16 and 4, respectively, then the frequency function is such that $f(0) - 0.01$, $f(1) = 0.42, f(2) = 0.37, f(3) = 0.16$ and $f(4) = 0.04$.

For a continuous distribution, the frequency function $f(x)$ is the function whose *integral from $x=a$ to $x=b$ equals the probability that the continuous random variable X takes a value in the interval $a \leqslant X \leqslant b$. Thus,

$$\Pr(a \leqslant X \leqslant b) = \int_a^b f(x)\,dx.$$

This is equivalent to saying that the probability equals the area under the curve $y = f(x)$ between $x=a$ and $x=b$. The probability that X takes a value between x and $x+\delta x$, where δx is small, equals an area close to $f(x)\delta x$ (*see* diagram (b)). Thus the frequency function $f(x)$ is a measure of the probability with which the variable takes values in the immediate neighbourhood of an individual value x. It gives the *probability density* of X at x.

A common alternative name for the frequency function of a continuous distribution is *probability density function*.

If the continuous distribution has *distribution function $F(x)$, then

$$f(x) = F'(x).$$

The graph of the frequency function is sometimes called the *frequency curve* and, since areas beneath the curve represent probabilities, the entire area between the curve and the x-axis must be equal to 1.

For example, suppose that the continuous variable X has frequency function $f(x)$ defined by

$$f(x) = \begin{cases} \frac{1}{9}x^2 & \text{for } 0 \leqslant x \leqslant 3, \\ 0 & \text{otherwise.} \end{cases}$$

The frequency curve is shown in diagram (c); the area between the curve and the x-axis equals 1. The probability that X takes a value between 0 and 1 is found by integration to equal $\frac{1}{27}$:

$$\Pr(0 \leqslant X \leqslant 1) = \int_0^1 \frac{1}{9}x^2\,dx = \left[\frac{1}{27}x^3\right]_0^1 = \frac{1}{27}.$$

The probabilities of X falling between 1 and 2 and between 2 and 3 are found to be $\frac{7}{27}$ and $\frac{19}{27}$, respectively. These values reflect the way the probability density increases as X takes

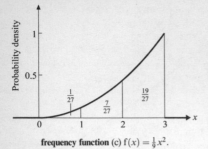

frequency function (c) $f(x) = \frac{1}{9}x^2$.

larger values. It is much more likely to take values near to 3 than values near to 1.

frequency polygon A figure obtained by joining the mid-points of the tops of the rectangles of a *histogram, in succession. *See* frequency curve.

frequency table A table that summarizes a set of observations by giving the *frequency (or relative frequency) with which each value or event occurs. It is sometimes extended to include cumulative frequencies (or cumulative relative frequencies).

For example, if the number of e-mails received each day over a 20-day period were

4, 1, 2, 0, 2, 4, 2, 5, 3, 3,
6, 1, 4, 5, 3, 2, 6, 2, 4, 1,

then the table of frequencies and cumulative frequencies is as in table (a). A table giving relative frequencies would be table (b).

Sometimes it is more useful or practical to group the data before constructing a frequency table. The table then gives the frequency with which observations fall into the (non-overlapping) groups. For instance, if the data were the ages of 2000 patients in a hospital, a large number of different ages might be recorded, and to form an impression of the age profile of the patients some form of grouping, e.g. 'under 5', '5 to 9', etc. is desirable (*see* grouped data).

See also contingency table.

frequential inference *See* Bayesian inference.

Friedman's test A *nonparametric test using *ranks for testing equality of treatment means in a *randomized blocks design involving three or more treatments or conditions. It is particularly useful where a two-way *analysis of variance is inappropriate, which is the case when data cannot be assumed to come from *normal distributions with equal *variances, or when data are available only in the form of ranks.

When there are $k \geqslant 3$ treatments and N groups of matched units (or N subjects in a *repeated measures design), the data for the test are ranks set out in an $N \times k$ table. Each row contains the responses of a block (or a subject) to the k treatments, ranked 1 to k. The *null hypothesis is that the columns of ranks are random samples from the same population and thus have the same means (and column totals).

To illustrate the procedure, suppose that a company's market researcher is trying to find the best advertisement for a product,

frequency table (a)

E-mails received in a day	0	1	2	3	4	5	6
Frequency	1	3	5	3	4	2	2
Cumulative frequency	1	4	9	12	16	18	20

frequency table (b)

E-mails received in a day	0	1	2	3	4	5	6
Relative frequency	0.05	0.15	0.25	0.15	0.2	0.1	0.1
Cumulative relative frequency	0.05	0.2	0.45	0.6	0.8	0.9	1.0

and asks five sales managers to independently rank three possible advertisements, A, B and C, in ascending order from 1 to 3. The results and the sums of the ranks in each column are given in the following table:

Manager	Advertisement		
	A	B	C
a	3	1	2
b	2	1	3
c	3	2	1
d	3	1	2
e	3	1	2
Column total (T)	14	6	10

The Friedman test statistic is often denoted by χ_r^2 and is calculated from this table using the formula

$$\chi_r^2 = \frac{12}{Nk(k+1)} \sum T^2 - 3N(k+1)$$

where k is the number of conditions or treatments, N is the number of subjects or groups of matched subjects and $\sum T^2$ is the sum of the squares of the column totals (T). In our example, $k = 3$, $N = 5$, and the column totals are 14, 6 and 10. Thus

$$\chi_r^2 = \frac{12}{5 \times 3 \times 4}(14^2 + 6^2 + 10^2) - 3 \times 5 \times 4$$
$$= 6.4$$

Significantly high values of χ_r^2 lead to rejection of the null hypothesis.

Under the null hypothesis, when N and/or k are reasonably large, the distribution of χ_r^2 is approximately a *chi-squared distribution with $k - 1$ degrees of freedom. So, for example, when N is large and $k = 3$, the chi-squared tables for $3 - 1 = 2$ degrees of freedom indicate that χ_r^2 needs to exceed 5.99 to be significant at the 5% level. However, for small values of N and k, tables of exact critical values of χ_r^2 are available. Some statistical packages will give *p-values for this test. In our example $N = 5$ and $k = 3$, and tables state that the least value for significance at the 5% level is 6.4 (its *p-value is 0.039). Thus the ratings of the advertisements differ significantly at the 5% level when assessed by rank totals. Advertisement A is rated the best, and B the worst.

Suppose that, before the experiment, the researcher predicted that advertisement A would be preferred to C, and C to B. To assess whether the data lend significant support to this hypothesis, a *trend test such as the *Page test is appropriate.

See also coefficient of concordance.

F-test A statistical test involving the *F-distribution. *See* variance ratio test.

FTSE share index A *Financial Times* share index, one of several *indices compiled by the newspaper, minute by minute during trading, from share prices on the London Stock Exchange. The *FTSE 100*, or '*Footsie 100*', is the weighted arithmetic *mean of the prices of the hundred largest quoted companies, with the current capital values of the companies as weights. The base point, when the index was set at 1000, is 3 January 1984. On 9 January 2004, the FTSE 100 closed at 4466.30. *See also* geometric mean.

FT30 Share Index *See* geometric mean.

function A rule or operation that associates with each element x of some *set X a unique element y of a set Y; this is written as $y = f(x)$, where f denotes the function. Thus the operation of squaring is a function that associates with each number x its square, the number x^2. The *factorial function associates, with each positive integer n, its factorial, the positive integer $n!$. There are various notations for functions, e.g. the square function might be referred to as

$$y = x^2 \quad \text{or} \quad x^2 \quad \text{or} \quad f : x \mapsto x^2$$

For a function $y = f(x)$, the set X is called

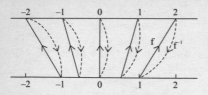

function The action of a function f and of its inverse function f^{-1}.

the *domain* and the set Y is called the *co-domain* of the function. The set of all the elements $f(x)$ is the *range* of the function. Such a function is called a *function of x*, and x is called the *independent variable* or *argument*, while y is called the *dependent variable*. Not all functions can be expressed algebraically. For example, the function 'word length' associates with each word the number of letters in it.

A graph consisting of the points with coordinates (x, y), where $y = f(x)$, is called the *graph* of the function f.

A function f, associating a unique element y with each element x, may have an *inverse function* f^{-1} which reverses the association. For example, the function f defined by $y = 2x$, which doubles each number x, has an inverse f^{-1}, defined by $y = \frac{1}{2}x$, which halves each number (*see* diagram).

Thus f associates with 6 the number 12, since $f(6) = 12$, while its inverse associates with 12 the number 6, since $f^{-1}(12) = \frac{1}{2} \times 12 = 6$.

However, not all functions have inverses. For example, the function 'word length' has no inverse since there is no unique word associated with any particular number of letters.

In statistics, the *normal distribution function $\Phi(z)$ gives the cumulative probability corresponding to a z-value. Thus the probability that z is less than or equal to 1.96 is given by $\Phi(1.96) = 0.975$. The inverse function Φ^{-1} gives the z-value corresponding to a cumulative probability. Thus the z-value whose cumulative probability is 0.9 is $\Phi^{-1}(0.9) = 1.6449$.

The idea of functionality extends to functions with two or more independent variables. For example, the area A of a rectangle is lb, where l is its length and b is its breadth. So A is a function of two variables. Here, l and b are the independent variables and A is the dependent variable.

See also continuous function; exponential function; linear function; polynomial function.

Gaussian distribution *See* normal distribution.

generalized linear model *See* model.

generating function *See* moment generating function; probability generating function.

GenStat *Abbreviation for* Generalized Statistical Package. *See* statistical software packages.

geographical coordinates Coordinates used to describe position on the Earth's surface with respect to the equator and the prime (Greenwich) meridian. The position of a point is specified by its latitude (angular distance from 0° to 90° north or south of the equator) and longitude (angular distance from 0° to 180° east or west of the Greenwich meridian).

geometric distribution A discrete *distribution in which the frequencies or probabilities of the values of the variable decrease in *geometric progression as the variable increases. For example, if a fair die is rolled repeatedly until a 6 is obtained, the chance of obtaining the 6 with the first throw is $\frac{1}{6}$. The chance that it takes 2 throws to obtain a 6 is $\frac{1}{6} \times \frac{5}{6}$; the chance that it takes 3 throws is $\frac{1}{6} \times \left(\frac{5}{6}\right)^2$; and, in general, the chance that it takes r throws to obtain a 6 is $\frac{1}{6} \times \left(\frac{5}{6}\right)^{r-1}$. These results are given in the following table and diagram. It can be seen that the probabilities are a geometric pro-

gression with first term $\frac{1}{6}$ and common ratio $\frac{5}{6}$.

Number of throws to obtain a 6	1	2	3	...	r	...
Probability	$\frac{1}{6}$	$\frac{1}{6} \times \frac{5}{6}$	$\frac{1}{6} \times \left(\frac{5}{6}\right)^2$	...	$\frac{1}{6} \times \left(\frac{5}{6}\right)^{r-1}$	...

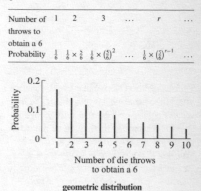

geometric distribution

This illustrates the general result that the number of trials, X, up to and including the first success in a series of *Bernoulli trials, has a geometric distribution. For if p is the probability of success in each trial and $q(= 1 - p)$ the probability of failure, then the probability that it takes r trials to obtain the first success is pq^{r-1}. So the random variable X has *frequency function

$$\Pr(X = r) = pq^{r-1}, \quad \text{where} \quad r = 1, 2, 3, \ldots,$$

and the distribution of X can be tabulated as follows:

Number of trials up to first success	1	2	3	...	r	...
Probability	p	pq	pq^2	...	pq^{r-1}	...

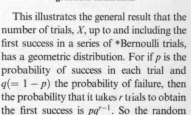

This distribution has *mean $1/p$ and *variance q/p^2. It is sometimes denoted by Geo(p). In our example, the number of throws needed to obtain a 6 has the distribution Geo($\frac{1}{6}$). The mean is $1 \div \frac{1}{6} = 6$, i.e. it takes an average of six throws to obtain a 6, and the variance is 30.

The number of failures, Y, before the first success also has a geometric distribution. The frequency function is

$$\Pr(Y = r) = pq^r, \quad \text{where} \quad r = 0, 1, 2, \ldots,$$

and the distribution of Y can be tabulated as follows:

Number of failures before first success	0	1	2	...	r	...
Probability	p	pq	pq^2	...	pq^r	...

This distribution has mean q/p and variance q/p^2. If the time one has to wait for the first success is measured by the number of failures that precede it, then Y can be regarded as the *waiting time* to the first success. For example, if a person repeatedly enters a lottery in which the probability of winning a prize is $\frac{1}{10}$ on each occasion, then the number of failures before the first win has the distribution given in the table at the foot of the page. Since $p = 0.1$ and $q = 0.9$, the mean is $0.9/0.1 = 9$. Thus the person should expect to fail 9 times before first winning a prize, i.e. a waiting time of 9 entries.

See negative binomial distribution.

geometric mean *See* mean.

geometric progression (geometric sequence) A *sequence in which the ratio of each term (except the first) to the preceding term is a constant, the *common ratio*. For example, the geometric progression whose first five terms are

$$3, 6, 12, 24, 48$$

has common ratio equal to 2.

In general, if the first term is a and the common ratio is r, then the progression takes the form

$$a, ar, ar^2, ar^3, \ldots$$

and the nth term is ar^{n-1}.

If $r \neq 1$, the sum of the first n terms is given by

$$\frac{a(1 - r^n)}{1 - r} \quad \text{or} \quad \frac{a(r^n - 1)}{r - 1}.$$

In our example, $a = 3$ and $r = 2$. The sum of the first 10 terms of the progression will be

$$\frac{3(2^{10} - 1)}{2 - 1} = 3069.$$

Compare arithmetic progression. *See* geometric distribution; Malthus model.

geometric series A *series of the form

$$a + ar + ar^2 + ar^3 + \cdots$$

whose terms are those of a *geometric progression with first term a and common ratio r. If $r \neq 1$ and the number of terms is n, the sum s_n is given by

$$s_n = \frac{a(1 - r^n)}{1 - r} \quad \text{or} \quad \frac{a(r^n - 1)}{r - 1}.$$

If it is an infinite series and $|r| < 1$, i.e. $-1 < r < 1$, then it is a *convergent series and its sum (or *sum to infinity*) is

$$\frac{a}{1 - r}.$$

geometric distribution

Number of failures before first win	0	1	2	...	r	...
Probability	0.1	0.1×0.9	$0.1 \times (0.9)^2$	...	$0.1 \times (0.9)^r$	...

Thus the infinite geometric series

$$1 + \frac{1}{3} + \frac{1}{9} + \frac{1}{27} + \cdots,$$

which has first term $a = 1$ and common ratio $r = \frac{1}{3}$, is convergent and its sum is

$$\frac{1}{1 - \frac{1}{3}} = \frac{3}{2} = 1\frac{1}{2}.$$

The sum of all the probabilities in the *geometric distribution Geo(p) is given by

$$p + pq + pq^2 + pq^3 + \cdots,$$

where $q = 1 - p$. This is an infinite geometric series with first term $a = p$ and common ratio $r = q$. It is convergent since $0 < q < 1$, and its sum is

$$\frac{p}{1 - q} = \frac{p}{p} = 1.$$

Gini coefficient A measure of the degree of inequality in the distribution of an economic quantity such as income or wealth. *See* Lorenz curve.

global maximum *See* maximum.

global minimum *See* minimum.

goodness of fit In general, the closeness of agreement between a set of observations and a hypothetical set obtained from a *model which attempts to fit the data. In particular, the term is used when fitting a theoretical distribution such as a *normal distribution to observations of one variable, and to the fitting of *regression lines to pairs of observations of two variables. The closeness of agreement is often measured by a quantity involving the squares of the differences between certain observed and theoretical values. When the model is chosen so that this quantity has a minimum value, the goodness of fit is said to be *best*, based on the least-squares criterion. *See* chi-squared test; least squares; line of best fit; Kolmogorov–Smirnov tests.

gradient The slope, i.e. the inclination to the horizontal. It is expressed in various ways, for example as the angle a line or plane makes with the horizontal, i.e. the slope angle. In mathematics it is usually taken to be the tangent of the slope angle, i.e. the vertical distance risen per horizontal distance travelled along the line or plane. In this sense, the gradient of the line passing through the points with coordinates (x_1, y_1), (x_2, y_2) is equal to

$$\frac{y_2 - y_1}{x_2 - x_1}.$$

For example, the line passing through $A(2, 1)$ and $B(4, 5)$ has gradient

$$(5 - 1)/(4 - 2) = 2,$$

so that the line rises 2 units for every unit travelled in the positive x-direction. The line passing through $A(2, 1)$ and $C(4, 0)$ has gradient

$$(0 - 1)/(4 - 2) = -\tfrac{1}{2}.$$

The negative sign indicates that the line *falls* half a unit for every unit travelled in the positive x-direction (*see* diagram).

The equation of a line with gradient m is expressible in the form $y = mx + c$, where c is some constant. For example, the equation

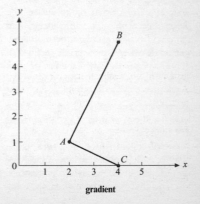

gradient

of AB, which has gradient 2, can be written as $y = 2x - 3$.

Parallel lines have equal gradients. A line parallel to the y-axis, i.e. a vertical line, is said to have infinite gradient. A line parallel to the x-axis, i.e. a horizontal line, has zero gradient.

The gradient of a curve at a particular point is equal to the gradient of the tangent to the curve at that point, if it has one. It is equal to the value of the *derivative at that point. So, for the curve with equation $y = x^3$ and derivative $dy/dx = 3x^2$, the gradient of the curve at the point $(2, 8)$ on it is equal to $3 \times 2^2 = 12$.

Graeco-Latin square A square *array of Greek letters $(\alpha, \beta, \gamma, \ldots)$ and Latin letters $(A, B, C, \ldots)$ in which each Greek or Latin letter occurs once in each row or column, and each Latin letter is paired once with each Greek letter. An example of a 4×4 square is:

$A\alpha$	$B\beta$	$C\gamma$	$D\delta$
$B\gamma$	$A\delta$	$D\alpha$	$C\beta$
$C\delta$	$D\gamma$	$A\beta$	$B\alpha$
$D\beta$	$C\alpha$	$B\delta$	$A\gamma$

In statistics, Graeco-Latin squares are used as an *experimental design which involves three possible sources of variation apart from the treatments. This is done by identifying the three sources with the rows, columns and Greek letters of the square, and the treatments with the Latin letters. Thus there is a *four-way classification* of observations. It is an extension of the method of *Latin squares from two sources of variation to three sources. Alternatively, it provides a design in which there are two independent treatments (Greek and Latin letters) and two sources of variation (rows and columns).

A problem is that for small squares the number of degrees of freedom of the error mean square in the *analysis of variance is low. This difficulty can be overcome by using more than one square. The restriction that each source of variation must have the same number of types as the treatments can present practical difficulties that may outweigh any benefits associated with the design.

grand mean *See* analysis of variance.

graph 1. A diagram showing a relationship between two *variables. It is usually drawn using a *Cartesian coordinate system with an x-axis and y-axis at right angles. If, for example, the y-axis is vertical and the x-axis is horizontal, the graph is sometimes called a *graph* (or *plot*) *of* y *against* x.

In two dimensions, the graph of an equation is a curve containing the points whose coordinates satisfy the equation. For example, the graph of the equation $y = x^2$ is the curve containing all the points, such as $(2, 4)$ and $(-1, 1)$, whose x- and y-coordinates satisfy the equation. A graph of a *function $f(x)$ is the graph of the equation $y = f(x)$.

A graph of an inequality, in two dimensions, is a region containing the points whose coordinates satisfy the inequality. Thus the graph of the inequality $y > x^2$ is the region containing all points, such as $(2, 5)$ and $(-1, 2)$, whose coordinates satisfy the inequality (*see* diagram (a)).

Graphs of equations (or functions) can be plotted by taking a number of values of x and calculating the corresponding values of y from the equation. The points are marked on *graph paper*, and a smooth curve is drawn through them. Graphs can also be drawn using the graphical package of a calculator or computer.

Although graphs are mostly drawn on squared graph paper, other types of paper or scaling are sometimes used. A *logarithmic* or *log–log graph* is one in which both axes are marked with a *logarithmic scale. An equation of the form $y = ax^n$, where a and n are constants, has a straight-line graph when plotted on *logarithmic paper* (*see* diagram (b)). A *semi-logarithmic graph* is one in

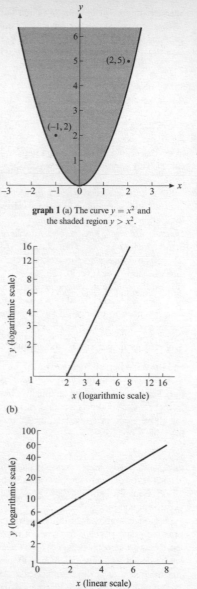

graph 1 (a) The curve $y = x^2$ and the shaded region $y > x^2$.

graph 1 (b) The log–log graph of $y = \frac{1}{4}x^2$
(c) The semi-logarithmic graph of $y = 4(1.4)^x$.

which one axis has a logarithmic scale and the other has a linear scale. An equation of the form $y = ab^x$, where a and b are constants, has a straight-line graph when plotted on semi-logarithmic paper (*see* diagram (c)).

See also bar chart; scatter diagram.

2. A set of points, called *vertices* or *nodes*, and a set of lines, called *edges*, connecting some or all of the vertices in pairs. An edge joining a vertex to itself is called a *loop*. The *degree* of a vertex is the number of edges containing it (*see* diagram (a)). A *connected graph* is one in which each vertex can be reached *via* the edges from every other vertex. A *directed graph* (*digraph*) or *network* is one in which the edges have directions and are called *arcs* (*see* diagram (b)).

See tree; tree diagram.

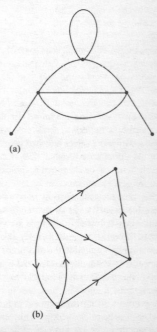

graph 2 (a) A graph with five vertices and one loop. (b) A network with four vertices.

grouped data Data consisting of the *frequencies (or relative frequencies) with which observed values of a variable fall into a set of non-overlapping intervals. These intervals are called *class intervals*, their endpoints are called *class boundaries*, and the number of values falling in a particular interval is the *class frequency*. For example, if the systolic blood pressure x mmHg (millimetres of mercury) is measured for 200 adults and five class intervals are used, the grouped data in the following table might be obtained.

Interval	Number of adults
$80 \leqslant x < 100$	2
$100 \leqslant x < 120$	46
$120 \leqslant x < 140$	112
$140 \leqslant x < 160$	37
$160 \leqslant x < 180$	3

Class intervals do not all need to be of the same width, though they often are, and sometimes have only one boundary, e.g. $x < 80$. With a suitable choice of intervals, grouped data can give an impression of the distribution underlying a sample. In this example, the distribution appears to be symmetrical, with most values bunched around a central value of approximately 130. In this form, the data can be illustrated graphically by means of a *histogram.

When data are available only in grouped form, estimates of the *mean, *variance and *standard deviation of the sample are still possible. These are obtained by taking each observation to be equal to the mid-point of the interval in which it falls. This mid-point is called the *mid-interval value*. So in our example, the 2 adults with pressures in the interval $80 \leqslant x < 100$ are assumed to have blood pressures of 90 mmHg. The other mid-interval values are 110, 130, 150 and 170, and the estimate of the mean blood pressure is

$$m = \frac{1}{120}(2 \times 90 + 46 \times 110 + 112 \times 130$$
$$+ 37 \times 150 + 3 \times 170)$$
$$= 129.3.$$

If it is assumed that the measurements are from a *normal distribution, then estimation of the variance is improved by subtracting $h^2/12$, where h is the interval width, from the estimate based on mid-interval values. This adjustment is known as *Sheppard's correction*.

Some care is needed when stating class intervals and calculating mid-interval values for data which have been rounded. For example, the ages, y years, of a sample of doctors might be grouped into classes '25 to 29', '30 to 34', etc. In this case the class intervals are $25 \leqslant y < 30$, $30 \leqslant y < 35$, etc., and the mid-interval values are 27.5, 32.5, etc. Similarly, the doctor's weights w kg (rounded to the nearest kg) might be grouped into classes such as '60 to 64', '65 to 69', etc. In this case the intervals are $59.5 \leqslant w < 64.5$, $64.5 \leqslant w < 69.5$, etc., and the mid-interval values are 62, 67, etc.

A grouped *cumulative frequency table* is obtained by calculating the *cumulative frequency for each of the class boundaries. For the above blood-pressure data, the following table is obtained:

Pressure	Cumulative frequency
80	0
100	2
120	48
140	160
160	197
180	200

A graph in which cumulative frequency is plotted against class boundaries is a *cumulative frequency polygon* (*see* diagram).

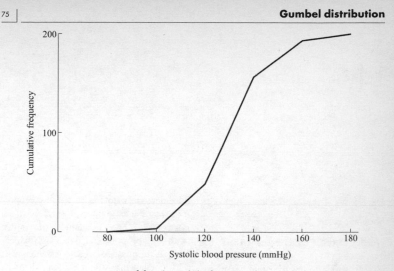

grouped data A cumulative frequency polygon.

Estimates of *quantiles, such as the *median and *quartiles, can be made from grouped data. In our example, the estimate of the median is the blood pressure corresponding to a cumulative frequency of 100 and clearly lies in the interval $120 \leqslant x < 140$. The estimate can be improved by linear *interpolation or by taking a reading from the cumulative frequency polygon.

grouping *See* grouped data; matched pairs; randomized blocks.

g-statistics The *statistics g_1, g_2, which are the sample equivalents of γ_1, γ_2, the population measures of *skewness and *kurtosis.

Gumbel distribution *See* extreme value distribution.

H

H₀, H₁ *See* hypothesis testing.

harmonic mean *See* mean.

Hartley's test An extension of the *variance ratio test to more than two samples. It is used to test the *null hypothesis that m (>2) random samples of equal size n are from *normal populations having equal variances, against the alternative hypothesis that at least one population has a different variance. It is based on the ratio of the largest and smallest sample variances. More formally, if the unbiased estimates of variance for each of the m samples are $s_1^2, s_2^2, \ldots, s_m^2$, then the test statistic H is given by

$$H = \frac{\max(s_1^2, s_2^2, \ldots, s_m^2)}{\min(s_1^2, s_2^2, \ldots, s_m^2)}.$$

A significantly high value of H leads to rejection of the null hypothesis. Tables of the distribution commonly give critical values for a comprehensive range of pairs of values of m and n. *See also* Bartlett's test; Levene's test.

heteroscedastic **1.** Describing a set of variables with unequal *variances.
2. Describing a *bivariate (or *multivariate) distribution in which no variable has constant variance for all fixed values of the other variable (or other variables). *Compare* homoscedastic.

histogram A graphical representation of *grouped data. The horizontal axis is divided into segments with lengths proportional to the class intervals, and, on these segments as bases, rectangles are drawn with areas proportional to the class frequencies, i.e. the numbers in each class interval. If all the class intervals are equal, then the heights of the rectangles are proportional to the class frequencies (*see* diagram (a)). When the class intervals are not all equal, the height of each rectangle is proportional to

$$\frac{\text{class frequency}}{\text{length of class interval}}.$$

In either case, the height of each rectangle represents a *frequency density*, i.e. the frequency with which data are falling in some standard length of interval.

To illustrate the case when the class intervals are not all equal, the table gives grouped data for the ages (x years) of 181 female cases of rubella in an epidemic, and the calculations of frequency density for the accompanying histogram (diagram (b)).

See also circular histogram; rose diagram.

Hodges–Ajne test A *nonparametric test used to investigate whether a sample of n *angular data, e.g. times of day or compass directions, comes from a *uniform distribution. The n observations are identified with points on the circumference of a circle, and the semicircle containing the least number of points (m) is found. Under the *null hypothesis that the distribution is uniform,

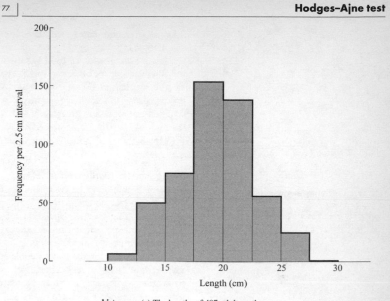

histogram (a) The lengths of 487 adult earthworms.

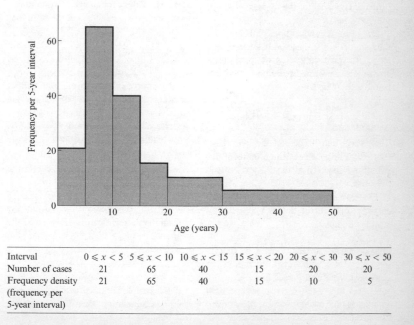

Interval	$0 \leqslant x < 5$	$5 \leqslant x < 10$	$10 \leqslant x < 15$	$15 \leqslant x < 20$	$20 \leqslant x < 30$	$30 \leqslant x < 50$
Number of cases	21	65	40	15	20	20
Frequency density (frequency per 5-year interval)	21	65	40	15	10	5

histogram (b) The ages of 181 female cases of rubella.

Hodges–Ajne test

the probability of obtaining m points or fewer is given by the formula

$$\frac{1}{2^{n-1}} \binom{n}{m} (n - 2m),$$

where $m < n/3$ and $\binom{n}{m}$ is a *binomial coefficient. A significantly low value of this probability leads to the rejection of the null hypothesis.

For example, the sample of 16 angular data shown in the diagram has $n = 16$ and $m = 2$. The probability that a sample of size 16 from a uniform distribution of points round a circle has $m \leqslant 2$ is

$$\frac{1}{2^{15}} \binom{16}{2} (16 - 4) = 0.0439.$$

This is less than 0.05, and the hypothesis that the sample comes from a uniform distribution is rejected at the 5% level of significance.

The test has been applied to data sets such as times of birth of babies and dates of suicide attempts.

homoscedastic 1. Describing a set of random variables with equal *variances. A basic assumption in F-tests (see F-distribution) and the *t-test for two independent samples is that the variables being sampled are homoscedastic. *See* variance ratio test; Bartlett's test; Hartley's test; Levene's test.

2. Describing a *bivariate (or *multivariate) distribution in which the variance of one variable is constant for all fixed values of the other variable (or other variables). The variable with constant variance is said to be homoscedastic in the other (or others). A common assumption in *regression is that the response variable is homoscedastic in the explanatory variable(s). *Compare* heteroscedastic.

hypergeometric distribution The *distribution of the number of 'successes' obtained when a *random sample is drawn *without replacement* from a finite population containing a number of items termed 'successes', the remainder being termed 'failures'.

More formally, suppose that a sample of size n is drawn without replacement from a population of N items, in which R items have some property and are 'successes', while the remaining $N - R$ items are 'failures'. Then the probability of obtaining r successes and $n - r$ failures in the sample is

$$\binom{R}{r} \binom{N - R}{n - r} \bigg/ \binom{N}{n},$$

where $\binom{R}{r}$, etc. are *binomial coefficients.

For example, if 7 cards are drawn without replacement from a pack of 52 playing cards, and drawing a heart is a 'success', we have $n = 7, N = 52$ and $R = 13$. The probability that 4 of the drawn cards are hearts, i.e. that $r = 4$, is

$$\binom{13}{4} \binom{39}{3} \bigg/ \binom{52}{7} = 0.049.$$

The general distribution has parameters n, R and N. The *mean is nR/N, and the *variance is

$$\frac{nR(N - n)(N - R)}{N^2(N - 1)}.$$

If the sample is drawn *with replacement* from this population, then the probability of obtaining r successes is given by the *binomial distribution $B(n, p)$, where

$p = R/N$ is the constant probability that a selected item is a success. When N is large compared with n, the hypergeometric distribution approaches this binomial distribution. This corresponds to the fact that sampling without replacement is approximately equivalent to sampling with replacement when the size of the population is large compared with the size of the sample.

hypothesis In statistics, a hypothesis is commonly an assertion about the *parameters or form of a population or populations. Three examples are (i) the hypothesis that two populations have equal *means, (ii) the hypothesis that a population has a *uniform distribution, and (iii) the hypothesis that there is no correlation between two random variables in a *bivariate distribution.

hypothesis testing (significance testing) A procedure for deciding whether a statistical *hypothesis, known as the *null hypothesis*, should be accepted or rejected in favour of another, the *alternative hypothesis*. The null hypothesis is denoted by H_0 or NH, and the alternative hypothesis by H_1 or AH. The decision is based on the value of a *test statistic* calculated from observed sample values. The range of possible values of this statistic is divided into an *acceptance region* and a *critical* (or *rejection*) *region* containing extreme values. The critical region is such that if H_0 is true there is a low probability α of the statistic falling in it, and the statistic is better explained if H_1 is true. Traditional values of α are 0.05, 0.01 and 0.001 (often referred to as 5%, 1% and 0.1%). If the test statistic falls in the acceptance region, then H_0 is accepted. If it falls in the critical region, then the statistic is said to be *significant* at *significance level* α, and H_0 is rejected in favour of H_1. Another form of terminology is to describe a result which is significant at the 0.05 level but not the 0.01 level as '*significant*', a result significant at the 0.01 level but not the 0.001 level as '*highly significant*',

and one significant at the 0.001 level as '*very highly significant*'.

The formation of the critical region takes into account the nature of the alternative hypothesis H_1. For example, if H_0 asserts that a parameter has a particular value, e.g. 'the population mean $\mu = 10$', then H_1 may be '$\mu > 10$'. This is called a *one-sided alternative*. The critical region then consists of one set of extreme values of the test statistic (called a *tail*), and the corresponding test is a *one-tail* (or *one-tailed*) *test*. If H_0 is true, the probability that the test statistic falls in this tail is α. On the other hand, H_1 may simply be '$\mu \neq 10$'. This is called a *two-sided alternative*. The critical region then consists of two sets of extreme values, i.e. two tails, on either side of the acceptance region, and the corresponding test is a *two-tail* (or *two-tailed*) *test*. If H_0 is true, the test statistic falls in each tail with probability $\frac{1}{2}\alpha$.

A value of the test statistic at the boundary between the acceptance region and the critical region is called a *critical value* at significance level α. Tables of critical values for one- and two-tail tests at the traditional levels such as $\alpha = 0.05, 0.01$, etc. are available for most of the commonly used tests such as the *t-test or *chi-squared test. A critical value for a two-tail test at level α will be identical to the critical value for a one-tail test at level $\frac{1}{2}\alpha$. They can be used to assess whether a particular calculated value of the test statistic is significant at one of the traditional levels. However, statistical packages on calculators and computers now make it possible to state the precise probability p of the test statistic having a value as extreme as or more extreme than the calculated value. This is called the *p-value* of the calculated value. When the value is significant, its p-value is said to give the *exact level of significance*. Thus, as well as saying that a particular value is 'significant at the 5% level', it is now possible to give a precise level of significance such as '$p = 0.015$'.

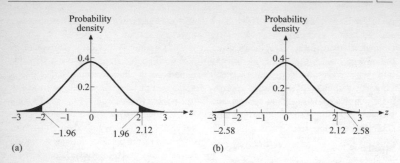

hypothesis testing where, under the null hypothesis, the test statistic z has the standard normal distribution. (a) A two-tail test for significance at the 5% level. The areas associated with the critical region are shaded and account for 5% of the distribution. The area above the acceptance region is unshaded. (b) A two-tail test for significance at the 1% level. The areas associated with the critical region are shaded and account for 1% of the distribution. The area above the acceptance region is unshaded.

As an illustration, suppose that a population is known to be *normally distributed, with *variance σ^2 equal to 16, and we wish to test whether the *mean μ is equal to 10. The appropriate null hypothesis is H_0: $\mu = 10$, and the alternative hypothesis is H_1: $\mu \neq 10$. Next, a random sample of 50 items is taken from the population and found to have a mean m equal to 11.2.

In such situations, a suitable test statistic is

$$z = \frac{m - \mu}{\sigma/\sqrt{n}},$$

where n is the sample size. The distribution of z is the standard normal distribution $N(0, 1)$. From the above data the value of z is

$$\frac{11.2 - 10}{4/\sqrt{50}} = 2.12.$$

As H_1 is two-sided, the critical region consists of two tails. To test for significance at the 5% level, the critical values for a two-tail test are found from tables to be $z = 1.96$ and $z = -1.96$, so the acceptance region is $-1.96 < z < 1.96$. The calculated value lies outside this region and falls in the critical region (see diagram (a)). It is thus significant at the 5% level, and H_0 is rejected at the 5% level of significance in favour of H_1: $\mu \neq 10$.

Since the critical values for significance at the 1% level are $z = 2.58$ and $z = -2.58$, the calculated test statistic of 2.12 fails to be significant at the 1% level (see diagram (b)). Alternatively, in view of the fact that H_1 is two-sided, the p-value of 2.12 is found to be $p = 0.034$. This again shows the result to be significant at the 5% level but not at the 1% level.

The structure of hypothesis tests is such that the null hypothesis H_0 may be rejected when it is in fact true. This is known as a *Type I error* or an *error of the first kind*. The probability of a Type I error is α, and thus depends on the chosen significance level. It is also possible that H_0 may be accepted when it is in fact false. This is known as a *Type II error* or an *error of the second kind*. The probability of a Type II error depends on the alternative hypothesis H_1, and for a particular H_1 is usually denoted by β. It follows that the probability of correctly rejecting H_0 when it is false is $1 - \beta$. This probability, $1 - \beta$, is called the *power* of the test.

Acceptance of a null hypothesis does not necessarily mean that it is true, only that we have insufficient evidence to be confident of rejecting it. Similarly, rejection of a null hypothesis does not necessarily mean that it is false, only that there is strong evidence that it might be false.

identity matrix *See* matrix.

illusory correlation *See* correlation.

improper integral *See* infinite integral.

incomplete Latin square An alternative name for a *Youden square.

increment A positive or negative change in a *variable. The term is usually used to mean a small change.

indefinite integral An *integral without any specified *limits, whose solution includes an undetermined constant (the constant of integration). For example, the integral $\int x^2 \, dx$, whose solution, $\frac{1}{3}x^3 + c$, includes the undetermined constant c is indefinite. *Compare* definite integral; *see* integration.

independence 1. Two *events are said to be *independent events* if the probability that one occurs is the same whether the other occurs or not. For example, if a fair die is thrown and an unbiased coin is tossed, the events 'the score on the die is a 6' and 'the coin comes down heads' are independent. The probability of a 6 is $\frac{1}{6}$, whether the coin comes down heads or tails. Similarly, the probability of heads is $\frac{1}{2}$, whatever the score on the die.

More formally, two events A and B are independent if the probability that both occur (the event 'A and B occur') is equal to the product of their separate probabil-

ities, i.e. if

$$Pr(A \cap B) = Pr(A)Pr(B).$$

In the above example, there are 12 equally likely possible outcomes when a fair die is thrown and an unbiased coin is tossed, so

$$Pr(\text{score of 6 and heads}) = \tfrac{1}{12}.$$

But also

$$Pr(\text{score of 6})Pr(\text{heads}) = \tfrac{1}{6} \times \tfrac{1}{2} = \tfrac{1}{12},$$

confirming that the events are independent.

An equivalent definition, using conditional *probabilities, is that events A and B are independent if $Pr(A) = Pr(A|B)$, or if $Pr(B) = Pr(B|A)$.

2. Two *random variables are said to be *independent random variables* if the values taken by one are not affected by the values taken by the other. For example, the scores on a pair of fair dice thrown together are independent random variables since the scores do not affect each other.

More formally, two discrete random variables X and Y are independent if

$$Pr(X = x, Y = y) = Pr(X = x)Pr(Y = y)$$

for all pairs of values (x, y).

Two continuous random variables with joint *frequency function $f(x, y)$ are independent if, for all pairs of values (x, y),

$$f(x, y) = f_1(x)f_2(y),$$

where $f_1(x)$ and $f_2(y)$, are the marginal

frequency functions of X and Y, respectively (*see* bivariate distribution).

independent events *See* independence.

independent random variables *See* independence.

independent variable *See* function; regression.

index (*plural* **indices**) **1. (index number)** In statistics, a number that indicates how the value of a variable, such as the price of a commodity, is varying over time in comparison with its value at some specific time, the *base period*, which is often a *base year*. The value b of the variable in the base period is usually given the index number 100 (sometimes 1000). The index number at other times is calculated by expressing the value x of the variable as a percentage of the value b in the base period. Thus the index number of x is $(x/b) \times 100$. A simple index of this kind is often called a *relative*.

For example, if the price of an item is 40 in the base year and 42 and 46 in the next two years, then the index numbers of the price in the three successive years are 100, $(42/40) \times 100$ and $(46/40) \times 100$, respectively, i.e. 100, 105 and 115.

In more complex situations, as when attempting to indicate changes over time in the cost of living, industrial production, or share prices on a stock exchange, an index will need to take into account and give appropriate weight to a number of relevant components, each with its own index. Thus, in such cases, most index numbers are *weighted index numbers*.

See weighted relatives index; weighted aggregate index; Laspeyres index; Paasche index; Retail Prices Index; FTSE share index.

2. *See* exponent.

3. *See* coefficient.

index notation *See* exponential notation.

index of determination *See* coefficient of determination.

index of discrimination *See* item analysis.

indices *Plural of* *index.

inequality A statement that one expression or quantity is greater or less than another in value. The following notation is used:

$$x > y \quad \text{for } x \text{ is greater than } y$$
$$x < y \quad \text{for } x \text{ is less than } y.$$

Clearly, $x > y$ is the same as $y < x$. The symbols $\geqslant$ for 'greater than or equal to' and $\leqslant$ for 'less than or equal to' are also used. To distinguish an inequality such as $x > y$ from $x \geqslant y$, the former is called a *strict inequality*.

inference *See* statistical inference.

infinite integral (improper integral) An integral in which one or both of the *limits is infinite or in which the integrand is infinite at some point in the range of *integration. An example of the first type is

$$\int_a^\infty f(x)\, dx,$$

which is short for

$$\lim_{b \to \infty} \int_a^b f(x)\, dx.$$

If the limit exists, the integral is said to be a *convergent integral*; if not, it is a *divergent integral*.

In statistics, this type of integral arises in connection with continuous distributions for which the *frequency function is non-zero over an infinite range, e.g. the *normal distribution. For example, the *exponential distribution has frequency function $f(x) = \lambda e^{-\lambda x}$ for $x \geqslant 0$, and is zero otherwise. The area under the frequency curve is

$$\int_0^\infty \lambda e^{-\lambda x}\,dx,$$

and this should be equal to 1. To verify this, we first calculate

$$\int_0^b \lambda e^{-\lambda x}\,dx = \left[-e^{-\lambda x}\right]_0^b = 1 - e^{-\lambda b}.$$

As $b \to \infty, (1 - e^{-\lambda b}) \to 1$. So the limit exists, and the infinite integral is convergent and is equal to 1. Similarly, infinite integrals of this type will be met when calculating the *mean and *variance of the distribution.

An integral of the second type, whose integrand $f(x)$ is finite for $a < x \leqslant b$, but infinite for $x = a$, is

$$\int_a^b f(x)\,dx,$$

which is short for

$$\underset{\delta \to 0}{\text{Lim}} \int_{a+\delta}^b f(x)\,dx,$$

where $\delta > 0$. If the limit exists, the integral is again said to be *convergent*; if not, it is *divergent*.

infinite sequence A *sequence that has an unlimited number of terms. *See* convergent sequence.

infinite series A *series that has an unlimited number of terms. *See* convergent series.

inflection (inflexion) *See* point of inflection.

integral 1. *See* integration.
2. Describing an integer.

integration The inverse process to *differentiation, i.e. the process of finding a function whose derivative is a given function. It is sometimes called *antidifferentia-*

tion. If $f(x)$ is the given function and $F(x)$ is a function which, when differentiated, gives $f(x)$, then $F(x)$ is said to be an *integral* (or *antiderivative*) of $f(x)$. So, for example, $\frac{1}{3}x^3$ is an integral of x^2, since

$$\frac{d}{dx}\left(\frac{1}{3}x^3\right) = x^2.$$

This is written as

$$F(x) = \int f(x)\,dx,$$

and is equivalent to

$$F'(x) = f(x).$$

The function $f(x)$ is the *integrand*.

If $F(x)$ is an integral of $f(x)$, then so is $F(x) + c$, where c is an arbitrary constant (since $dc/dx = 0$). An integral of this type is called an *indefinite integral, and c is the *constant of integration*. Some common integrals are given in Table 9 of the Appendix.

The difference between the values of an integral when evaluated for two values of the independent variable is a *definite integral. The notation is

$$F(b) - F(a) = \int_a^b f(x)\,dx.$$

The values $x = b$ and $x = a$ are called the *upper* and *lower limits* of the integral.

See also distribution function; expectation; frequency function.

interaction *See* factorial experiment.

intercept The distance from the origin to a point where a line or curve cuts a coordinate axis. An intercept with the y-axis is called a *y-intercept*, one with the x-axis is an *x-intercept*. For example, the straight line with equation $y + 2x = 4$ cuts the y-axis at $(0, 4)$ and the x-axis at $(-2, 0)$. The y-intercept is 4 and the x-intercept is -2. Sometimes the intercept is defined as the point of intersection rather than the distance of the point from the origin. *See* line.

interpolation When the values of a function $f(x)$ are known for several values of x, interpolation is the process of estimating from these data the value of the function for a value of x lying between two of the x-values for which f is known. For example, given that the typical stopping distances for cars travelling at 40 and 50 mph are 36 and 53 metres, estimating the stopping distance for a car travelling at 48 mph is a process of interpolation.

Suppose that $f(x)$ is known to equal $y_1, y_2, \ldots$ when x has values $x_1, x_2, \ldots$, and that an estimate y' is required when $x = x'$, where $x_1 < x' < x_2$. The simplest method of interpolation, *linear interpolation* assumes that the points with coordinates $(x_1, y_1), (x', y')$ and (x_2, y_2) lie on a straight line (*see* diagram). The estimate can then be calculated from the formula

$$y' = y_1 + \frac{(x' - x_1)(y_2 - y_1)}{(x_2 - x_1)}.$$

To use linear interpolation to estimate the stopping distance at 48 mph, we substitute $x_1 = 40$, $y_1 = 36$; $x_2 = 50, y_2 = 53$; and $x' = 48$. The formula gives

$$y' = 36 + \frac{(48 - 40)(53 - 36)}{(50 - 40)} = 49.6 \text{ metres.}$$

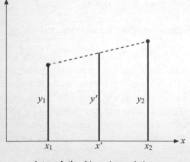

interpolation Linear interpolation.

In fact this will be an overestimate, because the relation between speed and stopping distance is not *linear.

The method is useful in connection with statistical tables. For example, the table of the standard *normal distribution function (*see* Table 1 of the Appendix) gives $\Phi(1.25) = 0.8944$ and $\Phi(1.26) = 0.8962$. Using linear interpolation, the value of $\Phi(1.254)$ is estimated to be, to four decimal places,

$$0.8944 + \frac{(1.254 - 1.25)(0.8962 - 0.8944)}{(1.26 - 1.25)}$$
$$= 0.8951.$$

More powerful methods use additional known values. In general, interpolation is based on the assumption that intermediate values will be consistent with the trend of the adjacent observations. Although they are useful and sometimes necessary, the estimates obtained by interpolation can be unreliable if wrong assumptions are made about trend.

Compare extrapolation; *see* line of best fit.

interquartile range A measure of the *dispersion of a set of *data, or of a *random variable, equal to the difference between the upper and lower *quartiles. For example, if the upper and lower quartiles of a set of observations are 56 and 38, respectively, then the interquartile range is $56 - 38 = 18$. It follows from this that the central 50% of the data lie in an interval of length 18.

A related measure of dispersion is the *semi-interquartile range* (or *quartile deviation*). This is equal to half the interquartile range. Thus, if the upper and lower quartiles are denoted by Q_3 and Q_1, respectively, then the semi-interquartile range is equal to $\frac{1}{2}(Q_3 - Q_1)$. It is equivalent to the average deviation of Q_1 and Q_3 from the *median. In the above example, the semi-interquartile range is equal to 9.

The interquartile range is a much more stable measure of dispersion than the *range. The latter relies on two observations only, the greatest and the least, and, in the presence of *outliers, can be misleading.

See box-and-whisker diagram; five-number summary; quantile.

intersection (meet, product) The intersection of two *sets A and B, denoted by $A \cap B$, consists of those elements that belong to both A and B. For example, if $A = \{2, 4, 6, 8\}$ and $B = \{4, 5, 6\}$, then $A \cap B = \{4, 6\}$. Two sets are said to be *disjoint if they have no elements in common, i.e. their intersection is empty. Thus if $C = \{1, 3, 5, 7\}$, then A and C are disjoint (but B and C are not disjoint).

The number of elements in the intersection of two sets is related to the number in their *union. Denoting the number of elements in a set A by $n(A)$, the relation for two sets A and B is

$$n(A \cap B) = n(A) + n(B) - n(A \cup B).$$

In our example, $A \cup B = \{2, 4, 5, 6, 8\}$. The numbers of elements in $A \cap B$, A, B and $A \cup B$ are 2, 4, 3 and 5, respectively, and, since

$$2 = 4 + 3 - 5,$$

the relation is satisfied.

The intersection of two *events E and F is the event 'both E and F occur'. It is represented by the intersection of the subsets of the *sample space corresponding to the events E and F. Thus $E \cap F$ represents the event 'both E and F occur'. Two events are said to be *mutually exclusive* if they cannot both occur, i.e. their intersection is empty. For example, suppose that a die is thrown, and event E is 'the score is even', event F is 'the score is odd' and event G is 'the score is divisible by 3' (*see* diagram).

The intersection $E \cap G$ is the event 'the score is even and divisible by 3', i.e. 'the score is 6'. Similarly, $F \cap G$ is the event

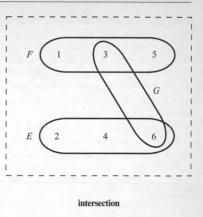

intersection

'the score is odd and divisible by 3', i.e. 'the score is 3'. However, the events E and F are mutually exclusive, as no score can be both even and odd simultaneously.

Compare union; *see* probability.

interval A set containing all numbers between two given numbers. These given numbers are the *end points* of the interval. If the interval contains the end points (a and b), so that it is the set of numbers x such that $a \leqslant x \leqslant b$, it is a *closed interval*, written as $[a, b]$. If the interval does not contain the end points, so that it is the set such that $a < x < b$, it is an *open interval*, written as (a, b). Intervals that are partly open (and partly closed) can be written using combinations of round and square brackets. Thus $(a, b]$ denotes the interval $a < x \leqslant b$, and $[a, b)$ denotes the interval $a \leqslant x < b$.

interval estimate *See* estimation.

interval scale *See* scale of measurement.

inverse function *See* function.

inversely proportional *See* variation.

inverse probability The approach to probability problems that attempts to find the *probability of an event (a cause) conditional on another event (a consequence or effect) having taken place. For example, finding the probability that a person has a disease given that they have tested positive for it is a problem of inverse probability because it involves finding the probability of a cause – having the disease – conditional on an effect – testing positive. *Bayes' theorem plays a key role in evaluating inverse probabilities.

The reverse approach, deducing the probability of an effect from the probabilities of its causes, is sometimes called *direct probability*.

item An individual question in a *test or *questionnaire.

item analysis The statistical analysis of the effectiveness of items in a *test.

The *facility* or *difficulty* of an item is the proportion of respondents who answer it correctly. Thus if 124 out of 200 students answer an item correctly, the facility of the item is $124/200 = 0.62$ (or 62%). A very easy item will have a facility close to 1. Difficult items will have low facilities near to zero.

The *discrimination* or *item discriminability* is the extent to which an item discriminates or differentiates between the individuals taking the test, i.e. how well it shows up the differences between them in the field of aptitude being tested. An item that discriminates well is thus one which is frequently answered correctly by respondents with high test scores and infrequently answered correctly by those with low total scores.

The standard *index of discrimination* (or *discrimination index*) defines the high-scoring respondents as those whose test scores are in the top 27%, and the weakest respondents as those in the bottom 27%. Then the index is $P_{high} - P_{low}$, where P_{high} is the proportion of the high-scoring group who answer the item correctly and P_{low} is the proportion of the low-scoring group who answer it correctly. The index has a value between -1 and $+1$. If an item is attracting a greater proportion of correct answers from the high-scoring group than

from the lower, the index will be positive and the item is said to *discriminate positively*. For example, when 200 students take a test, the high- and low-scoring groups each contain 27% of 200, i.e. 54 students. If 41 of the top group answer a certain item correctly and 5 of the low group answer it correctly, then

$$P_{high} = \frac{41}{54} \quad \text{and} \quad P_{low} = \frac{5}{54}.$$

The item's discrimination index is

$$\frac{41}{54} - \frac{5}{54} = \frac{36}{54} = 0.67,$$

indicating that the item discriminates positively.

The maximum value of the index, 1.00, occurs when an item is answered correctly by all the high group and by none of the low group.

An alternative measure of item discriminability is the *point biserial correlation coefficient* of the item. This is based on the scores of all individuals taking the test and gives the correlation between their responses to the item and the total scores on the test. Typically, correct and incorrect responses are scored 1 and 0, respectively. Like the discrimination index, this correlation coefficient has a value between -1 and $+1$. A positive value indicates that respondents who answer the item correctly tend to score highly on the whole test, while those who answer incorrectly tend to have low total scores – i.e. the item discriminates positively.

To assess the effectiveness of an item in a *multiple-choice test, a discrimination index (or correlation coefficient) can be based on the correct answer, the *key*, which ideally should be attracting more responses from the high-scoring respondents than from the low-scoring, and thus be positive. At the same time, indices can also be calculated for each of the incorrect alternatives, the *distractors*. These should ideally be attracting more responses from the low-scoring respondents than from high-scoring, and thus have negative indices or coefficients.

For example, in a trial of a test, an item with key *a* and distractors *b*, *c* and *d* might have the following responses from the high- and low-scoring groups, each containing 50 students:

Group	Response				
	a	*b*	*c*	*d*	Total
High scoring	42	6	0	2	50
Low scoring	7	4	19	20	50

Here, the key *a* has a discrimination index of

$$\frac{42}{50} - \frac{7}{50} = 0.7$$

and appears to be satisfactory. The distractors *b*, *c* and *d* have indices of 0.04, −0.38 and −0.36. On this evidence, distractor *b* seems less satisfactory than *c* or *d*.

item difficulty *See* item analysis.

item discriminability *See* item analysis.

J

jack-knife A method for estimating bias in a sample *estimator of a population parameter. In addition to the original *random sample of size n, the procedure works with n further samples. These are each of size $n - 1$, and each is obtained from the original sample by omitting one sample value, beginning with the first observation and continuing through to the nth. *See also* bootstrap; unbiased estimator.

join *See* union.

joint distribution A *distribution of two or more *random variables. *See* bivariate distribution; multivariate distribution.

Jonckheere–Terpstra test A *nonpara-ametric test for a predicted trend in the means of three or more independent samples. The *null hypothesis is that the samples come from the same population, or from populations with identical distributions and thus with equal means. The alternative hypothesis is that the population means differ and are in a certain specified order.

The simplest form of the test is when the samples contain the same number of observations. Then, when there are $k \geqslant 3$ samples with n observations in each, the data are set out in an $n \times k$ table. Each column contains the n observations in a sample, and the table is arranged so that, running left to right, the order of the columns corresponds

to the *predicted* ascending order of the means.

To illustrate the procedure, three dentists A, B and C, were each observed when extracting wisdom teeth on four occasions. It was predicted that C was the slowest and B the quickest at performing this operation. The times taken in minutes were as follows:

A	21	12	31	38
B	24	14	15	7
C	23	45	34	25

The predicted order of mean times is $B\,A\,C$, so the table of data is

B	A	C
24(5)	21(4)	23
14(7)	12(4)	45
15(7)	31(2)	34
7(8)	38(1)	25

Starting with the left-hand column, for each separate observation the number of observations greater than it in the columns to the right of it are recorded beside it in brackets, as shown. Thus for the observation 24, the number exceeding that observation is recorded as 5.

The test statistic is S, calculated from such a table by the formula

$$S = 2A - \tfrac{1}{2}k(k - 1)n^2,$$

where A is the sum of the bracketed numbers, k the number of samples and n the number of observations per sample.

For our data,

$$A = 5 + 7 + 7 + 8 + 4 + 4 + 2 + 1 = 38,$$

$k = 3$ and $n = 4$. The formula gives

$$S = 2 \times 38 - \tfrac{1}{2} \times 3 \times 2 \times 4^2 = 28.$$

Significantly high values of S lead to rejection of the null hypothesis that the means are equal. For small values of k and n, tables of critical values of S are available.

In our example, $k = 3$, $n = 4$ and $S = 28$. The critical values at the 5% and 1% levels are 24 and 32, respectively. Our value of S is greater than or equal to 24 and is significant at the 5% level. Thus the alternative hypothesis that B is quicker than A, and A faster than C, is accepted at the 5% level. The test can be adapted to the case where the samples are not all of equal size. Some statistical software packages provide *p-values associated with S-values.

See trend test. *See also* Kruskal–Wallis test; Page test.

K

Kendall's coefficient of concordance *See* coefficient of concordance.

Kendall's rank correlation coefficient *See* correlation coefficient.

Kendall's tau (τ) Kendall's rank correlation coefficient. *See* correlation coefficient.

Kolmogorov–Smirnov tests A set of *nonparametric tests for use with a single sample or with a pair of independent samples.

(1) The *one-sample test*, sometimes called the *Kolmogorov test*. A test of whether a *random sample has come from a population with a certain specified (cumulative) *distribution function. It is based on the maximum divergence between the distribution function of the sample and that of the population. A significantly high maximum leads to rejection of the *null hypothesis. It is thus a test of *goodness of fit*.

More formally, suppose that the sample consists of n observations,

$$x_1 \leqslant x_2 \leqslant \cdots \leqslant x_n,$$

of a variable X. The sample distribution function $S(x)$ is such that

$$S(x_i) = \Pr(X \leqslant x_i) = \frac{i}{n}.$$

If we denote the distribution function of the population by $F(x)$, the test statistic D is based on the values of $F(x_i) - S(x_i)$ and $F(x_i) - S(x_{i-1})$ for $i = 1$ to n. These are the differences between $F(x)$ and $S(x)$ at, and

just before, each data point. For a two-tail test, D is simply the magnitude of the largest difference. For a one-tail test, D is the magnitude of the largest difference *in the direction predicted* by the alternative hypothesis. Significantly high values of D lead to rejection of the null hypothesis that the distribution function of the population is $F(x)$.

To illustrate the method, consider the following sample of 10 'random numbers' generated by a pocket calculator and rearranged in ascending order:

0.266, 0.314, 0.361, 0.604, 0.621, 0.698, 0.731, 0.772, 0.827, 0.896.

We can call these numbers $x_1, x_2, \ldots, x_{10}$; the sample distribution function $S(x)$ then has $S(x_i) = i/10$ for $i = 1$ to 10. The manufacturer claims that the calculator generates random numbers with a *uniform distribution over the interval $(0, 1)$, so the popula-

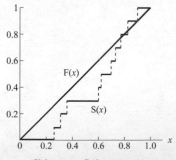

Kolmogorov–Smirnov tests (a)

x_i	$F(x_i)$	$S(x_i)$	$F(x_i) - S(x_i)$	$F(x_i) - S(x_{i-1})$
0.266	0.266	0.1	0.166	0.266
0.314	0.314	0.2	0.114	0.214
0.361	0.361	0.3	0.061	0.161
0.604	0.604	0.4	0.204	0.304
0.621	0.621	0.5	0.121	0.221
0.698	0.698	0.6	0.098	0.198
0.731	0.731	0.7	0.031	0.131
0.772	0.772	0.8	-0.028	0.072
0.827	0.827	0.9	-0.073	0.027
0.896	0.896	1.0	-0.104	-0.004

tion distribution function has $F(x) = x$ for $0 < x < 1$ (*see* diagram (a)).

We carry out a two-tail test, the alternative hypothesis being that the population distribution is not a uniform one. The table above gives values of $S(x)$ and $F(x)$, and the key differences. The largest difference is 0.304, so the test statistic $D = 0.304$.

Statistical software packages and tables are available to assess the value of D. Tables give minimum values for significance at various levels for small samples, e.g. of size $n = 5$ to 40. For higher values of n, the critical values at the 5% and 1% levels for two-tail tests are approximately $1.36/\sqrt{n}$ and $1.63/\sqrt{n}$, respectively.

In our example, $n = 10$ and $D = 0.304$, and the test is two-tailed. The minimum value for significance at the 5% level is 0.409. Our value of D is less than this, so the null hypothesis that the calculator is generating a uniform distribution of random numbers is retained.

(2) The *two-sample test*, sometimes called the *Smirnov test*. A test of whether two independent random samples have been drawn from identical populations (or from the same population). Sample distribution functions $S_1(x)$ and $S_2(x)$ are constructed (as in (1) above) for each sample. The test statistic is based on the difference between them. The null hypothesis is that the populations have identical distribution functions.

If the alternative hypothesis is that the populations are not identical, a two-tail test is appropriate, and the test statistic D is the *absolute value of the largest difference, i.e. $D = \max |S_1(x) - S_2(x)|$. If the alternative hypothesis is that one population generally contains larger values than the other, a one-tail test is appropriate, and the test statistic is the largest difference *in the predicted direction*. Thus if the first population is predicted to generally contain larger values than the second, then $D = \max(S_2(x) - S_1(x))$. High values of D lead to rejection of the null hypothesis.

As an illustration, suppose that the numbers of days absent from work in a year were calculated for random samples of two different groups of workers in order to test the idea that workers from group 1 were more likely to be absent than those from group 2. The sample data were:

Group 1	5	6	8	9	9
Group 2	1	2	4	5	7

Diagram (b) shows the distribution functions $S_1(x)$ and $S_2(x)$ of the two samples, where, for example, $S_1(5) = 0.2$ and $S_2(4) = 0.6$. For this one-tail test the test statistic $D = \max(S_2(x) - S_1(x))$. From a table of values or from the graph, it is found that $D = 0.6$.

Statistical software packages and tables are available to assess the test statistic. Tables give minimum values for significance at various levels for pairs of samples with small sizes, e.g. for n_1 and n_2 from 3 to 25.

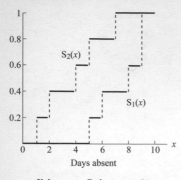

Kolmogorov–Smirnov tests (b)

In our example, $n_1 = n_2 = 5$ and $D = 0.6$, and the test is one-tailed. The minimum value for significance at the 5% level is $3/5 = 0.6$. Our value of D is equal to this, so the null hypothesis of no difference in absenteeism is rejected at the 5% level and the alternative hypothesis, that group 1 workers are more likely to be absent than group 2 workers, is accepted.

Kolmogorov test   An alternative name for the *Kolmogorov–Smirnov one-sample test.

Kruskal–Wallis test   A *nonparametric test of whether three or more independent *random samples come from populations with identical distributions and thus with equal *means (or *medians). It is particularly useful when a one-way *analysis of variance is inappropriate.

The first stage is to combine the samples, arrange all the observations in ascending order and replace them by their *ranks. When there are $k \geqslant 3$ samples and a total of N observations, these ranks will run from 1 to N. The data for the test are these ranks set out in k columns, each column containing the overall ranks of the observations in one of the samples. Under the *null hypothesis the columns of ranks are random samples from the same population (the numbers 1 to N) and thus have equal means.

To illustrate the procedure, consider a study of memory that presents a chess position with 26 pieces on the board to eight players, each having being rated as either 'expert', 'competent' or 'beginner' at chess. They are asked to memorize the position and then recall it. The numbers of pieces correctly recalled were as follows:

Expert	Competent	Beginner
24	19	13
20	11	8
23		10

When the observations have been ranked in ascending order, the following table of ranks is obtained:

	Expert	Competent	Beginner
	8	5	4
	6	3	1
	7		2
Column total (S_i)	21	8	7

The test statistic T is given by the formula

$$T = \frac{12}{N(N+1)} \sum_i \left(\frac{S_i^2}{n_i} \right) - 3(N+1),$$

where N is the total number of observations, n_i is the number of items in column i and S_i is the sum of the ranks in that column.

In this example, $N = 8$ and, numbering the columns as 1 to 3 from left to right, we have $n_1 = 3, S_1 = 21; n_2 = 2, S_2 = 8$; and $n_3 = 3, S_3 = 7$. The formula gives

$$T = \frac{12}{8 \times 9} \left(\frac{21^2}{3} + \frac{8^2}{2} + \frac{7^2}{3} \right) - (3 \times 9) = 5.56.$$

Significantly high values of T lead to rejection of the null hypothesis.

If k is greater than 3 and/or at least one sample has more than five items, then the distribution of T is approximately a *chi-squared distribution with $k - 1$ degrees of freedom. So, for example, when N is large and $k = 3$, the chi-squared tables for

$3 - 1 = 2$ degrees of freedom indicate that T needs to exceed 5.99 to be significant at the 5% level. However, when $k = 3$ and no sample contains more than five items, exact critical values of T are available. Tables are available giving critical values for all combinations of the three sample sizes up to 5, 5, 5. Some statistical software packages will give *p-values associated with T-values.

In our example, $k = 3$, the sizes of the three samples are 3, 3, 2, and $T = 5.56$. Tables state that the probability of obtaining a value of T as high or higher than 5.3611 is 0.032. Our value of T, 5.56, is greater than this and is thus significant at the 3% level. So the null hypothesis of no difference between the three groups is rejected.

It appears from the data that, on average, experts at chess recall more pieces than competent players, who, in turn recall more than beginners. To assess whether this apparent trend is significant, a test such as the *Jonckheere–Terpstra test is appropriate.

Kuder–Richardson formula One of a number of formulae which can be used to estimate a *reliability coefficient for a test.

kurtosis The degree of peakedness of a *frequency function near its *mode. The *normal distribution is taken as a standard. A distribution with the same degree of peakedness as the normal distribution is said to be *mesokurtic*, one less peaked is said to be *platykurtic* and one more peaked is *leptokurtic*.

If μ_i is the ith *moment about the mean, then one measure is γ_2, the *coefficient of kurtosis*, defined by

$$\gamma_2 = \frac{\mu_4}{\mu_2^2} - 3.$$

This is zero for a normal distribution, positive for a leptokurtic distribution and negative for a platykurtic distribution. For example, an extreme instance of a platykurtic distribution is a continuous *uniform distribution. This has a completely flat frequency curve, and $\gamma_2 = -1.2$.

An alternative measure of kurtosis is $\beta_2 = \mu_4 / \mu_2^2$. This is equal to, greater than, or less than 3 according to whether the distribution is mesokurtic (e.g. normal), leptokurtic or platykurtic.

See also g-statistics; *compare* skewness.

L

Laspeyres index A form of weighted *index number that uses base-year data as weights. For example, when used as a price index for a set of commodities, the Laspeyres index uses as weights the quantities of each commodity purchased in the base year. In this case and more precisely, if the prices of a set of k commodities are $p_{01}, p_{02}, \ldots, p_{0k}$ in the base year and $p_{n1}, p_{n2}, \ldots, p_{nk}$ in the nth year after the base year (year n), and if the quantities purchased in the base year are $q_{01}, q_{02}, \ldots, q_{0k}$, respectively, then the Laspeyres price index for year n, denoted by L_{0n}, is

$$L_{0n} = \frac{p_{n1}q_{01} + p_{n2}q_{02} + \cdots + p_{nk}q_{0k}}{p_{01}q_{01} + p_{02}q_{02} + \cdots + p_{0k}q_{0k}} \times 100,$$

or

$$L_{0n} = \left(\sum_i p_{ni}q_{0i} \Big/ \sum_i p_{0i}q_{0i} \right) \times 100.$$

For a simple illustration, suppose that in the base year the prices of three commodities were 20, 80 and 30, and the quantities purchased were 300, 150 and 200. If by the fifth year after the base year the prices have become 30, 90 and 25, respectively, then the Laspeyres price index for this set of commodities in the fifth year is

$$L_{05} = \frac{30 \times 300 + 90 \times 150 + 25 \times 200}{20 \times 300 + 80 \times 150 + 30 \times 200} \times 100$$

$$= 114.6.$$

In effect, the index compares the total cost of the base-year purchases at current prices with their actual cost at base-year prices.

Compare Paasche index.

Latin square A square *array of symbols in which each symbol occurs once in each row or column. An example of a 4×4 Latin square using the symbols A, B, C, D is

A	B	C	D
D	C	B	A
B	D	A	C
C	A	D	B

It can be used as a form of *experimental design which involves and takes account of two sources of variation apart from the treatments. This is done by identifying the two sources with the rows and columns of the square, and the treatments with the symbols. Thus there is a *three-way classification* of observations.

For example, if four plant varieties A, B, C and D are to be tested in greenhouse conditions with respect to two sources of variation, such as light intensity and temperature, each at four different levels, one could associate them with the rows and columns of a 4×4 square. So the design could take the form

Temperature level	Light intensity level			
	1	2	3	4
1	A	B	C	D
2	D	C	B	A
3	B	D	A	C
4	C	A	D	B

This design ensures that each variety is tested at each level of light intensity and each temperature. It involves 16 tests, and is more economical than testing each variety at every possible pair of levels – which would require a total of 64 tests.

Using a Latin square extends the method of *randomized blocks from one set of blocks to two (one for light intensity and one for temperature, in the above example) and is amenable to an *analysis of variance if the sources of variation are independent in their effects, i.e. in the absence of inter-actions (*see* factorial experiment). The restriction that each source of variation must have the same number of types as the treatments can lead to practical difficul-ties. For small squares, the degrees of free-dom of the *error mean square becomes low. This difficulty can be met by using more than one square, e.g. by using two 3×3 squares as shown:

	1	2	3			1	2	3
1	A	B	C		1	C	A	B
2	B	C	A		2	A	B	C
3	C	A	B		3	B	C	A

See also Graeco-Latin square; Youden square.

laws of exponents *See* exponent.

laws of indices *See* exponent.

laws of large numbers A group of theorems concerning the *limit as $n \to \infty$ of S_n/n, where

$$S_n = X_1 + X_2 + \cdots + X_n$$

is the sum of n independent random vari-ables.

For example, if the variables have identi-cal distributions with *mean μ, then

$$S_n/n \to \mu$$

with a probability equal to 1. Put more formally, for any fixed $\varepsilon > 0$,

$$\Pr(|(S_n/n) - \mu| < \varepsilon) \to 1 \quad \text{as } n \to \infty;$$

in words, the probability that S_n/n differs from μ by less than some fixed amount ε tends to 1 as n tends to infinity.

In particular, if the X_i are chosen from the same distribution, then S_n/n is the mean of a sample of size n. The above law states that as n tends to infinity, the sample mean tends to the population mean μ with prob-ability 1.

leading diagonal *See* matrix.

least squares A method of obtaining esti-mates of unknown parameters. The esti-mates are the values of the parameters that minimize a sum of squares formed from data values and the parameters. These values satisfy a set of simultaneous equa-tions known as the *normal equations*.

For example, suppose that when a quan-tity x of fertilizer is applied to a crop, the average of the crop yield y is believed to be given by a relation of the form $E(y) = \alpha + \beta x$, and that n pairs of data values (x_i, y_i) are known. The *least-squares estimators* of the unknown parameters α and β are the values $\alpha = a$ and $\beta = b$ that minimize the expression

$$(y_1 - \alpha - \beta x_1)^2 + (y_2 - \alpha - \beta x_2)^2 + \cdots + (y_n - \alpha - \beta x_n)^2.$$

The simultaneous equations that they sat-isfy, the normal equations, are

$$\sum_i y_i = n\alpha + \beta \sum_i x_i \quad \text{and}$$

$$\sum_i x_i y_i = \alpha \sum_i x_i + \beta \sum_i x_i^2.$$

In this case, the procedure leads to a fitted line $y = a + bx$ with the property that the sum of the squares of the deviations of the observed y_i from the fitted line measured parallel to the y-axis are less than the corresponding sum of squares that would result from any other values of a and b.

The method extends to more general situations involving multivariate data and any number of parameters.

See line of best fit; regression.

least-squares estimator An *estimator obtained by the method of *least squares.

left censored *See* censored data.

leptokurtic *See* kurtosis.

Levene's test A test of the *null hypothesis that m ($\geqslant 2$) random samples are from *normal populations having equal *variances, against the alternative hypothesis that at least one population has a different variance. *See also* Bartlett's test; Hartley's test.

life expectancy tables *See* life tables.

life tables Tables that give, for a particular population (e.g. English females) or group of individuals (e.g. doctors), the numbers of people who, out of a given number (e.g. 1000) born or living at a specific age (e.g. 25), live to successive higher ages, together with the numbers who die in the intervals. Although they are based on retrospective studies of populations or groups, life tables are used to predict the future life expectancy of individuals in similar populations or groups. Thus they are useful to actuaries who are deciding on the appropriate terms and premiums of life insurance policies for individuals of certain ages and occupations. They are also referred to as *life expectancy tables* or *mortality tables*.

likelihood function Suppose that a continuous *random variable X has a *distribution belonging to a family of distributions that involves a *parameter θ. This can be indicated by writing its *frequency function in the form $f(x, \theta)$. When considered as a frequency function, θ is fixed and x varies. However, if x is fixed and θ is allowed to vary, so that $f(x, \theta)$ is regarded as a function of θ, then this function is called the likelihood function of θ given x, and is written as $L(\theta) = f(x, \theta)$. It is so called because, for an observed value of x, say $x = x_i$, the value of (x_i, θ) varies with θ, and the greater the value of $f(x_i, \theta)$, the more 'likely' it is that this value x_i will be observed. The value of $f(x_i, \theta)$ for any particular value of θ is called the *likelihood*.

Now, suppose that we have a sample of n independent observations $x_1, x_2, \ldots, x_n$ from a distribution with frequency function $f(x, \theta)$, where θ is an unknown parameter. The independence condition implies that the joint frequency function is the product of the n functions $f(x_i, \theta)$. So the likelihood function of θ, given this sample, is

$$L(\theta) = f(x_1, \theta)f(x_2, \theta) \cdots f(x_n, \theta)$$

Clearly, if for two values θ_1 and θ_2 one finds that $L(\theta_2) < L(\theta_1)$, this implies that the sample has a smaller value of the joint frequency function if the unknown parameter is θ_2 rather than θ_1. This in turn implies that the sample is less likely to have come from a distribution where $\theta = \theta_2$ than from one with $\theta = \theta_1$. This argument leads to the principle of *maximum likelihood* as a method of estimating θ (*see* maximum likelihood estimation).

The concept of likelihood function may be extended to *discrete distributions and to distributions involving more than one parameter.

Likert scale *See* rating scale.

Lim *See* limit.

limit 1. (of a function) A value that is approached arbitrarily closely by the *function $f(x)$ when some restriction is placed on the independent variable x. For example, as x increases, $f(x) = 1/x$ decreases, becoming closer and closer to zero. The function $1/x$ is said to *tend to* zero as x

tends to infinity, and this is written as

$$\left(\frac{1}{x}\right) \to 0 \text{ as } x \to \infty.$$

Alternatively this can be expressed as 'the limit of $1/x$ as x tends to infinity is zero', written as

$$\operatorname{Lim}_{x \to \infty}\left(\frac{1}{x}\right) = 0.$$

If $f(x)$ always approaches a value l as x approaches a value a in any manner, then the notation is

$$f(x) \to l \text{ as } x \to a \text{ or } \operatorname{Lim}_{x \to a} f(x) = l.$$

For example, $x^2 + 2 \to 3$ as $x \to 1$, or

$$\operatorname{Lim}_{x \to 1}(x^2 + 2) = 3.$$

A function may become arbitrarily large as x tends to infinity or to some value a. In these cases the notation is $f(x) \to \infty$ as $x \to \infty$ and $f(x) \to \infty$ as $x \to a$. Similar notations are used for functions that tend to $-\infty$.

In analysing the behaviour of a function as x approaches a value a, it may be important to discuss separately the cases when x approaches a from the right (i.e. from ∞ to a) and when x approaches a from the left (i.e. from $-\infty$ to a). For example, in the case of the function $f(x) = (1/x)$ and $a = 0$, we have $(1/x) \to +\infty$ as x approaches zero from the right (through positive values) and $(1/x) \to -\infty$ as x approaches zero from the left.

See also continuous function; infinite integral.

2. (of a sequence) A number, A say, that the nth term, a_n, of an infinite *sequence $a_1, a_2, \ldots$ may approach arbitrarily closely as n increases indefinitely, i.e. tends to infinity. This is written as

$$a_n \to A \text{ as } n \to \infty \text{ or } \operatorname{Lim}_{n \to \infty} a_n = A.$$

For example, when $a_n = 1/2^n$, we have

$1/2^n \to 0$ as $n \to \infty$, or

$$\operatorname{Lim}_{x \to \infty} \frac{1}{2^n} = 0.$$

If a sequence has a finite limit it is said to be *convergent*, otherwise it is said to be *divergent*.

See also convergent series.

Lincoln index *See* capture–recapture sampling.

line A *straight line* is a curve that is completely determined geometrically by two of its points. In plane *coordinate geometry a line is a set of points that satisfies a *linear equation of the form

$$ax + by + c = 0,$$

where a and b are not both zero.

In Cartesian coordinates the equation of a straight line has various standard forms, including the following:

Gradient–intercept form. A line with the equation

$$y = mx + c$$

has *gradient m and an *intercept of c on the y-axis, i.e. it passes through the point $(0, c)$.

For example, the line $y = 2x + 3$ has a gradient of 2 and cuts the y-axis at the point $(0, 3)$.

Two-point form. A line passing through two known points (x_1, y_1) and (x_2, y_2) has an equation of the form

$$\frac{x - x_1}{x_2 - x_1} = \frac{y - y_1}{y_2 - y_1}.$$

For instance, the line passing through the points $(1, 3)$ and $(4, 6)$ has the equation

$$\frac{x - 1}{4 - 1} = \frac{y - 3}{6 - 3},$$

which simplifies to $y = x + 2$.

Point–gradient form. A line with gradient m passing through the known point (x_1, y_1)

has the equation

$$y - y_1 = m(x - x_1).$$

For example, the line with gradient -3 passing through the point $(1, 2)$ has the equation $y - 2 = -3(x - 1)$, which rearranges to $y + 3x = 5$.

A line with equation of the form $y = c$ has zero gradient (is horizontal) and passes through the point $(0, c)$. In particular, the x-axis has the equation $y = 0$.

A line with equation of the form $x = c$ is vertical and passes through the point $(c, 0)$. In particular, the y-axis has the equation $x = 0$.

linear Describing an equation, expression, etc. that is of the first *degree. A *linear equation* is one in which all non-constant terms have degree 1. For example,

$$2x + 3y = 6$$

is a linear equation in two variables.

It is also possible to apply the term 'linear' to particular variables in an expression. Thus $2xy^2$ is linear with respect to x.

linear function A *polynomial function of *degree 1. A linear function of one variable is of the form

$$f(x) = a + bx,$$

where a and b are constants. The graph of the function is a straight line with gradient b and intercept a on the y-axis.

linear hypothesis A statistical hypothesis about a *linear function of parameters. For example, a hypothesis that the difference between two population means μ_1 and μ_2 is zero is a linear hypothesis about the function $\mu_1 - \mu_2$.

linear interpolation *See* interpolation.

linear regression A *regression in which the expected value of the response variable is a *linear function of the parameters. For example, a simple linear regression model

of the relationship between the quantity of a commodity sold and its price takes the form

$$q = \alpha + \beta p,$$

where α and β are parameters, and q is the average quantity of the commodity sold when its price is p.

Similarly, a linear regression model of the relationship between stopping distance and car speed is

$$s = \alpha + \beta v + \gamma v^2,$$

where α, β, γ are parameters, and s is the average stopping distance of a car travelling at a given speed v. Here s is a nonlinear *quadratic function of v, but it is a linear function of the parameters and so the regression is linear.

linear scale The standard type of *scale used in drawing *graphs on which the distance of a marked value from the origin is proportional to the value. More generally, it is any scale on which a value is measured or recorded by a number which is proportional to it. *Compare* logarithmic scale.

line of best fit A line which, in some sense, best fits a set of points. Given a set of n points with coordinates (x_1, y_1), (x_2, y_2), $\ldots, (x_n, y_n)$, the line of best fit is often taken to be either the *regression line of y on x* or the *regression line of x on y*.

The regression line of y on x has the equation $y = a + bx$, where the constants a and b are determined from the data points by the method of *least squares. They are the values $\alpha = a$ and $\beta = b$ that minimize the expression

$$\sum_i (y_i - \alpha - \beta x_i)^2.$$

Geometrically, this choice of α and β minimizes the sum of the squares of the deviations of points from the line $y = \alpha + \beta x$ measured in the direction of the y-axis

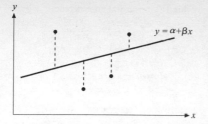

line of best fit (a)

(*see* diagram (a)). These deviations, i.e. $y_i - \alpha - \beta x_i$, are often called *residuals*.

The values of the constants a and b can be calculated from the formulae

$$b = \frac{n \sum_i x_i y_i - \sum_i x_i \sum_i y_i}{n \sum_i x_i^2 - \left(\sum_i x_i\right)^2} \quad \text{and}$$
$$a = \bar{y} - b\bar{x},$$

where

$$\bar{x} = \frac{1}{n}\left(\sum_i x_i\right) \quad \text{and} \quad \bar{y} = \frac{1}{n}\left(\sum_i y_i\right).$$

Such a line of best fit is appropriate if x is assumed to be the explanatory (error-free) variable and y is the response variable. It is often used to estimate the average value of y for an intermediate value of x, and thus provides a method of *interpolation.

Similarly, the regression line of x on y has equation $x = c + dy$, where the constants c and d can be calculated from the formulae

$$d = \frac{n \sum_i x_i y_i - \sum_i x_i \sum_i y_i}{n \sum_i y_i^2 - \left(\sum_i y_i\right)^2} \quad \text{and}$$
$$c = \bar{x} - d\bar{y}.$$

This line of best fit will be appropriate if y is assumed to be the explanatory variable and x the response variable. It is often used to estimate the average value of x for an intermediate value of y.

If s_x and s_y denote the standard deviations of the x- and y-values, and s_{xy} is their *covariance, then the equation of the regression line of y on x can be written as

$$y - \bar{y} = \frac{s_{xy}}{s_x^2}(x - \bar{x})$$

and, similarly, the equation of the line of regression of x on y is

$$x - \bar{x} = \frac{s_{xy}}{s_y^2}(y - \bar{y}).$$

In general, the two regression lines, of y on x and of x on y, are not the same. However, they both always pass through the point $(\bar{x}, \bar{y})$. The lines are useful for making predictions about the likely value of the response variable when the explantory variable has some *intermediate* value. Their use with values outside the range of the data (i.e. as a method of *extrapolation) should be treated with caution, as the relation between the variables may change considerably outside the known range.

As an illustration, the following table contains the results of six trials, giving the yield y when a crop was given a quantity x of fertilizer:

Crop yield (y)	18	24	36	51	63	69
Fertilizer quantity (x)	1	2	3	4	5	6

If we assume the yield y to be the response variable, we seek a line of best fit of the form $y = a + bx$. From the table, $n = 6$, $\sum_i x_i = 21$, $\sum_i y_i = 261$, $\sum_i x_i^2 = 91$ and $\sum_i x_i y_i = 1107$. Using the formulae, we obtain

$$b = \frac{6 \times 1107 + 21 \times 261}{6 \times 91 - (21)^2} = 11.057.$$

Next, $\bar{x} = 21/6 = 3.5$ and $\bar{y} = 261/6 = 43.5$, and finally

$$a = 43.5 - 11.057 \times 3.5 = 4.80.$$

Thus the line of best fit (the regression line of y on x) is

$$y = 4.80 + 11.06x$$

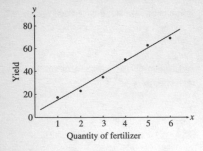

Quantity of fertilizer

line of best fit (b)

(*see* diagram (b)). We can use this to estimate that when the quantity of fertilizer $x = 4.5$, the average yield $y = 54.6$.

ln Natural logarithm. *See* logarithm.

local maximum *See* maximum.

local minimum *See* minimum.

location The position of a *frequency distribution or *sample. It is usually indicated by giving a central or typical value such as the *mean, *median or *mode. These are called *measures of location* or *central measures*. *See also* centrality.

logarithm (log) For a positive number x, the power y to which some number b must be raised to give x. The number b is the *base* of the logarithm. So if $x = b^y$, the logarithm of x to the base b is y, and this is written as $\log_b x = y$. For example, $100 = 10^2$, so the logarithm of 100 to the base 10 is 2, and this is written as $\log_{10} 100 = 2$.

Logarithms to the base 10 are called *common logarithms*, and, by convention, $\log_{10} x$ is usually written simply as $\log x$, e.g. on the keypads of calculators.

Logarithms to the base e $(2.718\ldots)$ are *natural logarithms* (also called *Napierian* or *hyperbolic logarithms*). Usually $\log_e x$ is written as $\ln x$.

The logarithm of 1 is zero, to any base. The logarithm of the *reciprocal of a number is the negative of the logarithm of the number. So, for example, $\log(1/100) =$

$-\log 100 = -2$ and, in general,

$$\log(1/n) = -\log n.$$

Certain *laws of logarithms* apply:
(i) $\log(mn) = \log m + \log n$;
(ii) $\log(m/n) = \log m - \log n$;
(iii) $\log(m^n) = n \log m$.

logarithmic coordinate system A *Cartesian coordinate system in which the axes are marked with *logarithmic scales. *See* graph.

logarithmic function The function $\ln x$ or $\log_e x$. It is defined for $x > 0$, and is such that $y = \ln x$ if $x = e^y$. Its *derivative is $1/x$. The graph of $y = \ln x$ intersects the x-axis at $(1, 0)$ and has an *asymptote, the y-axis (*see* diagram).

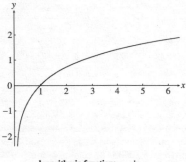

logarithmic function: $y = \ln x$.

logarithmic graph *See* graph.

logarithmic paper A form of graph paper on which both axes have *logarithmic scales. It is also called *log–log* or *double log paper*. Graph paper on which one axis has a *linear scale and the other has a logarithmic scale is called *semi-logarithmic* or *single log paper* (*see* diagram).

logarithmic scale A type of *scale used in drawing *graphs on which the distance of a marked value from the origin is proportional to the *logarithm of the value. The

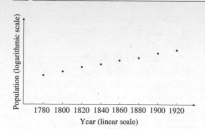

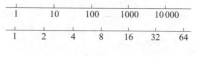

logarithmic paper A plot on semi-logarithmic paper of Swedish population data for 1780 to 1920. The points lie close to a straight line, which suggests that there was an exponential growth of population during that period.

origin is marked 1 since the logarithm of 1 is zero (to any base).

For example, the logarithmic scale with points at equal intervals marked 1, 10, 100, 1000, 10 000, … is commonly used. So also is the scale marked 1, 2, 4, 8, 16, 32, … (*see* diagram).

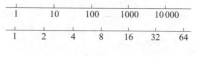

logarithmic scale

More generally, it is any scale on which a value is measured or recorded by a number that is proportional to the logarithm of the value. For instance, the Richter scale is a logarithmic scale for recording the magnitude of a seismic disturbance.

See logarithmic paper; *compare* linear scale.

logarithmic transformation A transformation of a positive random variable X into a variable Y where $Y = \ln X$. It is important because in some situations the distribution of Y is *normal, and so it transforms X into a variable with well-known properties. *See* lognormal distribution.

logistic curve *See* sigmoid curve.

logistic function *See* logistic regression.

logistic regression A linear *regression of the *logit of a proportion on explanatory variables of which at least one is continuous. For an example with one explanatory variable, suppose that an insecticide is applied at a series of increasing concentrations x_1, x_2, …, x_n to n independent groups of insects, and that the corresponding proportions dying in the groups are estimated to be p_1, p_2, …, p_n. The proportion dying increases as the concentration increases, and it is sometimes appropriate to assume that the average proportion p killed at concentration x is given by a *logistic function* of the form

$$p = \frac{1}{1 + \exp(-\alpha - \beta x)},$$

where α and β are constants. The graph of such a function, a *logistic curve*, has the shape of a *sigmoid curve. The equation given above can be shown to be equivalent to

$$\ln\left(\frac{p}{1-p}\right) = \alpha + \beta x.$$

This is a linear regression of $\ln(p/(1-p))$, the *logit* of p, on x, and is called a *logistic regression equation*.

Appropriate computer software will give *maximum likelihood estimates of the parameters α and β based on the n pairs of experimental values (p_i, x_i).

The method may be extended to more than one explanatory variable, and will be valid only if certain assumptions hold.

logit For a proportion p, where $0 < p < 1$, the quantity $\ln(p/(1-p))$. When p is a probability, its logit is equal to the logarithm of the *odds. It is sometimes called the *log-odds*. *See* logistic regression.

log–log graph *See* graph.

log–log paper *See* logarithmic paper.

lognormal distribution If a positive random variable X is such that the *logarithm of X has a *normal distribution, then X is said to have a *lognormal distribution*, or to be *lognormally distributed*. More formally, if $Y = \ln X$ and Y has a normal distribution, then X has a lognormal distribution. For example, studies have shown that the weight of vegetable marrows is approximately lognormally distributed.

lognormally *See* lognormal distribution.

log-odds *See* logit.

longitudinal data *See* longitudinal study.

longitudinal study A general term for studies in which observations are taken at different points in time. Data obtained in this way are called *longitudinal data*.

In a *cohort study*, a group of individuals, the *cohort*, is selected, and observations are made on samples of members of the cohort at intervals. For example, a longitudinal study of child development could use all children born in a particular year as the cohort.

In a *panel study*, a group of individuals, the *panel*, is selected, and observations are made on each member of the panel at intervals. For example, the British Household Panel Survey is of this form, using a representative sample of households as the panel and interviewing annually.

Compare cross-sectional study.

loop *See* graph.

Lorenz curve A graph that illustrates the sharing of economic quantities such as income, land or wealth among individuals. Usually it is a plot of the cumulative percentage (y) of the quantity earned (or

owned) against the cumulative percentage (x) of individuals earning (or owning) it. Thus it illustrates statements such as 'the poorest x percent of the people own y percent of the nation's wealth'.

More formally, let the amounts earned by n individuals be, in ascending order, $x_1, x_2, \ldots, x_n$, and the total amount earned be A. Then the amount owned by the first r individuals is $\sum_1^r x_i$, and the Lorenz curve is a plot of

$$y = \frac{1}{A} \sum_1^r x_i \times 100 \quad \text{against} \quad x = \frac{r}{n} \times 100.$$

For example, if a sample of ten individuals in a company have annual salaries, in £k, of 10, 11, 15, 17, 18, 27, 30, 35, 38 and 49, then the total is 250 and the cumulative amounts earned are 10, 21, 36, 53, 71, 98, 128, 163, 201 and 250. The cumulative amounts are converted into percentages of 250, and the Lorenz curve is then based on the table.

The series of points are usually joined, and a line joining $(0, 0)$ to $(100, 100)$ is com-

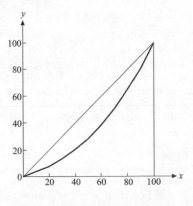

Lorenz curve

Cumulative % of individuals (x)	0	10	20	30	40	50	60	70	80	90	100
Cumulative % of salary total (y)	0	4	8	14	21	28	39	51	65	80	100

monly added. This line corresponds to the situation where all individuals earn or own the same amount and is sometimes called the *line of equality*.

The *Gini coefficient*, denoted by G, is a measure of the degree of inequality in earnings or ownership. It is based on the relative size of the area between the Lorenz curve and the line of equality, and is given by

$$G = \frac{\text{area between the Lorenz curve and the line of equality}}{\text{triangular area below the line of equality}}.$$

This lies between 0 and 1, with $G = 0$ representing perfect equality of distribution and a value close to 1 indicating an extreme degree of inequality. In the above example, $G = 0.28$.

lower quartile *See* quartile.

M

McNemar's test A *nonparametric test for differences in proportions in *matched pair samples. It is most often used when the observed variable is a *dichotomous variable, e.g. taking values 'yes' or 'no'. For example, samples might be formed from the responses 'cure' or 'failure' of matched pairs of patients to two medical treatments, or from the attitudes 'for' or 'against' of individuals before and after the debate of a motion.

In general, denoting the possible values of the variable by a and b, the test determines whether the proportion of pairs (a, b) differs significantly from that of (b, a). From the data the number of pairs of each type are counted and can be tabulated as shown below:

First sample value	Second sample value	
	a	b
a	P	Q
b	R	S

The test is concerned with the numbers Q and R, of pairs in which there is a difference or change in value. The test statistic X^2 is given by

$$X^2 = \frac{(|Q - R| - 1)^2}{Q + R},$$

where $|\ |$ is the *modulus sign.

The distribution of X^2 is approximately the *chi-squared distribution with 1 degree of freedom. Significantly high values of X^2

lead to rejection of the *null hypothesis that pairs (a, b) and (b, a) are equally likely.

For example, suppose that a random sample of 200 voters were asked for their attitude towards a party before and after a party political broadcast by its leader, and that the results were as follows:

Before	After	
	For	Against
For	80	12
Against	23	85

The null hypothesis is that voters who changed their attitude were equally likely to change in favour as to change against the party. The table shows 23 changed in favour and 12 changed against. The test statistic is given by

$$X^2 = \frac{(|12 - 23| - 1)^2}{35} = \frac{10^2}{35} = 2.86.$$

From Table 5 in the Appendix, the value of X^2 needs to exceed 3.84 to be significant at the 5% level. Since 2.86 is less than 3.84 (its *p-value is 0.091), we retain the null hypothesis that, on the evidence of this sample, there has been no swing for or against the party in question.

The test is an approximation to the *sign test for matched pairs applied to a situation where ties predominate and are ignored. The test statistic is a chi-squared approximation to the *binomial distribution with $p = 0.5$. In the above example, in which there are $12 + 23 = 35$ non-tied pairs, the approximation is close, but this would not be so if the number of non-tied pairs were very small.

main diagonal *See* matrix.

main effect *See* factorial experiment.

Malthus model *See* model.

Mann–Whitney test *See* Wilcoxon rank sum test.

marginal distribution *See* bivariate distribution.

marginal frequency function *See* bivariate distribution.

Markov chain A *stochastic process involving a succession of discrete *random variables $X_1, X_2, X_3, \ldots$ in which the conditional distribution (*see* bivariate distribution) of X_n depends only on the state (i.e. value) of X_{n-1}, for all $n \geqslant 2$.

For example, suppose that the weather on a particular day has one of two states: D (dry) or R (rainy). Suppose that if it is dry one day, then the probabilities that it is dry or rainy the next day are 0.5 and 0.5, respectively, and that if it is rainy then the probabilities that it is dry or rainy the next day are 0.4 and 0.6, respectively. Then the probabilities for the weather on a particular day are dependent only on the state of the weather the previous day. Let W_n denote the weather on day n; this is a random variable taking one of two values, D or R. As we have seen, the distribution of W_n is dependent only on the state of W_{n-1}. So we have a Markov chain: $W_1, W_2, W_3, \ldots$. The probabilities of a dry (or rainy) day, given that it was dry or rainy the previous day, are called *transition probabilities* and can be presented in a *matrix as follows. A matrix of transition probabilities is called a *transition matrix*.

Today

		Dry	Rainy
Previous day	Dry	0.5	0.5
	Rainy	0.4	0.6

In our example, the random variables have two possible states, and the transition probabilities form a 2×2 matrix in which the sum of the elements in each row is equal to 1. In general, when the random variables have k possible states, the transition probability p_{ij} is the probability of being in the jth state, given that the previous state was the ith state. The transition probabilities form a $k \times k$ transition matrix, the typical element p_{ij} lying in the ith row and jth column. Again, the sum of the elements in each row of the transition matrix is equal to 1.

matched groups procedure *See* matched pairs.

matched pairs Pairs of experimental units chosen to be as close as possible to each other in characteristics likely to affect their response to treatment. For example, in an experiment to compare the readability of a children's text in two different formats, pairs of children with the same reading age and general ability could be used as matched pairs.

When comparing two treatments A and B, a member of a pair is chosen at random to receive treatment A and the other member then receives treatment B. Carrying out this process for a number of matched pairs produces two samples of observations, one for treatment A and the other for treatment B. These are called *matched* (or *related*) *samples* or *matched pair samples*. The process is sometimes called the *matched pairs procedure*.

Pairs can also be obtained by using single units twice. In this case the two treatments are given in random order and with an appropriate interval between them. For example, to assess whether two tests of spatial ability were of the same difficulty, participants could take both tests a week apart. As above, the process produces two matched samples.

The procedure extends to the comparison of more than two treatments using matched groups of units or the repeated use of individual units. It again leads to *matched* (or *related*) *samples* for the treatments. For example, in a test of three growth hormones on piglets, taking three piglets from the same litter to form each matched group could help to reduce the effect of genetic differences on the response to treatment. The use of matched groups is sometimes called the *matched groups procedure*.

See also randomized blocks; sign test; *t*-test; Wilcoxon signed rank test.

matched samples *See* matched pairs.

matched samples design *See* randomized blocks.

matrix (*plural* **matrices**) An array of numbers arranged in rows and columns and enclosed in brackets.

A matrix with r rows and c columns is said to be of *order* $r \times c$ or to be an $r \times c$ *matrix*. The numbers in the matrix are called *elements* or *entries*. The standard notation for the element in the ith row and jth column of a matrix A is a_{ij}. Thus for the matrix

$$A = \begin{pmatrix} 3 & 2 & 6 \\ 1 & 0 & 4 \end{pmatrix} = \begin{pmatrix} a_{11} & a_{21} & a_{31} \\ a_{21} & a_{22} & a_{23} \end{pmatrix},$$

A is a 2×3 matrix, with $a_{11} = 3, a_{21} = 2$, etc.

A matrix consisting of only one row is a *row matrix* or *row vector*, and a matrix with only one column is a *column matrix* or *column vector*.

A *square matrix* has the same number of rows as columns. For a square matrix, the diagonal line from the top left corner to the bottom right corner is called the *leading diagonal* or *main diagonal*. The diagonal from top right to bottom left is the *secondary diagonal*. A *symmetric matrix* is symmetric in its leading diagonal, i.e. is such that $a_{ij} = a_{ji}$ for all i and j. For example,

$$\begin{pmatrix} 0 & 3 \\ 3 & -1 \end{pmatrix}$$

is symmetric. If all the elements not lying on the leading diagonal of a matrix are zero, then it is a *diagonal matrix*. For instance,

$$\begin{pmatrix} 2 & 0 \\ 0 & 1 \end{pmatrix}$$

is a diagonal matrix. An *identity* (or *unit*) *matrix* is a diagonal matrix in which all the elements on the leading diagonal are equal to 1. For example,

$$\begin{pmatrix} 1 & 0 \\ 0 & 1 \end{pmatrix} \quad \text{and} \quad \begin{pmatrix} 1 & 0 & 0 \\ 0 & 1 & 0 \\ 0 & 0 & 1 \end{pmatrix}$$

are identity matrices.

See correlation matrix; covariance matrix; stochastic matrix; transition matrix.

maximum (*plural* **maxima**) Greatest possible. The *maximum value* (or *global maximum*) of a function is the greatest value that it reaches. A function $f(x)$ has a *local maximum* when $x = a$, if $f(x) \leqslant f(a)$ for all values of x in the neighbourhood of a (it has a *strict local maximum* if $f(x) < f(a)$).

maximum likelihood estimation A procedure for estimating a *parameter by finding the value of it that maximizes the *likelihood function for a random sample of observations. As the *logarithm of the likelihood is also maximized by the same value of the parameter, and the calculations are simpler, it is common practice to work with the logarithm of the likelihood.

A simple example of the procedure's use is to estimate the parameter λ of the *exponential distribution, whose *frequency function is written in the form

$$f(x, \lambda) = \lambda e^{-\lambda x}.$$

Given a sample of n independent observations $x_1, x_2, \ldots, x_n$ from the distribution, the likelihood function is

$$L(\lambda) = \lambda e^{-\lambda x_1} \lambda e^{-\lambda x_2} \cdots \lambda e^{-\lambda x_n}$$
$$= \lambda^n e^{-\lambda(x_1 + x_2 + \cdots + x_n)}.$$

Taking logarithms to base e, we have

$$\ln L(\lambda) = n \ln \lambda - \lambda(x_1 + x_2 + \cdots + x_n).$$

To determine the value of λ, we differentiate $\ln L(\lambda)$ with respect to λ, equate the *derivative to zero and solve the resulting equation for λ. The equation obtained by differentiation is

$$n/\lambda - (x_1 + x_2 + \cdots + x_n) = 0,$$

and the solution is

$$\lambda = n/(x_1 + x_2 + \cdots + x_n).$$

It is easily verified that this value of λ gives $\ln L(\lambda)$ (and also $L(\lambda)$) its maximum value. Hence the maximum likelihood estimator of λ is the *reciprocal of the *sample mean.

The method extends to the estimation of more than one parameter, and usually leads to *estimators with desirable statistical properties such as being *unbiased.

maximum value See maximum.

mean 1. The *arithmetic mean* or *average* of a set of observations is their sum divided by the number of observations. Thus for the four observations 7, 10, 19, 24,

$$\text{arithmetic mean} = \frac{7 + 10 + 19 + 24}{4} = \frac{60}{4}$$
$$= 15.$$

In general, for a set of n observations $x_1, x_2, \ldots, x_n$, the mean is usually denoted

by $\bar{x}$ and may be expressed as

$$\bar{x} = \frac{x_1 + x_2 + \cdots + x_n}{n} = \frac{1}{n} \sum_i x_i.$$

It is common practice to omit the word 'arithmetic', so that the 'mean' of a set of observations is taken to indicate the arithmetic mean.

A *weighted mean* (or *weighted average*) is one in which a weight w_i is given to each observation x_i, and is equal to

$$\sum_i w_i x_i \Big/ \sum_i w_i.$$

For example, if the observations 7, 10, 19, 24 are given weights of 3, 2, 1, 1, respectively, then the weighted mean of the observations, $\bar{x}_w$, is calculated as

$$\bar{x}_w = \frac{3 \times 7 + 2 \times 10 + 1 \times 19 + 1 \times 24}{3 + 2 + 1 + 1} = \frac{84}{7}$$
$$= 12.$$

When data are recorded in a *frequency table in which each observation x_i has frequency f_i, the mean of the observations is given by

$$\bar{x} = \sum_i f_i x_i \Big/ \sum_i f_i.$$

For example, the following table records daily frequencies of e-mails:

E-mails received in a day (x_i)	0	1	2	3	4	5	6
Frequency (f_i)	1	3	5	3	4	2	2

The mean number of e-mails received per day is calculated as

$$\bar{x} = \frac{1 \times 0 + 3 \times 1 + 5 \times 2 + 3 \times 3 + 4 \times 4 + 2 \times 5 + 2 \times 6}{1 + 3 + 5 + 3 + 4 + 2 + 2}$$
$$= \frac{60}{20} = 3.$$

The mean of a sample or distribution is a standard measure of *centrality and *location.

2. The *geometric mean* of n positive quantities is the nth root of their product. Thus for two positive quantities it is the square root of their product; for three, the cube root; and so on. For the four observations 7, 10, 19, 24, the geometric mean is

$$\sqrt[4]{7 \times 10 \times 19 \times 24} = \sqrt[4]{31\,920} = 13.4.$$

In general, the geometric mean of the n quantities $x_1, x_2, \ldots, x_n$ is

$$\sqrt[n]{(x_1 x_2 \cdots x_n)}.$$

The geometric mean of a set of positive quantities is always less than or equal to their arithmetic mean (the *arithmetic–geometric mean inequality*). If a sample contains large *outliers, their influence on the sample mean can be reduced by using the geometric mean rather than the arithmetic mean. For example, the sample of five observations 12, 17, 19, 26, 91 has a large outlier, 91. The arithmetic mean is 33 and exceeds all but one of the observations. On the other hand, the geometric mean is 24.7. One of the earliest *FTSE share indices, the *FT30 Share Index*, was a geometric mean of the prices of 30 leading shares.

3. The *harmonic mean* of a set of non-zero quantities is the *reciprocal of the arithmetic mean of the reciprocals of the quantities. It is not widely used in statistics.

4. The mean of a *random variable X is its *expectation $E(X)$.

mean absolute deviation The mean of the *absolute values of the deviations of a set of observations from their *mean, or sometimes from their *median. It is a measure of *dispersion. The expression 'mean absolute deviation' is often shortened to *mean deviation*.

For example, the observations 1, 5, 6, 8, 15 have a mean of 7. Their deviations from the mean are $-6, -2, -1, +1, +8$, respectively, and the absolute values of these deviations are 6, 2, 1, 1, 8. The mean absolute

deviation about the mean is thus

$$\frac{6 + 2 + 1 + 1 + 8}{5} = \frac{18}{5} = 3.6.$$

Alternatively, their median is 6 and the mean absolute deviation about the median is

$$\frac{5 + 1 + 0 + 2 + 9}{5} = \frac{17}{5} = 3.4.$$

In general, for a set of n observations $x_1, x_2, \ldots, x_n$ with mean $\bar{x}$ and median m, the mean absolute deviation about the mean is given by

$$\frac{1}{n} \sum_1^n |x_i - \bar{x}|,$$

and the mean absolute deviation about median by

$$\frac{1}{n} \sum_1^n |x_i - m|.$$

It can be shown that the mean absolute deviation of a set of observations is least when measured about the median.

Compare mean square deviation.

mean deviation **1.** *Abbreviated form of* *mean absolute deviation.

2. The *mean of the deviations of a set of observations from some value. It is equivalent to the deviation of the mean of the observations from the given value. Thus the mean deviation of observations from their mean is always zero.

For example, suppose that a factory unit aims to produce 50 items per day and actually produces 48, 55, 51, 43, 56 items in a certain five-day week. The deviations from the daily production target of 50 are $-2, +5, +1, -7, +6$, respectively. The mean deviation is

$$(-2 + 5 + 1 - 7 + 6)/5 = 0.6.$$

This indicates that the average daily production was above target that week and was equal to 50.6 items.

mean square *See* analysis of variance; mean square deviation.

mean square deviation The *mean of the squares of the deviations of a set of observations from some value. For a set of n observations $x_1, x_2, \ldots, x_n$, the mean square deviation about the value a is

$$\frac{1}{n} \sum_{1}^{n} (x_i - a)^2.$$

The mean square deviation about the mean $\bar{x}$ is the *variance of the observations. Its square root, the *root mean square deviation* about the mean, is the *standard deviation. It can be shown that the mean square deviation is least when measured about the mean. *Compare* mean absolute deviation.

measurement The assignment of a number to an object or observation according to some system or *scale of measurement. For example, the height of one adult in a group of 20 might be measured as 1.92 metres, or assigned the number 5 if the adults are simply ranked on their heights from 1 (tallest) to 20 (shortest). The idea is sometimes extended to include the assignment of a category to the object of measurement. Thus an adult's eye colour might be placed in the category 'blue' and said to be 'measured as blue'. *See* data.

measurement scale *See* scale of measurement.

measures of dispersion *See* dispersion.

measures of location *See* location.

median For the five observations 2, 6, 8, 12, 17 arranged in ascending order, the median is the 'middle' value, 8. For the six observations 3, 9, 13, 15, 23, 30, the median is 14, the average of the two central values, 13 and 15. In general, if n observations are listed in ascending order, the median is the $\frac{1}{2}(n + 1)$th observation if n is odd, and the average of the $\frac{1}{2}n$th and the $(\frac{1}{2}n + 1)$th if n is even. Thus in the first example above, $n = 5$ is odd, and the median is the $\frac{1}{2}(5 + 1) = $ 3rd observation, 8. In the second example, $n = 6$ is even, and the median is the average of the 3rd and 4th observations, 13 and 15. The median is a useful measure of *centrality and location.

When observations are available only as *grouped data, an approximate median can be found from a *cumulative frequency table or graph by estimating the value whose cumulative relative frequency is 0.5.

For a continuous *random variable X with *distribution function $F(x)$, the median is the value m such that

$$\Pr(X \leqslant m) = F(m) = 0.5.$$

Thus the median is the 50th *percentile. If the frequency function is $f(x)$, then m is such that

$$\int_{-\infty}^{m} f(x)\,dx = 0.5.$$

For a discrete random variable X taking values $x_1 < x_2 < x_3 < \cdots$, the median is the value x_i if $\Pr(X \leqslant x_i) > 0.5$ and $\Pr(X \leqslant x_{i-1}) < 0.5$, and is taken to be $\frac{1}{2}(x_i + x_{i+1})$ if $\Pr(X \leqslant x_i) = 0.5$.

median test A *distribution-free test of whether two independent samples are from populations with equal *medians (or are from the same population). First, the samples are combined, and the median of the combined sample is calculated. Secondly a 2×2 *contingency table is formed, the rows corresponding to the separate samples and the columns containing the numbers of sample values above and below the combined median. Finally, *Fisher's exact test is used to test for differences in the proportions of sample values above and below the combined median. Significant differences indicate that the populations have different medians. Alternatively, if the total number of sample values is large, the *chi-squared test can be used.

To illustrate the procedure, the following data consist of the times in minutes taken by two groups of individuals to each complete a standard word-processing task. One group used a new computer, A, advertised to be faster than the computer, B, used by the other group. The median test is used to test the *null hypothesis that the median time for this task is the same on both computers against the alternative that the median time for computer A is less than that for B.

The results were:

Times for computer A	19	25	33	42		
Times for computer B	29	44	44	47	58	59

The median of the ten values in the combined sample is the average of 42 and 44, i.e. 43. The contingency table is thus:

	Above the median	Below the median
Sample for computer A	0	4
Sample for computer B	5	1

Fisher's exact test shows that the difference in proportions above and below the combined median is significant at the 5% level (the one-tail *p-value is 0.029). Thus the alternative hypothesis that the median time for this task is lower on computer A than on B is accepted.

A difficulty arises in forming the contingency table if some sample values are equal to the combined median. This can be met either by changing the second column heading from 'Below the median' to 'Less than or equal to the median', or, if the total number of sample values is large, by omitting these values from the analysis.

The median test can be extended to determine whether $k \, (>2)$ independent samples come from populations with equal medians (or the same population). The median of the combined samples is calculated, a $k \times 2$ contingency table formed, and an extension of the exact test or a chi-squared test carried out.

See also Wilcoxon rank sum test.

meet *See* intersection.

member *See* set.

mesokurtic *See* kurtosis.

meta-analysis An analytic procedure in which data from a number of separate experiments performed at different times and/or locations are combined and used to make *statistical inferences. In this way it is sometimes possible to establish that an effect is *significant when the individual experiments are too small for this to be achieved with single experiments, or to increase the *precision of estimates. However, care must be taken when combining measurements that are nominally similar if they have been made under different conditions in the separate experiments. For example, in comparisons of the cure rates for two drugs, in one experiment the drugs may have been given only to patients showing mild symptoms, whereas in a second experiment they were given only to those showing severe symptoms, and in a third experiment to patients showing a wide variety of symptoms. *See also* data mining; Simpson's paradox.

method of least squares *See* least squares.

metric (distance function) A procedure for finding, in some sense, a 'distance' between two items, or a measure of their 'closeness'. For example, for points in two dimensions the standard metric defines the distance $d(A, B)$ between two points A, B to be the length of the straight line joining them. If A and B have coordinates (x_1, y_1) and

(x_2, y_2), respectively, then

$$d(A, B) = \sqrt{(x_2 - x_1)^2 + (y_2 - y_1)^2}.$$

This is called the *Euclidean metric*, and is easily extended to pairs of points in spaces of three or more dimensions.

Another metric, the *taxicab* or *city-block metric*, defines $d(A, B)$ to be the shortest distance from one point to the other travelling parallel to the coordinate axes. In two dimensions,

$$d(A, B) = |x_2 - x_1| + |y_2 - y_1|,$$

where $| |$ is the *modulus sign. This also easily extends to pairs of points in higher-dimensional spaces.

For example, if A and B are the points $(2, 6)$ and $(5, 2)$, then the standard Euclidean metric calculates the distance between them to be $\sqrt{[(3)^2 + (-4)^2]} = \sqrt{25} = 5$, whereas the taxicab metric would calculate the distance to be $|3| + |-4| = 7$.

Similarly, suppose that $(4, 3, 6)$ and $(6, 7, 2)$ represent the scores of two individuals on three different tests. The Euclidean distance between these results is $\sqrt{[2^2 + 4^2 + (-4)^2]} = 6$. The taxicab distance is $|2| + |4| + |-4| = 10$.

More formally, a metric on a set of items gives to any two of them, a and b, a non-negative number $d(a, b)$ which is such that
(i) $d(a, a) = 0$;
(ii) $d(a, b) = d(b, a)$;
(iii) for any third item c,

$$d(a, b) + d(b, c) \geqslant d(a, c).$$

See cluster analysis.

m.g.f. *Abbreviation for* *moment generating function.

mid-interval value (mid value) *See* grouped data.

mid-parent *See* regression towards the mean.

mid-rank method *See* rank.

minimum (*plural* **minima**) Least possible. The *minimum value* (or *global minimum*) of a function is the least value that it reaches. A function $f(x)$ has a *local minimum* when $x = a$, if $f(x) \geqslant f(a)$ for all values of x in the neighbourhood of a (it has a *strict local minimum* if $f(x) > f(a)$).

minimum value *See* minimum.

MINITAB *See* statistical software packages.

mixed distribution *See* compound distribution.

modal class *See* mode.

mode For a sample, the mode is the observation with the greatest *frequency. Thus, for the sample

$$4 \quad 5 \quad 1 \quad 4 \quad 8 \quad 3 \quad 5 \quad 2 \quad 6 \quad 4$$

the mode is 4.

For data which are *grouped using equal class intervals, the *modal class* is the interval with the greatest class frequency. Sometimes a modal class is defined as a class whose class frequency is greater than those of either of its neighbours.

For a random variable X, the modes are the values of X corresponding to any *maxima of the *frequency function.

There may be more than one mode, in which case the sample or distribution is said to be *multimodal*. The term *bimodal* is used when there are two modes. The mode is a measure of *centrality and location.

model In general, a system of definitions, assumptions and equations set up to describe or study some natural phenomenon. A family of *distributions such as the *normal and *exponential distribution families are models that under appropriate assumptions describe the behaviour of observations of certain physical entities. For example, the distribution of heights of adult males can be described by a normal distribution with a suitable choice of parameters. When these parameters are unknown, the use of sample data to estimate them is a problem of *statistical inference.

Some models are entirely deterministic. A very simple example is the *Malthus model* of population growth, which asserts that human populations grow in *geometric progression, i.e. by a constant percentage each year. There are also models, called *stochastic models*, that are composed entirely of random elements or processes. These include, for example, models for queuing at supermarket checkouts or at airline check-in desks and are used to study the effects of changes in variables such as the rate at which customers join the queue, the speed at which they are served, or how the system behaviour might be changed by opening additional checkouts or desks. Stochastic models are also used to study the likely development of epidemics of contagious diseases.

Much statistical inference is concerned with models that contain both a deterministic and a random element. A commonly used model of this type is the *linear regression model. A more sophisticated group of models of this nature are the *generalized linear models*, which are prominent in advanced applications.

See regression.

modulus *See* absolute value.

modulus sign The symbol $|\ |$ used to denote the *absolute value of a number.

moment In general, the *mean or *expectation of a power of a variable (or a power of its deviation from some value).

For a random variable X, the expectation of X^r, i.e. $\mathrm{E}(X^r)$, is the rth *moment about the origin*. Thus the first moment about the origin is $\mathrm{E}(X)$, and equals the mean μ; the second moment is $\mathrm{E}(X^2)$, and so on. The rth moment about the origin is often denoted by μ'_r. Thus $\mu'_r = \mathrm{E}(X^r)$ and $\mu'_1 = \mu$.

Similarly, for a sample of n observations $x_1, x_2, \ldots, x_n$, the mean value of x_i^r, i.e. $(1/n)\sum_{i=1}^{n} x_i^r$, is the rth *sample moment about the origin*. Thus the first sample moment about the origin is $(1/n)\sum_i x_i$, and equals the sample mean $\bar{x}$; the second moment is $(1/n)\sum_i x_i^2$, and so on.

In general, the rth moment about a point a is $\mathrm{E}((X - a)^r)$ for a variable X, and $(1/n)\sum_{i=1}^{n} (x_i - a)^r$ for a sample. The most commonly used moments are those when a is the origin ($a = 0$) and when a is the mean.

For a random variable X, with mean μ, the expectation of $(X - \mu)^r$ is the rth *moment about the mean*. It is often denoted by μ_r. Thus

$$\mu_r = \mathrm{E}((X - \mu)^r).$$

The second moment about the mean, μ_2, is the *variance of X.

Similarly, for a sample of n observations x_i with mean $\bar{x}$, the mean value of $(x_i - \bar{x})^r$ is the rth *sample moment about the mean*. It is often denoted by m_r. Thus

$$m_r = \frac{1}{n} \sum_{i=1}^{n} (x_i - \bar{x})^r.$$

The second sample moment about the mean, m_2, is the sample variance. Moments about the mean are sometimes called *corrected moments*, moments about the origin being called *uncorrected moments*.

See product moment; moment generating function; kurtosis; skewness.

moment generating function (m.g.f.) For a *random variable X, the moment generating function is the *expectation of e^{tX}. It is usually denoted by $\mathrm{M}(t)$ or $\mathrm{M}_X(t)$; the variable t is arbitrary. The function is said to *generate* *moments since, if it has a *series expansion, the coefficient of $t^r/r!$ is the rth moment about the origin of X. It is also the value of the rth derivative of $\mathrm{M}(t)$ when $t = 0$. Thus $\mathrm{E}(X) = \mathrm{M}'(0)$,

$E(X^2) = M''(0)$, and so on. Also, $Var(X) = M''(0) - (M'(0))^2$.

For a simple example, suppose that X has a continuous *uniform distribution on the interval $[0, 1]$. Its frequency function $f(x)$ is equal to 1 when $0 \leqslant x \leqslant 1$, and zero otherwise. Then

$$M(t) = \int_0^1 e^{tx}.1 \, dx = \left[\frac{e^{tx}}{t}\right]_0^1 = \frac{e^t - 1}{t},$$

and, using the *exponential series, the series for $M(t)$ is found to be

$$M(t) = 1 + \frac{t}{2} + \frac{t^2}{6} + \frac{t^3}{24} + \cdots.$$

From this, the first moment $E(X) = \frac{1}{2} = M'(0)$, the second moment $E(X^2) = \frac{1}{3} = M''(0)$, and in general the rth moment is equal to $1/(r + 1)$. Also,

$$Var(X) = \frac{1}{3} - \left(\frac{1}{2}\right)^2 = \frac{1}{12}.$$

An important result is that if two random variables X and Y are independent, then the moment generating function of their sum $X + Y$ equals the product of their moment generating functions. Thus if $Z = X + Y$, then

$$M_Z(t) = M_X(t)M_Y(t).$$

For example, if X and Y both have uniform distributions on $[0, 1]$ (as described above) and are independent, then their sum Z has a *triangular distribution. Its moment generating function is given by

$$M_Z(t) = \frac{(e^t - 1)^2}{t^2}$$

$$= 1 + t + \frac{7}{12}t^2 + \frac{1}{4}t^3 + \cdots.$$

From this, the first three moments of Z are $1, \frac{7}{6}$ and $\frac{3}{2}$ respectively. The mean is 1 and the variance is $\frac{7}{6} - 1^2 = \frac{1}{6}$.

For a variable X, with mean μ, the moment generating function $M(t)$ – when

it exists – gives all the moments about the origin. The moment generating function giving all the moments about the mean is $e^{-\mu t} M(t)$.

See also probability generating function.

Monte Carlo methods Methods in which sampling experiments, usually carried out on computers using *random number generators, are used to solve a problem. Monte Carlo methods are applied widely to test mathematical *models in economics and science, since the data they provide exemplify what real data would be like if the assumptions of the model were correct. They are also used to provide estimates or approximate solutions to problems where an exact method is impractical or unknown.

mortality rate *See* death rate.

mortality tables *See* life tables.

moving average One of a sequence of values used in smoothing the fluctuations in a *time series. Given a set of observations $x_1, x_2, x_3, \ldots$ taken at equally spaced intervals of time, e.g. daily, a moving average is a *mean (usually a weighted mean) of a fixed number of neighbouring observations. It is associated with the time at the centre of the observations from which it is formed.

For example, a simple *three-point moving average* is $\frac{1}{3}(x_{i-1} + x_i + x_{i+1})$ for $i \geqslant 2$, and this is associated with the time of x_i. A three-point weighted average could be $\frac{1}{4}(x_{i-1} + 2x_i + x_{i+1})$. As an illustration, a sequence of eight daily maximum temperatures (°C) at a location is given in the table, and the associated sequence of simple three-point averages is shown in the diagram.

The choice of time span for the observations in a moving average is important. For example, given the monthly sales figures for a product, a six-point moving average may reveal seasonal trends in sales, but a twelve-point average will smooth out seasonal trends and indicate longer-term trends.

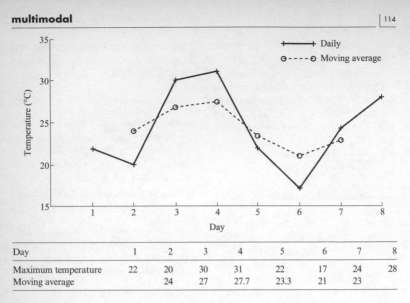

Day	1	2	3	4	5	6	7	8
Maximum temperature	22	20	30	31	22	17	24	28
Moving average		24	27	27.7	23.3	21	23	

moving average

multimodal *See* mode.

multinomial An algebraic expression that is the sum of two or more terms. *See also* polynomial.

multinomial distribution A generalization of the *binomial distribution. It gives the distribution for the results of n independent trials, at each of which there are $r (\geqslant 2)$ possible outcomes. Denoting the probabilities of the outcomes of one trial by $p_1, p_2, \ldots, p_r$, where $p_1 + p_2 + \cdots + p_r = 1$, the probabilities of the various outcomes of n trials are the terms of the *multinomial expansion* of $(p_1 + p_2 + \cdots + p_r)^n$. Thus the terms of the expansion of $(p_1 + p_2 + \cdots + p_6)^{12}$, where $p_1 = p_2 = \cdots = p_6 = \frac{1}{6}$, will be the probabilities of the various combinations of outcomes when a fair die is thrown 12 times. For example, the probability of obtaining 3 ones, 2 twos, 1 three, 2 fours, 3 fives and 1 six (in any order) corresponds to the term

$$\frac{12!}{3!2!1!2!3!1!} p_1^3 \, p_2^2 \, p_3^1 \, p_4^2 \, p_5^3 \, p_6^1.$$

This is equal to

$$\frac{12!}{144} \times \left(\frac{1}{6}\right)^{12} = 0.0015.$$

In general, if a single trial has r kinds of outcome, the ith kind having probability p_i, and the random variable X_i denotes the number of times the ith kind of outcome occurs in n such trials, then the variables $X_1, X_2, \ldots, X_r$ have a discrete *multivariate distribution with *frequency function

$$\Pr(X_1 = x_1, X_2 = x_2, \ldots, X_r = x_r)$$
$$= \frac{n!}{x_1! x_2! \cdots x_r!} p_1^{x_1} p_2^{x_2} \cdots p_r^{x_r},$$

where $0 \leqslant x_i \leqslant n$ and $\sum_1^r x_i = n$.

multinomial expansion The *expansion given by the *multinomial theorem.

multinomial theorem A generalization of the *binomial theorem that gives the expansion of a *multinomial raised to a positive integral power n. For example, it gives the expansion of an expression such as $(x + y + z)^5$.

More formally, it states that, when n is a positive integer,

$$(x_1 + x_2 + \cdots + x_r)^n$$
$$= \sum \frac{n!}{a!b! \cdots k!} x_1^a x_2^b \cdots x_r^k,$$

where the summation is for all possible combinations of integers $a, b, \ldots, k$ lying between 0 and n and such that

$$a + b + \cdots + k = n.$$

For example, the expansion of

$$(x + y + z)^5$$

will have terms of the form

$$\frac{5!}{a!b!c!} x^a y^b z^c,$$

where $a + b + c = 5$. The combination $a = 1, b = 1, c = 3$ gives the term

$$\frac{5!}{1!1!3!} x^1 y^1 x^3,$$

which simplifies to $20xyz^3$; the combination $a = 0, b = 5, c = 0$ gives the term y^5; and so on.

See multinomial distribution.

multiple-answer *See* multiple-choice question.

multiple bar chart A diagram that combines and compares visually two or more *bar charts by placing corresponding bars side by side or either side of the base line.

multiple-choice question (multiple-choice item) A question that asks the respondent to choose from a list of (more than two) responses. If only one response is permitted, then the question is in *single-answer* mode, for example

What is the colour of your eyes?
Blue
Brown
Grey/green
None of these

If more than one response is permitted, then the question is in *multiple-answer* mode, for example

Which of these communication devices did you use today?
Letter
E-mail
Telephone/mobile
Fax
None at all

Multiple-choice questions are a useful device in questionnaires designed to gather information.

In educational tests or aptitude tests, a multiple-choice question will usually have a single correct answer, the *key*. The remaining incorrect alternatives are called *distractors*. Thus, for instance, in the question

What is 50 divided by 0.5?			
a	b	c	d
10	100	250	25

the key is b and the distractors are a, c and d.

Compare dichotomous question. *See also* rating scale; item analysis.

multiple correlation coefficient The product moment *correlation coefficient between the observed values of the response variable in a *multiple regression and those predicted by the regression equation from the corresponding observed values of the explanatory variables.

For example, from a set of n observations (w_1, h_1, t_1), (w_2, h_2, t_2), $\ldots$, (w_n, h_n, t_n) of the weight w, height h and age t of a sample of female adults, a *least-squares equation for the regression of weight on height and age can be found. Then to each observed weight w_i there will be a corresponding weight $\hat{w}_i$ predicted by the regression equation and obtained by the substitution of h_i and t_i. The multiple correlation coefficient is the product moment correlation coefficient for the n pairs of values $(w_1, \hat{w}_1)$, $(w_2, \hat{w}_2), \ldots, (w_n, \hat{w}_n)$.

The multiple correlation coefficient is denoted by R. The quantity R^2 is called the *coefficient of multiple determination* or *coefficient of determination*. It expresses the proportion of the *variance of the response variable accounted for by the regression equation.

multiple determination, coefficient of *See* multiple correlation coefficient.

multiple linear regression *See* multiple regression.

multiple regression The *regression of a response variable on more than one explanatory variable. For example, a formula giving the average weight of an adult female of a given height and age.

The simplest form is a *multiple linear regression* in which y, the average value of the response variable when the values of the explanatory variables are fixed at $x_1, x_2, \ldots, x_n$, is given by an equation of the form

$$y = \beta_0 + \beta_1 x_1 + \beta_2 x_2 + \cdots + \beta_n x_n,$$

where $\beta_0, \beta_1, \beta_2, \ldots, \beta_n$ are constants.

multiplicative law *See* probability.

multistage sampling A sampling method in which the selection of the *sample is done in several stages. For example, in obtaining a random sample of households in a large country such as the USA, the entire country is first divided into regions, and each region is then divided into districts with about 500 households in each. The sample is obtained in three stages. First, a *random sample of regions is made; secondly, a random sample of districts in these regions is made; and finally, households are randomly selected from within these districts.

The groups of units from which the first random selection is made are called the *primary sampling units*. In the above example, the primary sampling units are the regions. The *secondary* and *ternary sampling units* are the groups of units from which the second and third random selections are made. In the example, the secondary sampling units are the districts in the chosen regions, and the ternary units are the households in the chosen districts.

See also cluster sample.

multivariate data *See* contingency table; data.

multivariate distribution A joint *distribution involving more than two *random variables. It describes or presents the frequency or probability with which sets of values of the variables occur. The concepts of marginal and conditional distributions associated with *bivariate distributions extend to multivariate distributions. A *multivariate normal distribution* is a continuous multivariate distribution in $p \, (> 2)$ variables in which, for any set of fixed values of $p - 1$ variables the other random variable has a *normal distribution. *See* multinomial distribution.

multivariate normal distribution *See* multivariate distribution.

multiway table *See* contingency table.

mutually exclusive *See* intersection; probability.

Napierian logarithm *See* logarithm.

natural logarithm *See* logarithm.

negative binomial distribution The *distribution of the number of failures, *X*, before the *k*th success in a sequence of *Bernoulli trials. If *p* is the probability of success in each trial and *q* (= 1 − *p*) the probability of failure, then *X* has *frequency function

$$\Pr(X = r) = \binom{r + k - 1}{r} p^k q^r,$$

where $r = 0, 1, 2, \ldots,$

and $\binom{n}{r}$ is the *binomial coefficient. This formula gives the probability that *r* failures precede the *k*th success. The *mean of the distribution is kq/p, and the *variance is kq/p^2. The special case when $k = 1$ is a *geometric distribution.

For example, in a sequence of tosses of a fair coin, the number of tails, *X*, before the third head will have a negative binomial distribution. Here $p = q = 0.5$ and $k = 3$, and the formula takes the form

$$\Pr(X = r) = \binom{r + 2}{r} (0.5)^3 (0.5)^r.$$

Probabilities for low values of *X* are given in the table. The mean is 3 and the variance is 6.

The distribution is called 'negative binomial' because the probabilities are the terms of a *binomial expansion with a negative index.

See also binomial distribution.

negative correlation *See* correlation.

negatively skewed (skew) *See* skewness.

negative skewness *See* skewness.

network *See* graph.

NH *Abbreviation for* null hypothesis (*see* hypothesis testing).

NNT *Abbreviation for* *number needed to treat.

node *See* graph.

nominal data *See* scale of measurement.

nominal measurement *See* scale of measurement.

nominal scale *See* scale of measurement.

nominal variable *See* categorical variable.

nonparametric method A method for making *statistical inferences from samples that does not assume the sample to come from any specific underlying family of distribu-

negative binomial distribution

Number of tails before third head (x)	0	1	2	3	4	5	6	...	10	...
Probability		0.13	0.19	0.19	0.16	0.12	0.08	0.05	...	0.008	...

tions such as the *normal distribution, and makes no assumptions about any population *parameter. The term is widely taken to be equivalent to *distribution-free methods, though in fact nonparametric methods are not only distribution free but 'parametric assumption free'. The distinction is of no great practical importance, but the adjective 'nonparametric' is sometimes used where 'distribution-free' would be more appropriate.

See coefficient of concordance; correlation coefficient; Friedman's test; Jonckheere–Terpstra test; Kolmogorov–Smirnov tests; Kruskal–Wallis test; median test; Page test; permutation test; runs test; sign test; Tukey's quick test; Wilcoxon rank sum test; Wilcoxon signed rank test. *Compare* parametric method.

nonsense correlation *See* correlation.

normal Having a *normal distribution.

normal approximation The use of a *normal distribution as an approximation to a given distribution. If the given distribution is of a *discrete random variable, a *continuity correction will be necessary when making a normal approximation.

For example, under certain conditions a satisfactory approximation to a *binomial distribution can be made by a normal distribution with the same mean and variance. More precisely, if both np and nq are large enough (e.g. 5 or more), the binomial distribution $B(n, p)$ can be approximated by the normal distribution $N(np, npq)$. Similarly, if λ is large enough (e.g. 15 or more), the *Poisson distribution with mean λ can be approximated by the normal distribution $N(\lambda, \lambda)$.

As an illustration, the number of heads, H, obtained when a fair coin is tossed 16 times has a binomial distribution with $n = 16$ and $p = q = \frac{1}{2}$. It has mean $np = 8$ and variance $npq = 4$, and $nq = 8$. The normal approximation $N(8, 4)$ can be used to estimate the probability of obtaining more than 10 heads as

$$\Pr(H > 10) \approx 1 - \Phi\left(\frac{10.5 - 8}{\sqrt{4}}\right)$$
$$= 1 - \Phi(1.25) = 0.106.$$

The exact value, using the binomial distribution, is 0.105 to 3 places of decimals.

normal curve *See* normal distribution.

normal distribution In general, the *distribution of a continuous variable X with *mean μ and *variance σ^2 (standard deviation σ), whose *frequency function is

$$\frac{1}{\sigma\sqrt{2\pi}}\exp\left(-\frac{(x - \mu)^2}{2\sigma^2}\right).$$

This distribution is denoted by $N(\mu, \sigma^2)$. The statement that X has this distribution is sometimes shortened to 'X is $N(\mu, \sigma^2)$' or to '$X \sim N(\mu, \sigma^2)$'. The normal distribution is sometimes called the *Gaussian distribution*.

The frequency curve is symmetric about the line $x = \mu$, is *bell-shaped* and is called a *normal curve* (*see* diagram (a)). Approximately 68% of values lie within one standard deviation of the mean, 95.4% within two standard deviations and 97.7% within three.

The transformation $Z = (X - \mu)/\sigma$ is said to *standardize* the variable X, converting it into the *standard normal variable Z*, whose distribution has mean 0 and variance 1, i.e. is $N(0, 1)$. Under this transformation each value x has a corresponding value z called its *standardized score, standard score* or *z-score*. The standard normal distribution has frequency function denoted by $\phi(z)$, where

$$\phi(z) = \frac{1}{\sqrt{2\pi}}\exp\left(-\frac{1}{2}z^2\right),$$

and its graph is the *standard normal curve*. Its distribution function, denoted by $\Phi(z)$, gives $\Pr(Z \leqslant z)$. This probability is represented by the area under the curve from $-\infty$ to z (*see* diagram (b)).

Tables and statistical packages are available giving values of $\Phi(z)$. Thus a probability such as $\Pr(Z \leqslant 2)$ is found from Table 1 in the Appendix to be $\Phi(2) = 0.9772$, from which the complementary probability $\Pr(Z > 2) = 1 - 0.9772 = 0.0228$. Tables are also widely available giving upper *percentage points for the standard normal distribution. These are particular values of Z exceeded by some percentage of the dis-

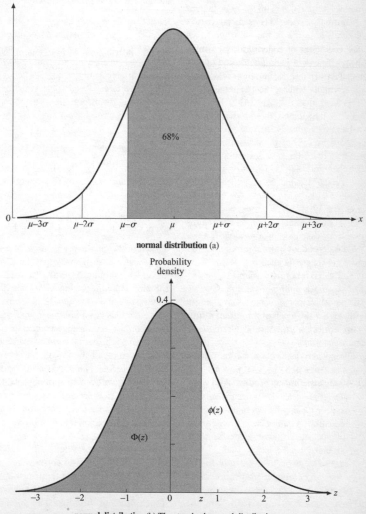

normal distribution (a)

normal distribution (b) The standard normal distribution.

tribution. For example, Table 2 in the Appendix gives $z = 1.960$ as the upper $2\frac{1}{2}\%$ point, i.e. $\Pr(Z > 1.960) = 0.025$. These *critical values* are useful when constructing *confidence intervals or in *hypothesis testing.

Standardization enables inferences about any normal distribution to be referred to the standard normal distribution. For example, if a normal variable X has mean 16 and standard deviation 5, then a value x will have a corresponding standardized score z, where $z = \frac{1}{5}(x - 16)$. Then, finding the probability that X is less than 22, say, is equivalent to finding the probability that z is less than $\frac{1}{5}(22 - 16) = 1.2$. But $\Phi(1.2) = 0.885$, and this is the required probability. Similarly, to find the value x exceeded by 25% of the distribution of X, one first finds the corresponding value z such that $\Phi(z) = 0.75$. Tables or a package give $z = 0.6745$, and solving the equation $0.6745 = \frac{1}{5}(x - 16)$ gives the required value, $x = 19.4$.

A random variable having a normal distribution is called a *normal variable*. If X and Y are independent normal variables and a and b are constants, then

(i) $aX + b$ is a normal variable;

(ii) $aX + bY$ is a normal variable.

An important consequence of the second result is that the mean of a random sample of size n drawn from a normal distribution is a normal variable.

The normal distribution is important in statistics because

(i) many experiments produce data which are approximately normally distributed, e.g. lengths of mass-produced industrial components, weights of humans of the same gender and age-group;

(ii) means of large, or even only moderately large, samples from non-normal distributions are approximately normally distributed (*see* central limit theorem);

(iii) under certain conditions, other important distributions, e.g. the *binomial distribution and *Poisson distribution, are approximated by a normal distribution.

See normal approximation; normalizing transformation.

normal equations *See* least squares.

normalizing transformation A transformation $Y = \mathrm{f}(X)$ of a random variable X into a variable Y with a *normal distribution. The transformation is said to *normalize* the variable X. For example, when X is a positive variable, $Y = \ln X$ is sometimes a normalizing transformation. In such an event, X is said to have a *lognormal distribution*.

normally distributed (normal) Having a *normal distribution.

normal number *See* Champernowne's number.

normal population A *population consisting of values having a *normal distribution.

normal probability paper A form of graph paper scaled in such a way that the (cumulative) *distribution curve of a *normal distribution is a straight line. One axis has a *linear scale and is for values of the variable. The other axis has a nonlinear scale and is for recording *cumulative percentages. To investigate whether a random sample is from a normal distribution, a table of cumulative frequencies is made from the sample data and then plotted on normal probability paper. The closeness of the graph to a straight line indicates whether the sample is from a distribution that is approximately normal.

For example, the lengths of a random sample of 487 adult earthworms were measured, and the cumulative frequencies given in the table were obtained. The diagram shows a plot of this table. The points are close to a line, which suggests that the lengths of earthworms are approximately normally distributed.

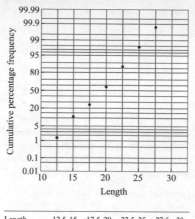

Length (cm)	12.5	15	17.5	20	22.5	25	27.5	30
Cumulative frequency (%)	1.4	11.7	27.1	58.5	86.7	97.9	99.8	100.0

normal probability paper

normal variable A *random variable having a *normal distribution.

not significant (n.s.) *See* hypothesis testing.

null distribution In a hypothesis test, the *distribution of the test statistic when the null hypothesis is assumed to be true (*see* hypothesis testing).

null hypothesis (NH) *See* hypothesis testing.

null result An outcome of an experiment that is not significant. *See* hypothesis testing.

null set (empty set) The *set with no members, usually denoted by $\emptyset$ or { }. *Compare* universal set.

number needed to treat (NNT) A measure of the effectiveness of a medical treatment. It equals the average number of individuals needed to participate in a treatment for it to be effective on one individual. For example, if mammogram screening proves life saving for 1 in 1000 women who participate, the NNT (to save one life) is 1000. NNT is also used as a measure of the harmfulness of treatments. For example, if 1 in 7000 women taking a certain oral contraceptive suffer from thromboembolism (blockage of blood vessel by a clot), the NNT (to suffer from thromboembolism) is 7000. The measure can also be used to compare treatments. Thus one measure of the superiority of a treatment *A* over another treatment *B* of the same condition would be the number needed to treat for *A* to cure one more patient than *B*.

O

octile The octiles of a *distribution are the seven values that divide the range of values of the variable into eight intervals having equal frequencies. *See* quantile.

odd permutation A *permutation that is equivalent to an odd number of *transpositions. For example, 321 is an odd permutation of 123 since it is equivalent to the single transposition (13). Similarly, 9678 is an odd permutation of 6789 since it is equivalent to three transpositions, e.g. (98) then (97) then (96). *Compare* even permutation.

odds When an event E has probability p of occurring and $q = 1 - p$ of not occurring, the 'odds on E' is the ratio of p to q, or p/q. For example, if $p = \frac{2}{3}$, the odds on E are $\frac{2}{3}$ to $\frac{1}{3}$, or 2, spoken as 'two to one on'. If $p = q = \frac{1}{2}$, the odds become 'one to one on', which is usually called 'evens'.

When $p < q$, it is common practice to talk of the 'odds against E'. This is the ratio of q to p. For example, when $p = \frac{1}{10}$, $q = \frac{9}{10}$, and the odds *against* E are $\frac{9}{10}$ to $\frac{1}{10}$, spoken as 'nine to one against'. The odds *on* E are 'one to nine on'.

ogive An alternative name for the *distribution curve (cumulative frequency curve). The term literally implies an S-shaped or *sigmoid curve, and the distribution curves of the *normal distribution and others are indeed of this shape. However, there are many distributions, e.g. the con-tinuous *uniform distribution, with distribution curves that are far from being S-shaped and for which the term seems inappropriate.

one-sided alternative *See* hypothesis testing.

one-tail test (one-tailed test) *See* hypothesis testing.

one-way classification *See* analysis of variance.

open-ended question A question which can be responded to freely, as compared with a *closed question*, which is answered by selecting from a range of specific responses. For example,

Why are you reading this book?

is an open-ended question, whereas

Are you a student? Yes/No

is a closed question. *See also* multiple-choice question.

opportunity sample *See* convenience sample.

order 1. (of a derivative) The number of times *differentiation is performed on a function. For example, differentiating a function twice produces its derivative of order two, or second-order derivative. **2.** (of a matrix) The dimensions of a *matrix.

3. (of a polynomial) The *degree of a *polynomial.

ordered alternative hypothesis (ordered alternative) In a *hypothesis test involving two or more samples, an alternative hypothesis stating that the population means (or medians) form an ordered sequence. *See* trend test.

order effects *See* randomized blocks.

order statistics When a sample of observations such as 4, 15, 9, 19, 11, 5, 2 is rearranged in ascending order as 2, 4, 5, 9, 11, 15, 19, then 2 is said to be the first *order statistic*, 4 the second order statistic, and so on. The *median of the sample of seven observations will be the fourth order statistic and is equal to 9.

In general, when a set of n observations $x_1, x_2, \ldots, x_n$ is rearranged in ascending order, the ith value is the ith order statistic and is labelled $x_{(i)}$. Thus $x_{(1)}$ is the least value, $x_{(n)}$ is the greatest, and, if n is odd, the $\frac{1}{2}(n+1)$th order statistic is the median.

ordinal data *See* data; rank; scale of measurement.

ordinal measurement *See* scale of measurement.

ordinal scale *See* scale of measurement.

ordinal variable *See* categorical variable.

ordinate The y-coordinate, measured parallel to the y-axis in a *Cartesian coordinate system.

outcome *See* sample space; event.

outcome variable *See* regression.

outlier An observation that seems very unusual and does not fit the general pattern of other values in a sample. For example, in the set of values 14, 6, 12, 11, 19, 60, 13, the observation 60 is an outlier. Outliers may arise from errors in measuring or recording values, or from some genuine irregularity in connection with the variable or variables being measured. For instance, in an experiment, 16 subjects were briefly shown a short text and then asked to recall it. The diagram shows a plot of the percentage of text correctly recalled by each subject against the time taken.

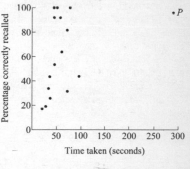

outlier

The data point P is an outlier. In this case there were no errors of measurement or plotting – the subject concerned simply took an exceptionally long time to complete an excellent response.

See trimming; winsorization.

P

Paasche index A form of weighted *index number that uses current-year data as weights. For example, when used as a price index for a set of commodities, the Paasche index uses as weights the quantities of each commodity purchased in the current year. In this case and more precisely, if the prices of a set of k commodities are $p_{01}, p_{02}, \ldots, p_{0k}$ in the base year and $p_{n1}, p_{n2}, \ldots, p_{nk}$ in the nth year after the base year (year n), and if the quantities purchased in year n are $q_{n1}, q_{n2}, \ldots, q_{nk}$, respectively, then the Paasche price index for year n, denoted by P_{0n}, is

$$P_{0n} = \frac{p_{n1}q_{n1} + p_{n2}q_{n2} + \cdots + p_{nk}q_{nk}}{p_{01}q_{n1} + p_{02}q_{n2} + \cdots + p_{0k}q_{nk}} \times 100,$$

or

$$P_{0n} = \left(\sum_i p_{ni}q_{ni} / \sum_i p_{0i}q_{ni} \right) \times 100.$$

For a simple illustration, suppose that in the base year the prices of three commodities were 20, 80 and 30, and that in the fifth year after the base year the prices have become 30, 90 and 25, respectively, and the quantities being purchased are 250, 220 and 180. The Paasche price index for this set of commodities in the fifth year is

$$P_{05} = \frac{30 \times 250 + 90 \times 220 + 25 \times 180}{20 \times 250 + 80 \times 220 + 30 \times 180} \times 100$$

$$= 113.6.$$

In effect, the index compares the total cost of purchases in the current year at current prices with their cost at base-year prices.

Compare Laspeyres index.

Page test (Page's L trend test) A *nonparametric test using *ranks which tests for a trend in treatment *means in a *randomized blocks design involving three or more treatments or conditions.

When there are $k \geqslant 3$ treatments and N groups of matched units (or N subjects in a *repeated measures design), the data for the test are ranks set out in an $N \times k$ table. Each row contains the responses of a block (or a subject) to the k treatments, ranked 1 to k. The *null hypothesis is that the columns of ranks are random samples from the same population and thus have equal means (and column totals). The alternative hypothesis is that the columns differ and that there is a specified trend in their means (and column totals).

To illustrate the procedure, suppose that a company's market researcher has three possible advertisements A, B and C for a product, and predicts that A is better than C, and C is better than B. To test these predictions, four customers are asked to independently rank the advertisements in ascending order from 1 to 3. The test results are as in table (a).

Next, the sum of the ranks in each column is found, and the table rearranged so that, running from left to right, the order of

Page test (a)

Customer	Advertisement		
	A	B	C
a	3	2	1
b	3	1	2
c	3	1	2
d	2	1	3

the columns corresponds to the *predicted* ascending order of column totals. Thus the column with the lowest predicted total, B, is on the left, and that predicted to have the largest, A, is on the right. The result is as in table (b). The test statistic is Page's L, calculated from such a table and the formula

$$L = 1 \times T_1 + 2 \times T_2 + \cdots + k \times T_k,$$

where T_i is the column total for column i, and there are k columns in all.

For our data, the column totals are 5, 8 and 11. Thus

$$L = 1 \times 5 + 2 \times 8 + 3 \times 11 = 54.$$

Significantly high values of L lead to rejection of the null hypothesis. When N and/or k are reasonably large, the distribution of L is approximately *normal with mean $Nk(k + 1)^2/4$ and variance $N(k^3 - k)^2/[144(k - 1)]$. However, for small values of N and k (e.g. $N \leqslant 12$, $k \leqslant 6$), tables of exact critical values of L are available.

In our example, $k = 3$, $N = 4$ and $L = 54$. Tables state that the probability of obtain-

Page test (b)

Customer	Advertisement		
	B	C	A
a	2	1	3
b	1	2	3
c	1	2	3
d	1	3	2
Column number	1	2	3
Column total (T_i)	5	8	11

ing a value of L as high or higher than 54 is less than 0.05. Thus the alternative hypothesis that A is preferred to C, and C to B, is accepted at the 5% level.

See trend test; *see also* Jonckheere–Terpstra test.

paired observations *See* matched pairs.

panel *See* longitudinal study.

panel study *See* longitudinal study.

parameter 1. A *constant or *variable that distinguishes special cases of a general mathematical expression. For example, the general form of the equation of a straight line,

$$y = mx + c,$$

contains two parameters, m and c, representing the gradient and the y-intercept of any specific line. Setting $m = 2$ and $c = 5$ gives the particular case $y = 2x + 5$.
2. In statistics, a parameter is a constant appearing in the *frequency function of a family of *distributions. For example, the general form of the *binomial distribution has two parameters: n, the number of independent trials, and p, the probability of success in a trial. Giving n and p values produces a particular binomial distribution. Similarly, the *normal distribution has parameters μ and σ^2 (mean and variance), the *Poisson distribution has parameter λ (mean), the *chi-squared and *t-distributions have parameter ν (degrees of freedom) and the *F-distribution has parameters ν_1 and ν_2 (degrees of freedom).

The term is also used for a constant that determines the specific form of a *model. For example, the linear *regression model

$$E(Y|x) = \alpha + \beta x$$

involves two parameters, α and β.

parametric method A method for making *statistical inferences that assumes that samples come from a known family of *distributions, as distinct from *distribution-free or *nonparametric methods. For example, *t-tests or the method of *analysis of variance assume that samples are drawn from distributions that are *normal distributions (or approximately so), and so these are parametric methods. The adjective 'parametric' is given to these methods because *parameters occur in the general specification of the known distributions.

When samples are from continuous distributions, parametric inference is often based on the normal distribution, *exponential distribution, *uniform distribution or an *extreme value distribution. When samples are from discrete distributions, parametric inference is often based on the *binomial distribution, *Poisson distribution, *negative binomial distribution, uniform distribution or *multinomial distribution.

Compare distribution-free method; nonparametric method.

Pareto curve *See* Pareto distribution.

Pareto distribution A *distribution of a positive continuous random variable with frequency function of the form

$$f(x) = Ax^{-(1+\alpha)},$$

where A and α are positive constants. If $x \geqslant k > 0$, then $A = \alpha k^{\alpha}$.

It first arose in a *model for the distribution of income x in a population, but the term is now given to any distribution of this form. A *Pareto curve* is the *frequency curve of a Pareto distribution.

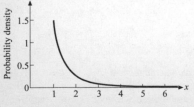

Pareto distribution with $\alpha = 1.5$ and $k = 1$.

partial correlation coefficient A measure of the *correlation between two variables when the effects of one or more other related variables have been removed.

For example, if X_1 represents mathematical ability, X_2 musical ability and X_3 general intelligence of a group of people, a high correlation between X_1 and X_2 may be partly a reflection of high positive correlations of each with X_3. The partial correlation coefficient removes, or is said to *partial out*, the effect of intelligence. It can be thought of as a measure of association between mathematical and musical ability for people with the same level of general intelligence.

When correlation is measured by the product moment correlation coefficient, the partial correlation coefficient between X_1 and X_2 when the effect of X_3 has been removed is denoted by $r_{12.3}$. For a sample of data this coefficient can be calculated from the coefficients between the three pairs of variables by using the formula

$$r_{12.3} = \frac{r_{12} - r_{13}r_{23}}{\sqrt{(1 - r_{13}^2)(1 - r_{23}^2)}},$$

where, for example, r_{12} denotes the product moment correlation coefficient between X_1 and X_2.

As an illustration, suppose that a study of mathematical and musical ability has produced the following *correlation matrix:

	Mathematics	Music	Intelligence
Mathematics	1	0.54	0.66
Music	0.54	1	0.62
Intelligence	0.66	0.62	1

Here $r_{12} = 0.54$, $r_{13} = 0.66$ and $r_{23} = 0.62$. The formula gives

$$r_{12.3} = \frac{0.54 - 0.66 \times 0.62}{\sqrt{(1 - 0.66^2)(1 - 0.62^2)}} = 0.22.$$

Thus the result of removing the association with intelligence has been to replace the coefficient of 0.54 between mathematical and musical ability by the much weaker partial coefficient of 0.22. When the data consist of *ranks, a *partial rank correlation coefficient* can be calculated from a formula analogous to the one above. When *Spearman's rank correlation coefficient is used, then $r_{12.3}, r_{12}, \ldots$ are replaced by $\rho_{12.3}, \rho_{12}, \ldots$; and when *Kendall's rank correlation coefficient is used they are replaced by $\tau_{12.3}, \tau_{12}, \ldots$.

partial out *See* partial correlation coefficient.

partial rank correlation coefficient *See* partial correlation coefficient.

participant *See* experimental design.

Pascal's triangle A triangular arrangement of numbers as shown below:

$$
\begin{array}{ccccccccccccc}
 & & & & & & 1 & & & & & & \\
 & & & & & 1 & & 1 & & & & & \\
 & & & & 1 & & 2 & & 1 & & & & \\
 & & & 1 & & 3 & & 3 & & 1 & & & \\
 & & 1 & & 4 & & 6 & & 4 & & 1 & & \\
 & 1 & & 5 & & 10 & & 10 & & 5 & & 1 & \\
1 & & 6 & & 15 & & 20 & & 15 & & 6 & & 1 \\
\end{array}
$$
etc.

Each row has 1 for its first and last number. Other numbers are equal to the sum of the two numbers immediately above them, for example, $5 = 1 + 4$ and $10 = 4 + 6$. This property can be used to generate the triangle. So, for instance, the next row contains the numbers 1, 7, 21, 35, 35, 21, 7 and 1. The numbers in each row give the coefficients in the *binomial expansions of expressions such as $(1 + x)^n$ or $(p + q)^n$. The first row is for $n = 0$, the second for $n = 1$, the third for $n = 2$, etc. For example, to expand $(1 + x)^2$ the third row is used to give

$$(1 + x)^2 = 1 + 2x + 1x^2 = 1 + 2x + x^2.$$

Similarly, using the fourth row,

$$
\begin{aligned}
(p + q)^3 &= 1p^3 + 3p^2q + 3pq^2 + 1q^3 \\
&= p^3 + 3p^2q + 3pq^2 + q^3.
\end{aligned}
$$

See also binomial distribution.

p.d.f. *Abbreviation for* *probability density function.

Pearson's correlation coefficient (Pearson's r) The product moment correlation coefficient (*see* correlation coefficient).

percent Indicating hundredths. Thus 2% is 2 hundredths or $\frac{2}{100}$.

percentage A proportion or fraction expressed in hundredths. A fraction can be expressed as a percentage by multiplying it by 100. For example, $\frac{1}{5}$ is $100 \times \frac{1}{5} = 20$ percent, and so a probability equal to $\frac{1}{5}$ is sometimes referred to as 'a 20 percent chance'.

percentage bar chart A *bar chart in which the lengths of the bars are proportional to the percentages of the total frequency or magnitude being represented.

percentage decrease *See* percentage increase.

percentage error The quantity

$$\frac{\text{absolute error}}{\text{true value}} \times 100,$$

often applied to a *mean or other measure. For instance, if the true value of a population mean is 50 and an estimate of it is 52.7, then the percentage error is

$$\frac{52.7 - 50}{50} \times 100 = 5.4\%.$$

percentage increase The quantity

$$\frac{\text{increase in value}}{\text{original value}} \times 100,$$

often applied to a price or other measure. For example, if the population of a small town increases from 2000 to 2500, then the percentage increase is

$$\frac{2500 - 2000}{2000} \times 100 = 25\%.$$

Similarly, a *percentage decrease* is defined to be

$$\frac{\text{decrease in value}}{\text{original value}} \times 100.$$

For instance, if the price of an item is reduced from £2500 to £2000, then the percentage decrease is

$$\frac{2500 - 2000}{2500} \times 100 = 20\%.$$

percentage point The *p% percentage point* of a *distribution is the value of the variable with a cumulative relative frequency (*see* cumulative frequency) of $p/100$. So *p%* of the distribution is less than or equal to this value. For example, the 90% percentage point of the standard *normal distribution is 1.2816. In other words, 90% of this distribution is less than or equal to 1.2816.

The *q% upper percentage point* of a distribution is the value of the variable exceeded by *q%* of the distribution. For example, 1.960 is the 2.5% upper percentage point of the standard normal distribution. This is the value of the standard normal variable *Z* that is exceeded by 2.5% of the distribution (*see* diagram).

Table 2 in the Appendix gives further upper percentage points of the standard normal distribution.

For *continuous* distributions, a *p%* percentage point is identical to a $(1-p)\%$ upper percentage point. Thus 1.2816 is both a 90% percentage point of the standard normal distribution and a 10% upper percentage point.

See also p-value; significance level.

percentile (centile) The percentiles of a *distribution are the 99 values that divide the range of values of the variable into 100

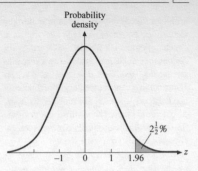

percentage point The 2.5% upper percentage point of the standard normal distribution is 1.96.

intervals with equal frequencies. For $r = 1$, 2, ..., 99, the *r*th percentile is the value of the variable such that *r%* of the distribution is less than or equal to it. Thus 53% of the distribution is less than or equal to the 53rd percentile. The 25th, 50th and 75th percentiles are the lower *quartile, *median and upper quartile, respectively.

In practice, approximate percentiles for a set of data can be found by *interpolation in a *cumulative frequency table or from a *cumulative frequency graph; the *r*th percentile being the value associated with a cumulative relative frequency of $r/100$ (or *r%*).

For a continuous random variable *X* with (cumulative) *distribution function $F(x)$, the *r*th percentile is the value *x* such that $\Pr(X \leqslant x) = F(x) = r/100$. Percentiles for a discrete random variable can also be defined in terms of its distribution function,

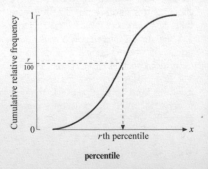

percentile

using a procedure similar to that used in the definition of its *median.

The percentiles define 100 intervals. Sometimes these intervals are referred to as 'percentiles'. For example, test scores lying between the second and third percentile are said to be 'in the third percentile', and a score above the 99th percentile to be 'in the 100th percentile'. The same is said of the individuals with such scores.

See decile; quantile.

permutation If the letters L, E and O are arranged in some order there are six possible orders or *permutations*: LEO, LOE, ELO, EOL, OEL and OLE.

In general, if n distinct objects are arranged in order, then the number of possible orders or *permutations* is $n(n-1)(n-2)\ldots 3 \times 2 \times 1$, i.e. $n!$ (n *factorial). Thus in the case of 3 objects the number of permutations is $3 \times 2 \times 1 = 3! = 6$, as we saw above.

More generally, if there are n distinct objects and r of them are selected and arranged in order, then the number of possible orders or permutations is $n(n-1)\cdots(n-r+1)$. This is equal to $n!/(n-r)!$. It is usually denoted by ^nP_r and often spoken as 'n perm r'. Thus if 2 letters are selected from A, B, C and D and arranged in order, then $n=4$ and $r=2$, and there will be $^4P_2 = 4!/2! = 4 \times 3 = 12$ permutations. They are AB, BA, AC, CA, AD, DA, BC, CB, BD, DB, CD and DC. Similarly, if 3 prizewinners are selected from 12 entrants in a contest and awarded first, second and third prize, then there are $^{12}P_3 = 12 \times 11 \times 10 = 1320$ different ways in which the prizes can be awarded.

When some objects are identical or indistinguishable, adjustments are necessary. For example, the 4 distinct letters A, B, C and D have $4! = 24$ permutations, but the 4 letters A, B, B and A have only 6 permutations: ABBA, ABAB, AABB, BAAB, BABA and BBAA.

In general, if in a set of n objects, a group of s are identical, another group of t are identical, and so on, then the number of distinct permutations of the n objects is $n!/s!t!\ldots$. Thus in the above example we had $n=4$, $s=2$ and $t=2$, and the formula gives $4!/2!2! = 6$ permutations. Similarly, the number of permutations of the 7 letters of the word ANAGRAM is also equal to $7!/3! = 840$.

Compare combination.

permutation test One of a class of *distribution-free tests in which the inference is based on equally likely alternatives to the sample data.

For example, suppose that two independent samples of sizes 7 and 8 have means differing by 2, and the *null hypothesis is that they are drawn from identical populations. A permutation test would begin by pooling the 15 observations and generating all possible pairs of samples of sizes 7 and 8. There are $^{15}C_7 = \binom{15}{7} = 6435$ such pairs (*see* combination). A two-tail test would then consider the proportion of pairs whose means differ by 2 or more. If, for instance, it was found that 130 pairs had means differing by 2 or more, then the proportion is $130/6435 = 0.02$. So the test result is significant at the 2% level, and there are grounds for rejecting the null hypothesis.

A test of this kind is often called a *Pitman test*. The names *Fisher–Pitman test* and *raw data test* are also used. Permutation tests based on raw data tend to involve large numbers of calculations, but appropriate computer software will now carry out such tests quickly.

A permutation test can also be performed on data in the form of *ranks. For example, suppose that 8 patients are being treated for some condition, and that instead of the standard treatment a new drug, predicted to be more effective, is given to 3 of them selected at random. After several weeks the patients are ranked 1 (good) to 8 (poor) for improvement, and those receiving the new drug are ranked 1, 2, 4. Here a permutation test could be based on the fact that under the null hypothesis of no difference between the treatments, each of the $8! = 40\,320$ ways of giving ranks 1 to 8 to the patients is equally likely. The proportion of these rankings in which the selected patients receive ranks 1, 2, 4, whose sum is 7, or (even better) 1, 2, 3, whose sum is 6, is $1/28 = 0.04$. So the result of the trial is significant at the 4% level; the new drug does appear to be more effective.

Permutation tests are also called *randomization tests*, but some writers reserve this alternative name for a restricted class of permutation tests.

perpendicular **1.** At or forming a right angle. Thus *perpendicular lines* are lines that are at right angles to one another.
2. A line or plane that is at right angles to another line or plane. For example, the perpendicular from a point A to a line l is the line through A that is at right angles to l.

Petersburg problem An alternative name for the *St Petersburg paradox.

Petersen estimator *See* capture–recapture sampling.

p.g.f. *Abbreviation for* *probability generating function.

phi coefficient (phi correlation coefficient) A measure of the degree of association between two *binary variables. For example, the answers given by students to two items (1 and 2) testing the same topic, the values being 'correct' and 'incorrect', are two such variables. A set of results for a sample of 200 students can be summarized in a 2×2 table of frequencies as follows:

Item 2	Item 1	
	Correct	Incorrect
Correct	78	42
Incorrect	29	51

When the cell frequencies are $\begin{matrix} a & b \\ c & d \end{matrix}$, the phi coefficient, denoted by ϕ, is given by

$$\phi = \frac{ad - bc}{[(a + b)(a + c)(b + d)(c + d)]^{1/2}}.$$

The coefficient takes a value between -1 and $+1$. It is equivalent to the product moment *correlation coefficient between the variables (when they are represented by variables taking numerical values 0 and 1). A value near to zero indicates a low or negligible degree of association. In the above example, $a = 78$, $b = 32$, $c = 29$ and $d = 51$. From these values, $\phi = 0.28$.

When the number of pairs of observations (n) is large, the distribution of $n\phi^2$ is approximately the chi-squared distribution with 1 degree of freedom. This fact (or an appropriate software package) can be used to decide whether there is a significant degree of association between the variables. In our example, $n = 200$ and $n\phi^2 = 15.95$, and there is very strong evidence to support a hypothesis that the responses to the two items are closely related.

The phi coefficient is sometimes called the *fourfold point correlation*, and described as a *coefficient of association*.

phi correlation coefficient *See* phi coefficient.

pictogram A pictorial form of *bar chart illustrating frequencies or amounts for each of several categories. A suitable symbol or *icon* is used to represent some standard unit of measurement, and each frequency or

January					
February					
March					
April					

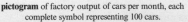

pictogram of factory output of cars per month, each complete symbol representing 100 cars.

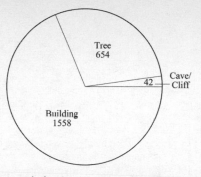

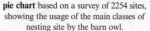

pie chart based on a survey of 2254 sites, showing the usage of the main classes of nesting site by the barn owl.

amount is then represented by an appropriate number of symbols. A fraction of a unit is represented by a part symbol (*see* diagram).

pie chart (circular chart) A circle divided into sectors whose areas (or angles) represent the proportions of a set of observations falling into each of several categories or classes. If, for example, 35 out of 150 observations fall into a certain category or class, then the corresponding sector has an angle of $(35/150) \times 360° = 84°$.

placebo A preparation that has no medicinal or pharmacological effect. In trials of drugs, it is common practice for the *control group to be given a placebo and to be unaware of or *blind* to this. This group can nevertheless respond to the knowledge that treatment is being given, e.g. have feelings of well-being or anticipation of improvement in their condition. This response to the administration of a placebo is known as a *placebo effect*. In such *experimental designs, the control and experimental groups experience the psychological effects of believing that they are receiving treatment. Thus a possible source of bias is removed. *See* blinding.

platykurtic *See* kurtosis.

plot *See* experimental design; graph; scatter diagram.

p.m.f. *Abbreviation for* probability mass function (*see* frequency function).

point biserial correlation coefficient *See* correlation coefficient.

point estimate *See* estimation.

point of inflection (point of inflexion) A point on a curve at which the *gradient changes from increasing to decreasing or vice versa, e.g. the mid-points of the letter S or the sign ∫, or a chicane on a racing circuit. The bell-shaped curve of the standard *normal distribution has two points of inflection, when $z = +1$ and $z = -1$.

Poisson distribution The *distribution of a discrete variable X taking integer values 0, 1, 2, 3, ... with probability

$$e^{-\lambda}, \quad \lambda e^{-\lambda}, \quad \frac{\lambda^2}{2!} e^{-\lambda}, \quad \frac{\lambda^3}{3!} e^{-\lambda}, \quad ...,$$

where λ is a positive constant. In general,

$$\Pr(X = r) = \frac{\lambda^r}{r!} e^{-\lambda},$$
$$\text{where } r = 0, 1, 2, 3, ...$$

In this expression $r!$ denotes *factorial r, and e^x is the *exponential function.

The *mean and the *variance are both equal to λ. The Poisson distribution with mean λ is sometimes denoted by Po(λ).

As an example, the distribution with $\lambda = 2.3$ can be tabulated and graphed as in the table and diagram (on the next page). For small values of λ, the distribution is skewed positively (*see* skewness) as shown in the diagram. However, when λ is large enough (e.g. 15 or more), the Poisson distribution can be approximated by the *normal distribution with the same mean and variance, i.e. N(λ, λ).

Examples of data that approximately follow a Poisson distribution include (i) the annual numbers of outbreaks of war from

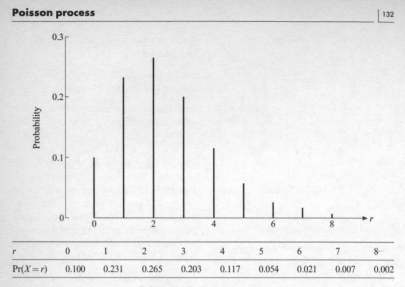

r	0	1	2	3	4	5	6	7	8
$\Pr(X = r)$	0.100	0.231	0.265	0.203	0.117	0.054	0.021	0.007	0.002

Poisson distribution with mean 2.3.

1500 to 1931 (432 observations with a mean of 0.69) and (ii) the number of times the letter z appears on each page of the novel *A Life* by Italo Svevo (300 observations with a mean of 0.90).

It can be proved that if np remains fixed but $n \to \infty$ and $p \to 0$, then the *binomial distribution $B(n, p)$ tends to the Poisson distribution with mean $\lambda = np$. A consequence of this is that $B(n, p)$ can be approximated well by $\text{Po}(np)$ when n is large enough (e.g. 50 or more) and p is sufficiently small for np to be less than 5.

A random variable having a Poisson distribution is called a *Poisson variable*. If X and Y are independent Poisson variables with means λ and μ, then their sum $X + Y$ is a Poisson variable with mean $\lambda + \mu$. For example, suppose that the number of e-mails received per working day in an office is believed to be a Poisson variable with mean 8, and the number of faxes arriving per day is believed to be a Poisson variable with mean 4.5. If e-mails and faxes are arriving independently, then the total number of

e-mails and faxes received per day will be a Poisson variable with mean 12.5.

See Poisson process.

Poisson process A random process in which (i) events occur at random in time, or in space, (ii) events occur independently, (iii) events occur singly and not simultaneously and (iv) events occur at a uniform rate in the sense that the expected number of events occurring in a given interval is proportional to the size of that interval.

Under these conditions, the number of events occurring in an interval of size t will have a *Poisson distribution with mean λt, where λ is some positive constant. There are many situations in which these conditions are reasonably met. For example, the emission of α-particles from the radioactive element polonium is a Poisson process, and in an experiment the number of particles emitted in a 12.5 second interval might be found to have a Poisson distribution with mean 3.87 (*see* diagram). Similarly, the appearance of faults such as bubbles

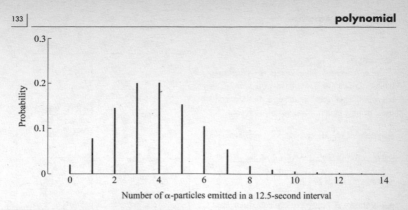

Number of α-particles emitted in a 12.5-second interval

Poisson process

in standard sized sheets of glass can be taken to be a Poisson process, as can the passage of traffic past a point on one lane of a motorway in a period of uniform traffic flow (a vehicle passing the point being an event).

In a Poisson process, the time between successive events (the *waiting time* or *wait time*) has an *exponential distribution. Thus in one of the above examples, the time interval between the emission of successive α-particles will have an exponential distribution.

polar angle *See* polar coordinate system.

polar axis *See* polar coordinate system.

polar coordinate system A *coordinate system in which the position of a point is determined by the length of the line segment from a fixed origin to the point together with the angle or angles that this line segment makes with a fixed line or lines. The origin is called the *pole*, and the line segment is the *radius* or

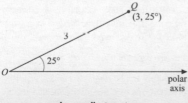

polar coordinate system

radius vector (r). In two dimensions, one axis is needed and is called the *polar axis*. The angle θ between the polar axis and the radius is called the *polar angle* or *vectorial angle*. By convention, positive values of θ are measured in an anticlockwise sense from the polar axis, negative values in a clockwise sense. The coordinates of the point are then given as (r, θ). For example, the point Q with polar coordinates $(3, 25°)$ is a distance 3 from the origin O, and OQ is rotated 25° anticlockwise from the polar axis (*see* diagram)

pole *See* polar coordinate system.

polynomial A mathematical expression that is the sum of terms, each term being the product of a constant and a non-negative power of a variable or variables. For one variable, the general form is

$$a_0 + a_1 x + a_2 x^2 + \cdots + a_n x^n.$$

The highest power (n) of the variable is the *degree* or *order* of the polynomial. Polynomials are described as linear, quadratic, cubic, etc., when their degree is 1, 2, 3, etc. The constants $a_1, a_2, \ldots, a_n$ are the *coefficients* of $x, x^2, \ldots, x^n$ in the polynomial, and a_0 is called the *constant term*. For example, $2 + 4x - x^3$ is a cubic polynomial (of degree 3). The constant term is 2, and the coefficients of x, x^2 and x^3 are 4, 0 and -1, respectively.

A *polynomial function* is a *function whose values are given by a polynomial. A *polynomial equation* is an equation formed by setting a polynomial equal to zero.

polynomial equation *See* polynomial.

polynomial function *See* polynomial.

pooled estimate *See* t-test.

population A complete collection of individuals or items about which statistical information is desired. Examples of populations include all children currently attending a primary school, all whales world-wide, all words in a particular book, and the digits of π, i.e. 3, 1, 4, 1, 5, 9, 2, 6, 5, 3, 5, 8, ... A population can be finite or infinite.

The *mean of the values of some variable, e.g. weight, calculated for all members of a population is called the *population mean* and is often denoted by the Greek letter μ. Similarly, the *variance of the values for the entire population is the *population variance* and is often denoted by σ^2. In these circumstances it is a common practice to refer also to the complete set of values as a 'population'. Thus it might be said that the marks obtained by 2500 students in a statistics exam formed an 'approximately normal population', rather than that the marks obtained from the population (of students) had an approximately *normal distribution.

population mean *See* population.

population proportion *See* proportion.

population pyramid A graphical representation of the age distribution of a population in the form of a *histogram with age measured vertically and frequency or relative frequency horizontally. When data for males and females are available, the histo-

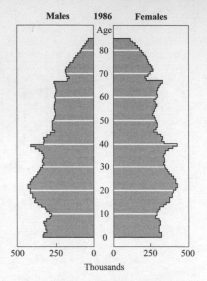

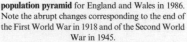

population pyramid for England and Wales in 1986. Note the abrupt changes corresponding to the end of the First World War in 1918 and of the Second World War in 1945.

grams may be drawn back to back with a common vertical axis (*see* diagram).

population variance *See* population.

positive correlation *See* correlation.

positively skewed (skew) *See* skewness.

positive skewness *See* skewness.

posterior probability (*a posteriori probability*) *See* prior probability.

posterior distribution (posterior probability distribution) *See* Bayesian inference.

power 1. (of a number) *See* exponent.
2. (of a test) The probability of correctly rejecting the null hypothesis when it is indeed false (*see* hypothesis testing).

Pr *See* probability.

precision 1. The degree to which repeated observations of a quantity conform to one another. The closeness of an observation to

the quantity it is measuring is its *accuracy*.
2. A quality associated with the *dispersion or spread of repeated observations of some single quantity. It is often measured by the *variance of the observations, a low variance indicating high precision and a high variance low precision. Alternatively, the *reciprocal of the variance can be used, a high (or low) reciprocal indicating high (or low) precision.

For example, if repeated measurements of the boiling point of a certain liquid are 111.1°C, 110.5°C, 110.8°C, 111.2°C, 110.9°C then the variance is 0.06. This is low and indicates a good degree of precision.

The precision of an *estimator is measured in terms of its standard error, a low (or high) standard error indicating high (or low) precision. In general, the standard error can be reduced and precision improved by increasing the number of observations on which the estimator is based.
See efficiency.

predicted variable *See* regression.

predictor variable *See* regression.

primary sampling unit (PSU) *See* cluster sample; multistage sampling.

principal component analysis In many experiments in the natural and social sciences, a number of characteristics are measured on each experimental unit. For example, a psychologist may score each of ten participants on each of three tests, one to test manual dexterity, one to test the ability to recognize shapes and the third to test reading ability. In this situation all three measured variables are likely to be *correlated. Principal component analysis is a procedure designed to replace the original variables by *linear functions of them (called *principal components*) that are uncorrelated with one another. These are chosen so that the first component accounts for as much of the total variability as possible, the

second for as much of the remaining variability as possible, and the final one for any variability not accounted for by the earlier components. The hope is that (i) fewer than three principal components will account for the bulk of the variability and (ii) the components will be easier to interpret in psychological terms than the original test scores, e.g. perhaps by indicating whether differences in the performances of individuals can be attributed largely to differences in overall ability, and any remaining differences to manual dexterity being greater in those who perform worse on the two mental tasks, and vice versa.

The method may be applied with any number p (≥ 2) of variables. The number of experimental units or participants n must exceed p, and in practice, for satisfactory results, n should be appreciably greater than p. Except in trivial cases, appropriate computer software is needed to carry out the analysis. An alternative procedure that is sometimes more successful in providing interpretations is *factor analysis.

prior distribution (prior probability distribution) *See* Bayesian inference.

prior probability (*a priori* probability) The probability given to an *event before an experiment has been conducted (*see* trial). The *posterior probability* or *a posteriori probability* is the probability given to the event after the experiment has been conducted, and may be calculated using *Bayes' theorem. *See* Bayesian inference.

probability The probability of an *event A is a number lying in the interval $0 \leq p \leq 1$. It is usually denoted by $\Pr(A)$ or $P(A)$. The probability of an impossible event is 0 and of a certain event is 1. If the probability of an event A is p, then the probability of the complementary event 'A does not occur' is $1 - p$. For instance, if the probability of a train arriving on time is

0.84, then the probability of it not arriving on time is $1 - 0.84 = 0.16$.

Probabilities are assigned to events in different ways:

(1) If the event can be thought of as resulting from an experiment with n equally likely possible outcomes, and the event A corresponds to r of them, then $\Pr(A) = r/n$, i.e. the number of outcomes corresponding to event A divided by the total number of possible, equally likely outcomes. For example, suppose that a number is chosen at random from 1, 2, 3, 4, 5, 6 and 7, and A is the event 'the chosen number is even'. Here there are 7 equally likely outcomes, and event A, the outcome being even, corresponds to 3 of them. Thus $n = 7$ and $r = 3$, and $\Pr(A) = \frac{3}{7}$. The probability of the complementary event 'the chosen number is odd' is $1 - \frac{3}{7} = \frac{4}{7}$.

(2) If an experiment can be repeated a large number of times (n), and the number of times event A occurs is r, then r/n is the *relative frequency* of event A. If this tends to a limit as n tends to infinity, then this limit is $\Pr(A)$. For example, an irregular biased die might be thrown 1000 times and a score of 2 recorded on 80 occasions. The relative frequency is $80/1000 = 0.08$ and, on this evidence, $\Pr(2)$ is estimated to be 0.08.

(3) A number is given to the event which expresses the observer's degree of belief that it will occur, as in 'I feel there is a 30% chance that it will rain tomorrow' or 'The instructor thinks the probability that Richard will pass his driving test is 0.4'. Since observers may differ in their beliefs and prior knowledge, a probability given to an event in this way is sometimes called a *subjective probability*.

Probabilities can also be given to *compound events* such as 'A or B (or both) occur', denoted by $A \cup B$, and 'A and B occur', denoted by $A \cap B$. Two events A and B which cannot both occur are said to be *mutually exclusive*. Then $\Pr(A \cap B) = 0$, and the *addition law* of probability holds, namely

$$\Pr(A \cup B) = \Pr(A) + \Pr(B).$$

For example, when a number is chosen at random from the numbers 1, 2, 3, 4, 5, 6 and 7, the events A, 'the number is even', and B, 'the number is 5', are mutually exclusive – they cannot both occur. $\Pr(A) = \frac{3}{7}$ and $\Pr(B) = \frac{1}{7}$, and the probability of $A \cup B$, 'the number is even or 5', is $\frac{3}{7} + \frac{1}{7} = \frac{4}{7}$.

However, when the events are not mutually exclusive then

$$\Pr(A \cup B) = \Pr(A) + \Pr(B) - \Pr(A \cap B).$$

For example, the events A, 'the number is even', and B, 'the number is less than 5', are not mutually exclusive – they can both occur. The probability of $A \cap B$, 'the number is even and less than 5', is $\frac{2}{7}$. Here $\Pr(B) = \frac{4}{7}$ and, using the above rule, the probability of $A \cup B$, 'the number is even or less than 5', is $\frac{3}{7} + \frac{4}{7} - \frac{2}{7} = \frac{5}{7}$.

The probability of an event B occurring after another event A has occurred is called the *conditional probability* of B given A. It is denoted by $\Pr(B \mid A)$. In the above example, the probability of the number 2 being chosen, given that an even number is chosen, is $\frac{1}{3}$, since the number 2 is one of the three equally likely even outcomes 2, 4 and 6. More formally, when $\Pr(A)$ is non-zero,

$$\Pr(B \mid A) = \frac{\Pr(A \cap B)}{\Pr(A)}.$$

This leads to the following general *multiplicative rules* for the probability of $A \cap B$,

$$\Pr(A \cap B) = \Pr(A) \, \Pr(B \mid A) \quad \text{and}$$
$$\Pr(A \cap B) = \Pr(B) \, \Pr(A \mid B).$$

Two events A and B are said to be *independent* if the probability that one occurs is the same regardless of whether the other occurs. This is equivalent to saying that $\Pr(B \mid A) = \Pr(B)$ or $\Pr(A \mid B) = \Pr(A)$. For two independent events, the probability of $A \cap B$, i.e. the event 'A and B occur', is given by

$$\Pr(A \cap B) = \Pr(A)\Pr(B),$$

which is sometimes called the *multiplicative law* of probability.

See independence; tree diagram; prior probability; Bayes' theorem.

probability density function (p.d.f.) A common alternative name for the *frequency function of a continuous *distribution. The shorter form, *density function*, is also used. *See* frequency function.

probability distribution A specification of the probabilities with which values of a variable occur. *See* distribution.

probability function *See* probability mass function.

probability generating function (p.g.f.) For a discrete *random variable X whose probabilities of taking the values $0, 1, 2, 3, \ldots$ are $p_0, p_1, p_2, \ldots$, the probability generating function is the *function whose series *expansion is $p_0 + p_1 t + p_2 t^2 + \cdots$. It is usually denoted by $G(t)$ or $G_X(t)$; the variable t is arbitrary.

The series can be written as $\sum_r p_r t^r$ and is equivalent to $E(t^X)$, the *expectation of t^X. The function is said to *generate* probabilities because when it is expanded as a series, the coefficient of t^r is p_r, the probability that $X = r$; so it generates all of X's probabilities.

For example, when X is the score on a fair die, $p_1 = p_2 = \cdots = p_6 = \frac{1}{6}$, and $p_r = 0$ otherwise. So the probability generating function is $\frac{1}{6}t + \frac{1}{6}t^2 + \cdots + \frac{1}{6}t^6$ as a series, and this is the expansion of

$$G(t) = \frac{1}{6} \frac{t(1 - t^7)}{(1 - t)}.$$

Similarly, when X has the *binomial distribution $B(n, p)$, then

$$G(t) = (q + pt)^n, \quad \text{where } q = 1 - p,$$

for, when expanded,

$$(q + pt)^n = q^n + \binom{n}{1} q^{n-1} pt + \cdots + p^n t^n,$$

and the coefficient of t^r is $\binom{n}{r} q^{n-r} p^r$, the binomial probability that $X = r$.

It can be shown that

$$E(X) = G'(1) \quad \text{and}$$
$$\text{Var}(X) = G''(1) + G'(1) - [(G''(1)]^2,$$

where $G'(t)$ and $G''(t)$ are the first and second *derivatives of $G(t)$. For the binomial distribution,

$$G'(t) = np(q + pt)^{n-1} \quad \text{and}$$
$$G''(t) = n(n - 1)p^2(q + pt)^{n-2}.$$

Substituting $t = 1$ gives

$$G'(1) = np \quad \text{and} \quad G''(1) = n(n - 1)p^2.$$

Hence

$$E(X) = np \quad \text{and}$$
$$\text{Var}(X) = n(n - 1)p^2 + np - (np)^2$$
$$= np(1 - p) = npq.$$

If two discrete random variables X and Y are *independent, then the probability generating function of their sum $X + Y$ equals the product of their probability generating functions. Thus if $Z = X + Y$, then

$$G_Z(t) = G_X(t).G_Y(t)$$

For instance, if X and Y are independent scores on two fair dice, then their sum Z is a discrete variable taking values $2, 3, \ldots, 12$. Its probability generating function is given by

$$G_Z(t) = \frac{1}{6} \frac{t(1 - t^7)}{(1 - t)} \times \frac{1}{6} \frac{t(1 - t^7)}{(1 - t)}$$
$$= \frac{1}{36} \frac{t^2(1 - t^7)^2}{(1 - t)^2}.$$

See also moment generating function.

probability mass function (probability function) (p.m.f.) A common alternative name for the *frequency function of a discrete distribution. *See* frequency distribution.

probability paper Graph paper scaled in such a way that the (cumulative) distribution curve of a certain type of distribution is a straight line (*see* distribution function). One axis has a *linear scale and is for values of the variable. The other axis has a non-linear scale for recording cumulative percentages. To investigate whether a sample is from a specified type of distribution, a *cumulative frequency table is prepared and then plotted on the appropriate form of paper. The closeness of the cumulative frequency graph to a straight line provides a visual indication of whether the sample is from that type of distribution. Types of distribution for which probability paper of this kind has been specially made include the *normal distribution and the *lognormal distribution. Other forms of probability paper have been made for the analysis of data in connection with the *binomial distribution and the *Poisson distribution. *See* normal probability paper.

probable error The probable error of the *sampling distribution of a *statistic is the deviation from the *mean which is exceeded by 50% of the distribution. When the distribution is assumed to be *normal, then the probable error is 0.6745 times the *standard error of the statistic. This is the case when the statistic is the mean of a large sample. The number 0.6745 is used since 50% of a normal distribution with standard deviation σ deviates from its mean by more than 0.6745σ. In other words, 0.6745σ and -0.6745σ are the upper and lower *quartiles of the normal distribution.

Current practice is to quote either the *standard error or a *confidence interval (usually 95%) associated with a statistic rather than the probable error.

problem of coincidences A celebrated problem in the history of probability which recurs in various forms. For example, a secretary puts n addressed letters into n addressed envelopes at random; calculate the probability that no letter is placed in its correct envelope. The solution is

$$\frac{1}{2!} - \frac{1}{3!} + \frac{1}{4!} - \frac{1}{5!} + \cdots + \frac{(-1)^n}{n!},$$

where $r!$ is *factorial r. As n increases, this sum rapidly approaches $1/e = 0.368$. For example, when $n = 5$, the probability is 0.367 (to 3 decimal places).

The problem is also known as *de Montmort's problem* or the *Treize problem* ('Thirteen' problem). These names comes from the form of the problem in which it was first solved by P. R. de Montmort in 1708. A well shuffled suit of 13 playing cards is dealt one card at a time, and the dealer simultaneously calls out the suit in rank order: Ace, $2, 3, \ldots$, King. The probability that no card is dealt and called at the same time is the case $n = 13$ of the above formula.

See also Banach's matchboxes; birthday problem; de Méré's problem; problem of points.

problem of points (division problem) An old recurrent problem in the history of probability. Two people A and B are playing a game in which they have an equal chance of winning each play and scoring a point. The first to reach a certain number of points wins. The game is interrupted and abandoned when they need, respectively, a and b points to win the game. Calculate a fair division of the stake money.

A fair division is based on the probabilities of A or B winning the game if it had continued to the end. Blaise Pascal and Pierre de Fermat developed methods for finding the correct probabilities in this and in other, more complex problems. For example, when $a = 2$ and $b = 3$, the correct division is in the ratio $11:5$. The numbers can be derived from the fourth line of *Pascal's triangle, in that $11 = 1 + 4 + 6$ and $5 = 4 + 1$.

See also Banach's matchboxes; birthday problem; de Méré's problem; problem of coincidences.

product moment For a *bivariate distribution of random variables X and Y, a product *moment is the *mean or *expectation of a product of powers of the variables, or of powers of the deviations of the variables from fixed values (usually their means).

For example, the first product moment about the origin is $E(XY)$. If X and Y have means μ_x and μ_y, the first product moment about their means is $E((X - \mu_x)(Y - \mu_y))$. This is the *covariance of X and Y.

Similarly, for a sample of n pairs (x_i, y_i), sample product moments can be defined. For example, the first sample product moment about the origin is

$$\frac{1}{n} \sum_1^n x_i y_i.$$

The definition of product moments is easily extended to *multivariate distributions.

product moment correlation coefficient *See* correlation coefficient.

proper subset *See* subset.

proportion A fraction or percentage. Some statistical studies are designed to find the *proportion* of a *population that have a certain characteristic or fall into a certain category. For example, studies of left-handedness in humans and of the germination rate of flower seeds can be of this type. The proportion of a population having the characteristic in question, e.g. being left-handed or germinating, is called the *population proportion*. Similarly, the proportion of a sample having the characteristic is called a *sample proportion*. If the proportion of the population having the characteristic is denoted by π, then the sample proportion

for samples of size n is, for large n, approximately *normally distributed with mean π and variance $\pi(1 - \pi)/n$. Thus the sample proportion (p) of a random sample can be used as an *estimator for the population proportion π. Also, by estimating the variance as $p(1 - p)/n$, a *confidence interval can be established. Thus an approximate 95% confidence interval for π has limits

$$p \pm 1.96 \sqrt{\left(\frac{p(1 - p)}{n}\right)}.$$

For example, if an exit poll records that 450 voters out of a random sample of 1000 stated that they voted 'Yes' in a referendum, then the sample proportion voting 'Yes' is $450/1000 = 0.45$. The population proportion voting 'Yes' is estimated to be 0.45 or 45%, and 95% confidence limits for it are

$$0.45 \pm \sqrt{\frac{0.45 \times 0.55}{1000}} = 0.45 \pm 0.03.$$

Hence a 95% confidence interval for the proportion voting 'Yes' is '42% to 48%'.

proportional to *See* variation.

pseudo-random numbers *See* random numbers.

PSU *Abbreviation for* primary sampling unit (*see* cluster sample; multistage sampling).

***p*-value** In a *hypothesis test, the *p*-value of a calculated test statistic is the probability, under the null hypothesis, of the statistic taking a value as extreme as or more extreme than the one calculated. For example, if a test statistic of 5.1 has a *p*-value of 0.06, then there is a 6% chance of the statistic having a value as extreme as or more extreme than 5.1. Such a *p*-value is often written as '$p = 0.06$'. In determining *p*-values, account must be taken of the alternative hypothesis: whether it is a *one-sided* or *two-sided alternative*. *See also* significance level; percentage point.

Q

quadrat A grid or lattice, usually square, used in *area sampling. The term is also used for an individual sub-area or unit of the grid.

quadratic Describing a mathematical expression of the second *degree, i.e. one in which the term of highest degree has degree 2. For example, $x^2 + x - 6 = 0$ is a quadratic equation, and $3x^2 + 7$ is a quadratic *polynomial.

A *quadratic function* of x is a *function whose values are given by a quadratic polynomial. Its graph is a *quadratic curve*.

quality control The use of statistical methods to monitor and maintain the quality of a process or product. It includes the use of *acceptance sampling, *control charts and *cusum charts to indicate whether processes or items produced are meeting certain standards and to give a warning when remedial action is necessary.

quantile The pth quantile of a *distribution is the value of the variable such that a fraction p ($0 < p < 1$) of the distribution is less than or equal to it. For a *random variable X, the pth quantile is denoted by x_p and is such that $\Pr(X \leqslant x_p) = p$.

If $p = 0.5$, then half the distribution is less than or equal to x_p, so $x_{0.5}$ is the *median. Similarly, $x_{0.25}$ and $x_{0.75}$ are the lower and upper *quartiles, respectively.

Often percentages are used as fractions for quantiles. If $p = r/100$, where $r = 1, 2,$ ..., 99, then x_p is the rth *percentile. So, for example, $x_{0.43}$ is the 43rd percentile.

Sometimes tenths are used. If $p = r/10$, where $r = 1, 2,$ ..., 9, then x_p is the rth *decile.

Occasionally eighths or fifths are used; then there are 7 *octiles* or 4 *quintiles*.

quartile For a set of observations of a variable listed in ascending order, the quartiles are the three values that divide the set into four equal parts. In ascending order they are the *first* or *lower quartile*, the *second quartile* (or *median) and the *third* or *upper quartile*. For example, the set of 11 observations

2 6 8 12 17 24 25 25 42 51 52

has 8, 24 and 42 as the first, second and third quartiles. In general, for a set of n observations the quartiles are commonly taken to be the $\frac{1}{4}(n+1)$th, $\frac{1}{2}(n+1)$th and $\frac{3}{4}(n+1)$th observations. For example, when $n = 11$ they are the 3rd, 6th and 9th observations, as above. When $n + 1$ is not divisible by 4, it is usual to take an *average of two observations, but another practice is to simply take the nearest observation. For example, if $n = 12$ the lower quartile is the $3\frac{1}{4}$th observation by the above rule. If the third and fourth observations are 8 and 12, then the first quartile will be estimated to be 10 (the average of 8 and 12) or 8 (the nearest observation), or even 9 (a weighted average of 8 and 12).

For *grouped data, estimates of quartiles can be found by *interpolation in the *cumulative frequency table or from the *cumulative frequency polygon, the rth quartile being the value with a cumulative relative frequency of $r/4$ (or $25r\%$).

The first, second and third quartiles are often denoted by Q_1, Q_2 (or M) and Q_3, respectively.

For a continuous *random variable X with (cumulative) *distribution function $F(x)$, the rth quartile is the value x such that $\Pr(X \leqslant x) = F(x) = r/4$. Quartiles for a discrete random variable can also be defined in terms of its distribution function, using a procedure similar to that used in the definition of its *median.

The quartiles of a *distribution divide the range of values of the variable into four intervals. Sometimes these intervals are referred to as 'quartiles'. For example, test scores lying between the first quartile and the median are said to be 'in the second quartile', and a score above the third quartile is said to be 'in the top quartile'. The same is said of the individuals with such scores.

See percentile; decile; quantile; interquartile range.

quartile deviation An alternative name for the semi-interquartile range. *See* interquartile range.

questionnaire A set of questions designed to gather information about a subject or number of subjects from respondents. *See* openended question; multiple-choice question; rating scale.

queuing theory The study of situations where participants queue for a service, e.g. airline passengers checking in for a flight, people telephoning a busy call-centre, or cars arriving at toll booths on a bridge or motorway. These situations are treated as *stochastic processes in which the interval between the arrivals of participants at the queue and the time taken in actually serving them are random elements with specified *distributions. Aspects of interest include the average length of queues, the average time a participant spends waiting in a queue for service, and the effects of changing the number of servers.

quintile The quintiles of a *distribution are the four values that divide the range of values of the variable into five intervals having equal frequencies. *See* quantile.

quota sample A *sample in which the units are not randomly selected but consist of specified numbers of units (the *quota*) chosen by the researcher in each of several categories. It is common practice to make the numbers proportional to the population sizes for the categories. For example, in a survey of student opinion about study facilities in a college with 600 arts, 400 science and 300 business students and a 50:50 gender ratio, the interviewer could be required to find and obtain the opinions of 13 female and 13 male students with 6, 4 and 3 in each group studying arts, science and business respectively.

The method is widely used in market research and opinion polls. Leaving the choice of units to the interviewer is a possible source of bias. In the above example, an interviewer who chose from students entering the college library might obtain a sample which reflected the opinions of the more studious students rather than the student body as a whole.

Compare stratified sample.

R

radius vector *See* polar coordinate system.

random In statistics, describing something that is not simply unpredictable, but can be described in terms of probability. Thus to say that a person has been 'chosen *at random* from a group of 50' is to say that the choice was not merely unpredictable, but that each person in the group had a 1 in 50 chance of being chosen. *See* error; random numbers; random sample; random variable; random walk.

random error *See* error.

randomization The arrangement of a set of objects in a random order. *See* randomized blocks; permutation test.

randomization test *See* permutation test.

randomized blocks (block design) A widely used *experimental design in which the experimental units are grouped into *blocks* so that all units in a block are as similar as possible in response to the treatments, and the treatments are applied randomly.

In a *balanced block design* all the blocks are of the same size and each treatment occurs equally often. If, in addition, each treatment is applied equally often within each block, then it is a *completely balanced block design*. To achieve this, the number of units in each block must equal (or be a multiple of) the number of treatments. Then each treatment is applied to one unit (or to an equal number of units) in each block. Treatments are allocated to units within a block at random.

In agricultural experiments, for example tests of several types of seed or fertilizer, a block might be a set of adjacent plots (= units) of land with similar fertility or soil condition. In comparing several tests of logical reasoning in groups of children, blocks might consist of children of the same age and general ability. The following table shows a completely balanced design for five treatments, *A*, *B*, *C*, *D* and *E*, using three blocks, *I*, *II* and *III*:

Block	Allocation of treatments				
I	*E*	*D*	*B*	*C*	*A*
II	*E*	*A*	*C*	*B*	*D*
III	*C*	*D*	*E*	*A*	*B*

When a two-way *analysis of variance is performed on the results, the variability between the blocks is subtracted from the residual mean square before calculating the error mean square. The effect is to remove any systematic variability between the blocks and focus better on the variability between the treatments. A nonparametric test for use with randomized blocks is *Friedman's test.

Since the results of the treatments are samples obtained from blocks of matched or related units, the design is sometimes called a *matched samples design* or *related samples design*.

A block may consist of the responses of a single individual or item to several treatments. For example, suppose that four students, *I, II, III* and *IV*, take five numeracy tests, *a, b, c, d* and *e*, over a period of 5 days. To allow for fatigue and possible bias, the order of testing for each student could be randomized by a completely balanced design in which each block consists of tests for one student:

Student	Day				
	1	2	3	4	5
I	*a*	*b*	*e*	*d*	*c*
II	*c*	*a*	*e*	*b*	*d*
III	*d*	*b*	*c*	*a*	*e*
IV	*e*	*d*	*b*	*c*	*a*

This is an example of a *repeated measures* or *within-subjects design* since the responses are taken repeatedly from the same individuals. Randomization is used to counteract any *order effects*, such as fatigue or learning effects. An analysis of variance may be used to see whether there are significant differences between the tests and/or between the mean scores of the students.

If the number of units in each block is less than the number of treatments, then the design is *incomplete*. However, if each treatment occurs equally often and every pair of treatments occurs together in the same number of blocks, then the design is a *balanced incomplete block design*. For example, in dietary experiments using as blocks animals from the same litter to reduce the effects of genetic differences, litter size may be less than the number of treatments being tested. For four treatments, *A, B, C* and *D*, on four litters with three animals in each, a balanced incomplete design could be as shown below.

Here each treatment is replicated three times and each pair occurs together in two blocks. As before, the treatments are allocated at random to the blocks and applied within the blocks at random.

Litter	Allocation of treatments		
1	*A*	*B*	*C*
2	*B*	*C*	*D*
3	*A*	*C*	*D*
4	*A*	*B*	*D*

In general, if there are *t* treatments replicated *r* times, and *b* blocks of *k* units (where $k < t$), and each pair occurs λ times, then $tr = bk$ and $\lambda = r(k-1)/(t-1)$.

See also Latin square; Graeco-Latin square; Youden square.

random numbers In its simplest form, a sequence consisting of the decimal digits 0 to 9 occurring at *random with equal probability. The occurrence of a particular digit at a particular place in the sequence cannot be predicted from the digits that precede it, nor is it a guide to the digits that follow it. The first 20 digits in such a sequence are

9 7 7 3 8 2 3 9 0 1 1 1 1 0 6 8 6 8 6 4 5.

A sequence of this type can be produced using ten balls numbered 0 to 9 in a container by repeatedly withdrawing a ball, noting its number and returning it to the container.

Procedures have been developed which enable computers and calculators to generate sequences of random digits or blocks of digits that are apparently random. Such sequences are described as *pseudo-random numbers*, for although they may pass a range of tests for randomness, they are nevertheless generated by procedures which are deterministic (i.e. not random). Random numbers are widely used in the selection of *random samples, and in allocating treatments in *designed experiments (*see* experimental design). For a table of random numbers see Table 7 in the Appendix.

See also Monte Carlo methods; simulation.

random sample A *sample drawn from a population in such a way that every possible sample of the same size has an equal chance of being chosen. If each item of the population can occur only once in a sample, the procedure is called sampling *without replacement*. If, however, immediately after selection an item is returned to the population and becomes available for reselection, then the procedure is sampling *with replacement*. In sampling with replacement an item may occur more than once in a sample. In both sampling with and without replacement, if each item eligible for selection at any stage has an equal probability of selection, then the procedure produces a *simple random sample*. *See* cluster sample; multistage sampling; stratified sample.

random variable (variate) A *variable that takes values in an unpredictable way, e.g. the number of aces in a bridge hand or the height of a randomly selected adult human.

More formally, a variable that takes discrete, isolated values, each with an associated probability or relative frequency, is a *discrete random variable*. The probabilities associated with each value are given by the *frequency function of the variable. For example, the number of aces in a bridge hand is a discrete random variable taking the values 0, 1, 2, 3 and 4 with probabilities 0.304, 0.439, 0.213, 0.041 and 0.003, respectively, and the number of girls in a family with three children is a discrete random variable taking the values 0, 1, 2, and 3 with probabilities $\frac{1}{8}$, $\frac{3}{8}$, $\frac{3}{8}$, and $\frac{1}{8}$, respectively.

A random variable that can take all values in an *interval is a *continuous random variable*. In this case, the frequency function associates with each value a *probability density* – a measure of the probability with which the variable takes values in its neighbourhood.

The standard convention is to denote random variables by capital italic letters, e.g. X and Y, and to denote general values of them by lower-case letters, e.g. x and y. Suffixes are often used when denoting several values of a variable. For example, three values of a random variable X could be denoted by x_1, x_2 and x_3.

See distribution.

random walk A path in one or more dimensions followed by an object taking steps whose size and/or direction are determined by a *random process. A simple form is the path of a particle that moves along a straight line, taking steps of one unit forwards or backwards with equal probability (*see* diagram). Since the position of the object at any stage is conditional only on its previous position, the positions reachable in a random walk form a *Markov chain.

A walk ends if the object reaches an *absorbing barrier*. This is a position that cannot be left. For example, consider a gambler who starts with capital of 10 units and repeatedly plays a game in which he wins or loses 1 unit with probabilities 0.4 and 0.6, respectively. The gambler's fortunes can be represented by a random walk along an x-axis. The walk starts at the point where

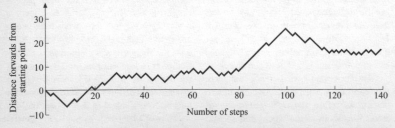

random walk The first 140 steps of a random walk.

$x = 10$ and involves a step of 1 unit in the positive direction whenever he wins a game and 1 unit in the negative direction whenever he loses. At any stage the x-coordinate of the position reached represents the gambler's current capital. There is an absorbing barrier at the point where $x = 0$, for here the gambler cannot afford to play any more and the random walk must end. If the bank starts with capital of, say, 200 units, then there is also an absorbing barrier at $x = 210$.

range 1. (of a data set) The difference between the largest and smallest values in a set of numerical *data. For example, the set of observations 23, 12, 35, 22, 23, 19 and 47 has a range of $47 - 12 = 35$. The range provides an elementary measure of *dispersion.
2. (of a variable) The set of values taken by a *variable.
3. (of a function) The set of values that can be taken by the dependent variable of a *function.

rank A set of objects is said to be *ranked* when it is arranged in order according to some criterion. For example, six finalists in a piano competition would be ranked on quality of performance, and professional golfers ranked according to the amount of prize money they win in a year.

The *rank* of an object is a number indicating its relative position when the objects have been arranged in ascending (or descending) order. For example, when the observations 4.5, 6.7, 2.1 and 11.4 are arranged in ascending order, their ranks are 2, 3, 1 and 4, respectively. This is tabulated as follows:

Observation	4.5	6.7	2.1	11.4
Rank	2	3	1	4

If a group of objects are equal in value or indistinguishable, they are said to be *tied* and to have *tied ranks*. The standard practice, sometimes called the *mid-rank method*, is to give each member of such a group a rank equal to the *mean of the ranks the group would have had if they had been ordered and in this position. Such a rank is called a *tied rank*. For instance, a sample of observations arranged in ascending order as 12, 14, 17, 17, 17, 18, 21 and 21 has two groups of tied values. The three values of 17 share the ranks 3, 4 and 5, and are each given a rank of 4. Similarly, the two values of 21 are given a rank of 7.5, the mean of 7 and 8. The result is:

Observation	12	14	17	17	17	18	21	21
Rank	1	2	4	4	4	6	7.5	7.5

In some cases ranked data are collected directly in the form of ranks; in others, ranked data are obtained by ranking sets of measured values. Many *nonparametric methods are based on ranks and usually have special procedures for dealing with sets of ranks that contain tied ranks.

rank correlation coefficient A measure of the *correlation between two sets of *ranks. *See* correlation coefficient.

rating scale A device for differentiating the responses to questions or statements. Rating scales provide for a flexibility of response denied by the simpler *dichotomous question in which only two responses are possible, e.g. yes/no or good/bad, and are widely used in surveys and questionnaires.

A *Likert scale* provides a range of responses to a question or statement as, for example, in the following:

Voting in elections should be compulsory				
Strongly disagree	Disagree	Neither agree nor disagree	Agree	Strongly agree

It is important that the responses are mutually exclusive, i.e. do not overlap, and that they exhaust the range of possible responses.

A *semantic differential scale* is a rating scale with an adjective at one end and its opposite at the other as, for example, in the following:

How difficult did you find mathematics at school?

Hard	1	2	3	4	5	6	Easy

A scale offering n alternative responses is called an *n-point scale*. The examples above are instances of a 5-point and a 6-point scale. Expert wine-tasters use a 9-point scale to record their impression of the sweetness/dryness of white wine. An important distinction between scales with odd and even numbers of points is that the former have a mid-point ('neither agree nor disagree' in the first example), whereas the latter force the respondent to make a response which is nearer to one extremity than to the other.

ratio scale *See* scale of measurement.

raw data test *See* permutation test.

reciprocal The number or expression produced by dividing 1 by the number or expression. Thus the reciprocal of 5 is $\frac{1}{5}$, and the reciprocal of $x + 1$ is $1/(x + 1)$.

rectangular distribution *See* uniform distribution.

reference axis *See* axis.

regression A statistical *model that predicts the *mean value of a *random variable when one or more other variables are fixed in value; for example, an equation giving the average stopping distance of cars travelling at a given speed, or a formula giving the average weight of a child of a given height and age.

More formally, let the mean value of a random variable Y for a fixed value of a variable x be denoted by $E(Y|x)$, i.e. the mean of Y *conditional on* x. Then the *regression of Y on x* is an equation expressing $E(Y|x)$ in terms of x. This is called a *regres-sion equation* and predicts the average value of Y for a given value of x. The random variable Y is called the *response* (or *dependent*) *variable*; other terms used include *effect*, *predicted* and *outcome variable*. The variable x is called the *explanatory* (or *independent*) *variable*; other terms used include *causal*, *controlled*, *criterion*, *experimental*, *predictor*, *regressor* and *treatment variable*. $E(Y|x)$ is sometimes abbreviated, in this context, to y_x, or simply y.

A simple case is when the average value of Y is a *linear function of x, so that

$$E(Y|x) = \alpha + \beta x,$$

where α and β are parameters. Such parameters are called *regression coefficients*, and a main task of *regression analysis* is to estimate values for these parameters from experimental data. If Y is assumed to have a *normal distribution with constant *variance σ^2 for each value of x, then from a sample of n independent pairs of values (x_i, y_i) the method of *least squares gives the best estimates of α and β. These estimates, a and b, are provided by most calculators and software packages. They can be directly calculated from the formulae

$$b = \frac{n \sum_i x_i y_i - \sum_i x_i \sum_i y_i}{n \sum_i x_i^2 - (\sum_i x_i)^2} \quad \text{and}$$
$$a = \bar{y} - b\bar{x},$$

where

$$\bar{x} = \frac{1}{n} \sum_i x_i \quad \text{and}$$
$$\bar{y} = \frac{1}{n} \sum_i y_i.$$

The line with equation $y = a + bx$ is then called the *regression line* of y on x.

An alternative, equivalent formulation of the above regression equation

$$E(Y|x) = \alpha + \beta x$$

is

$$Y = \alpha + \beta x + \varepsilon,$$

where ε is a *random component, independent of x, with zero mean and constant variance σ^2.

Models in which the equation is linear in the parameters are called *linear regression models*, and those with more than one explanatory variable are *multiple linear regression models*. For example, in economics, the 'demand equation'

$$q = \alpha + \beta x + \gamma p$$

is a multiple linear regression model predicting q, the average quantity of a commodity bought when its price is p and the consumer's income is x. Here, q is equivalent to $E(Q|x,p)$ in our notation. The parameters are α, β and γ. Similarly, on the basis of more than 1000 observations made in 1903, a multiple linear model estimated the regression of a son's height (in centimetres) on the heights of both parents to be

$$s = 35.76 + 0.41f + 0.43m,$$

where f and m are the heights of a given father and mother, and s is the predicted height of a son.

When the regression equation is not linear in the explanatory variables, the regression is said to be *curvilinear*. For instance, in some studies of fungicides a useful regression equation for the average number of spores killed, y, when the concentration of an applied fungicide is fixed at x is

$$y = \alpha + \beta \log x.$$

The regression of numbers of spores killed on concentration is curvilinear.

See line of best fit; logistic regression; multiple regression; regression towards the mean.

regression analysis *See* regression.

regression coefficient *See* regression.

regression equation *See* regression.

regression line *See* regression; line of best fit.

regression towards the mean The observation that in *regression analyses of bivariate *data, the average value y of the response variable for a given value x of the explanatory variable tends to deviate from its overall mean by fewer *standard deviations than x deviates from its *mean. This is a reflection of the fact that the *least squares line of regression of y on x,

$$y - \bar{y} = \frac{s_{xy}}{s_x^2}(x - \bar{x}),$$

can be rewritten in the form

$$\frac{y - \bar{y}}{s_y} = r\left(\frac{x - \bar{x}}{s_x}\right),$$

where r is the product moment *correlation coefficient. In this equation, the left-hand side and the bracketed term on the right express the deviations of y and x from their means in terms of their standard deviations, i.e. represent their *standardized scores. Since, in practice, $|r| < 1$, the standardized score of the predicted value y must be less than that of x in magnitude.

The phenomenon is a consequence of the methods of linear regression and was first observed in studies of heredity. For example, data giving the *median height of parents (the *mid-parent* height) and the average height of their adult children show that the adult children of tall parents tend to be shorter on average than the mid-parent height and therefore closer to the mean. Conversely, children with short parents tend to be taller on average than the mid-parent height and, again, are closer to the mean. In other words, the dependence of adult children's height on mid-parent height is such that the dependent variable 'reverts' or 'regresses' towards the mean. This phenomenon should not be taken to mean that over time people who are very tall or short will become rarer. In fact, sufficient numbers of such people will continue to be born naturally for the stability of the distribution of height to be maintained.

regressor variable *See* regression.

rejection region *See* hypothesis testing.

related samples *See* matched pairs.

related samples design *See* randomized blocks.

relative efficiency *See* efficiency.

relative error The quantity

$$\frac{\text{absolute error}}{\text{true value}},$$

often applied to approximations and estimates. For example, if the true population of a town is 27 456 and an estimate of it is 25 000, then the absolute error is 2456 and the relative error is $2456/27\,456 = 0.09$, or 9%. *See also* percentage error.

relative frequency *See* frequency.

reliability 1. In psychological and educational *tests, a general term for the dependability of a test, i.e. the extent to which it records genuine, relevant differences between individuals as distinct from error effects, which vary from sample to sample. Thus a reliable test can be expected to produce similar results if given to similar groups of individuals, or to the same group at suitably spaced times.

The degree to which a test is reliable can be approached and assessed by a number of methods, such as the following:

(1) The same test is administered to the same group twice (or more times), with appropriate intervals between the testing sessions, and the scores are compared. This assesses *test–retest reliability*.

(2) A second test containing *items which are similar in type and difficulty is given, and the scores are compared with those on the original test. This assesses *alternate forms reliability* (also called *equivalent* or *parallel forms reliability*).

(3) The test is given to two (or more) similar groups, and the scores are compared. This assesses *sample reliability*.

(4) The test is divided into two halves and a comparison made of the scores obtained by individuals on the two halves of the test. This assesses *split-half reliability* and indicates the *internal consistency* of the test. The *correlation between the scores on the two halves can be converted into an estimate of the reliability of the complete test by means of the *Spearman–Brown formula.

(5) An attempt is made to estimate the proportion of the *variance in the total scores on the test attributable to genuine differences between individuals rather than to random error effects. This may involve the use of a *Kuder–Richardson formula or the formula for the *alpha reliability coefficient.

2. A term used in connection with the lifetime of scientific or industrial components or equipment. If the lifetime t of a component has *distribution function $F(t)$, then the reliability of the component is the probability that it has a lifetime greater than t, and this is equal to $1 - F(t)$. For example, a component with a 5% probability of failing in the first 400 hours of operation has a 95% chance of running for more than 400 hours; it is thus 95% reliable for a lifetime of 400 hours.

reliability coefficient (coefficient of reliability) A measure of the *reliability of a psychological or educational *test. It is commonly a *correlation coefficient expressing the degree of relationship between two sets of scores obtained from two testing sessions with the same test or with two equivalent tests. The correlation coefficient is often given a descriptive name depending on the aspect of reliability being measured. If *test–retest reliability* is being assessed, the coefficient is a *coefficient of

reliability coefficient (a)

Student	Item								Total Score
	1	2	3	4	5	6	7	8	
a	1	1	1	1	0	1	1	1	7
b	1	1	0	0	0	0	0	0	2
c	1	1	1	1	0	1	0	1	6
d	0	0	0	1	0	1	0	0	2
e	1	1	0	1	0	1	0	1	5
p	0.8	0.8	0.4	0.8	0.0	0.8	0.2	0.6	

stability. If an assessment is made using *alternate* or *parallel forms* of a test, a *coefficient of equivalence* is obtained. An assessment of *split-half reliability* leads to a *coefficient of internal consistency*.

Reliability coefficients can also be estimated directly from a single administration of a test to a group of individuals. In the case of a test with n *items, an estimate of the reliability coefficient is given by a *Kuder–Richardson formula* such as

$$\frac{n}{n-1}\left(1 - \frac{1}{s^2}\sum pq\right),$$

where s^2 is the *variance of the total test scores, p is the proportion of correct or satisfactory responses to an item, $q = 1 - p$, and the summation is over all the n items in the test.

For example, in a trial of a test with 8 items made with 5 students, and answers to items are scored 1 if correct and 0 if wrong, the results in table (a) might be obtained. Here $n = 8$ and $s^2 = 4.24$, and

$$\sum pq = 0.8 \times 0.2 + 0.8 \times 0.2 + 0.4 \times 0.6$$
$$+ 0.8 \times 0.2 + 0 \times 1 + 0.8 \times 0.2$$
$$+ 0.2 \times 0.8 + 0.6 \times 0.4$$
$$= 1.28$$

Using the formula, the reliability coefficient is found to be

$$\frac{8}{7}\left(1 - \frac{1.28}{4.24}\right) = 0.80.$$

Alternatively, an estimate can be made using the *split-half method. Here the test is split into two comparable halves and a correlation coefficient r between the scores on the two halves is calculated. This measure of split-half reliability can be converted into an estimate of the reliability of the complete test by means of the *Spearman–Brown formula in the form

$$\frac{2r}{1 + r}.$$

In the above example, if the eight items are similar, it may be appropriate to use the total scores on the odd and even items. These are as in table (b). The product moment *correlation coefficient r for the five pairs is 0.62. This is the coefficient of internal consistency and measures the reliability of parallel subtests of four items. From the Spearman–Brown formula with $r = 0.62$ the estimate of the reliability coefficient for the full test is found to be 0.77.

For tests containing items on which a variety of scores are possible, rather than being scored correct or incorrect, a reliability coefficient known as the *alpha reliabil-

reliability coefficient (b)

Student	Total score	
	Odd items	Even items
a	3	4
b	1	1
c	2	4
d	0	2
e	1	4

ity coefficient (*Cronbach's alpha*) can be estimated.

repeated measures A form of *experimental design in which observations are made on the same units at two or more points in time. *See* randomized blocks.

replication 1. In a *designed experiment, the application of a treatment to a number of different units under identical experimental conditions. When comparing treatments, or comparing a treatment with a *control, it is often desirable (though not essential, and not always feasible) to have equal numbers of units receiving each treatment; this is called *equal replication*. *See* experimental design.
2. The reproduction or duplication of an entire experiment as precisely as possible, i.e. using the same treatments under the same conditions on a similar set of units. In this sense, the aim of a replication is to see if the same results are obtained as in the earlier experiment.

representative sample A *sample which in some sense is typical of the *population from which it is drawn. *See* cluster sample; quota sample; random sample; sample survey; stratified sample; systematic sample. *Compare* convenience sample.

residuals The differences between observed values and the values predicted by a *model. For example, from a sample of pairs of observations (x_i, y_i), $i = 1, 2, \ldots, n$, a *regression line of y on x, $y = a + bx$, can be obtained. For each value x_i, this linear regression model predicts the value $a + bx_i$ for y. This predicted value is sometimes denoted by $\hat{y}_i$. The actual observed value is y_i, so for this model the residuals are $y_i - a - bx_i$, sometimes given as $y_i - \hat{y}_i$. *See* residual variation; line of best fit.

residual variance *See* residual variation.

residual variation The variability not systematically accounted for by a *model. It is

estimated from the *residuals. For example, in a simple *linear regression model

$$Y = \alpha + \beta x + \varepsilon,$$

the expression $\alpha + \beta x$ represents the systematic variation of the random variable Y in terms of the variable x, and the term ε represents the uncontrolled residual variation. It is usually assumed that ε has zero *mean and a constant unknown *variance σ^2 independent of x. This variance is called the *residual variance* in the model. If, from a sample of n independent pairs of observations (x_i, y_i), a *regression line of y on x with equation $y = a + bx$ is obtained, then the residuals are $y_i - a - bx_i$. The *unbiased estimate of the residual variance σ^2 is

$$\frac{1}{n-2} \sum_{1}^{n} (y_i - a - bx_i)^2.$$

In an *analysis of variance, residual variation is measured by the error mean square. In the case of a linear regression based on n pairs of values, this approach also results in the above estimate of the variance, the number of *degrees of freedom being $n - 2$.

response variable *See* regression.

Retail Prices Index (RPI) An *index number based on the retail prices of a range of goods and services. In Britain it is calculated monthly and used to show changes in the cost of living. The index involves a large number of items classified in five groups: (1) food and catering, (2) alcohol and tobacco, (3) housing and household expenditure, (4) personal expenditure and (5) travel and leisure. The items in each group are weighted according to the proportion of expenditure currently spent on them by the average household, and a weighted index number is calculated for each group. Finally, the overall RPI is obtained by calculating a weighted *mean of these five indices.

Retail Prices Index

		Group			
	Food	Alcohol & tobacco	Housing	Personal	Travel & leisure
Weight	203	119	341	110	227
Index	112.1	111.3	123.2	110.9	113.4

The base point is 13 January 1987, at which time all indices were 100. As an illustration, the table above gives the weights and indices for the five groups shortly afterwards, on 15 August 1989. The sum of the weights is 1000. From these data we have

$$RPI = (112.1 \times 203 + 111.3 \times 119$$
$$+ 123.2 \times 341 + 110.9 \times 110$$
$$+ 113.4 \times 227)/1000$$
$$= 116.0$$

An annual survey of households is made to monitor the weights and take into account changes in patterns of expenditure. For example, in Britain the proportion of expenditure on tobacco products has fallen, and the weighting given to it has been decreased accordingly.

It is conventional to change the base point from time to time, and reset the RPI at 100. In recent times the base point was reset on 1 January 1974 and 13 January 1987.

Since December 2003, another index, the Consumer Prices Index (CPI), has begun to be published alongside the RPI. The CPI differs from the RPI by excluding a number of items, mainly related to housing, and by classifying items into twelve instead of five groups.

right censored *See* censored data.

robustness Some statistical procedures are more sensitive than others to departures from the assumptions on which they are based, or to the presence of *outliers in the data to which they are applied. For example, given a *random sample from a

*normal distribution, the sample *mean is generally preferred to the sample *median as an estimator of the population mean because it is more *efficient. However, if the data are contaminated by the presence of an outlier, the sample median or a *trimmed mean will generally give a more reliable estimate of the population mean.

Consider the ordered data set

2.7   2.8   2.9   4.5   4.6   5.1   5.5   6.0
6.1   6.9   7.6.

The sample mean is 4.97 and the sample median is 5.1. If the observation 4.5 were incorrectly recorded as 45, the mean for the amended data set would be 8.65, but the median would increase only to 5.6. Clearly, the median, being the *middle* value of the ordered data set, is moved at most to an immediate neighbouring value if one observation is mis-recorded as an outlier, whereas the mean can be substantially affected as a measure of location.

For strict validity, the *t-test for two independent samples requires the assumption that the samples are from normal distributions with equal *variances. The test is little affected by small departures from the assumption of equal variances, but if they differ substantially (e.g. by a factor of 2 or more) the test is likely to be less efficient than the *Wilcoxon rank sum test. The latter test may also be more efficient in the presence of outliers, and in these circumstances is said to be more *robust*.

More generally, tests based on assumptions of normality tend not to be very robust when samples are from skew distributions (*see* skewness) such as the

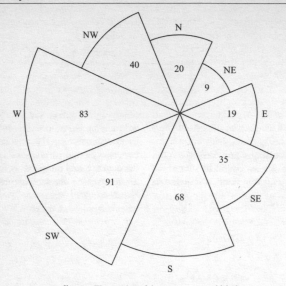

rose diagram The number of days per year on which the prevailing wind at a location was from a certain direction.

*exponential distribution, or from *symmetrical distributions with substantial tails such as the *Cauchy distribution. In these circumstances procedures that take account of the specific type of distribution from which the samples are taken may be appropriate, but many of these are not very robust against the failure of the assumptions on which they are based. In general, because they tend to involve fewer assumptions, nonparametric methods tend to be more robust than their parametric counterparts.

root mean square The positive square root of the *mean square deviation. When a deviation is measured from the *mean, it is the *standard deviation.

rose diagram A form of representation of grouped *angular data. The frequency f associated with an angular interval of size θ is represented by a circular sector of angle θ whose area is proportional to f. When the angular intervals are all equal, proportion-

ality is most easily achieved by making the radius of each sector proportional to the square root of the associated frequency. *See also* circular histogram.

rounding Replacing a number by the nearest number with a certain number of decimal places or *significant figures. For example, 4.529 is 4.53 when rounded to two decimal places, and 4.529 is 4.5 to two significant figures. A commonly used rule for rounding is that if the first digit to be dropped is 5 or more the preceding digit is increased by 1, and if the first digit to be dropped is less than 5 the preceding digit is unchanged. For instance, rounded to two decimal places, 2.6053 is 2.61, and 2.6049 is 2.60. It is standard practice to present results rounded to an appropriate degree.

The act of rounding produces a *rounding error* equal to the difference between the rounded value and the original value. For a simple example of the possible effect of rounding errors, suppose that three candidates in an election receive 200, 355 and 445 votes. Their percentages of the total poll are 20%, 35.5% and 44.5%, which sum to 100%. However, if the percentages are announced rounded to the nearest whole number they become 20%, 36% and 45%. These sum to 101% because, in this instance, the rounding errors (each of 0.5%) introduced by rounding 35.5 and 45.5 up to 36 and 46, reinforce rather than cancel each other.

When calculations are carried out on data that have been rounded, substantial errors can occur. In general, it is advisable to perform statistical calculations on raw numerical data and leave rounding to the final stages when presenting the results. A common practice is to report *means to one more significant figure than the data, and *standard deviations to two more; the inclusion of further digits usually gives a spurious impression of accuracy.

rounding error *See* rounding; uniform distribution.

row vector (row matrix) A *vector (or *matrix) having a single row of elements, for example the vector

$$(2 \quad -1 \quad 9).$$

Compare column vector.

RPI *Abbreviation for* *Retail Prices Index.

run An element or succession of elements of a certain specified type within a sequence which is followed or preceded by a different type of element or by no element at all. The length of a run is the number of elements it contains.

For example, the sequence of symbols

M M F F F F M F F F

contains four runs of identical symbols, MM, FFFF, M and FFF, of lengths 2, 4, 1 and 3, respectively. Similarly, the sequence of digits

2 8 9 3 5 7 8 8 6 9

contains two runs of even digits and two of odd digits.

A succession of numbers that are strictly increasing is called an *up run*, and one that is strictly decreasing is called a *down run*. In the above sequence of digits there are three up runs, '2 8 9', '3 5 7 8' and '6 9', and two down runs, '9 3' and '8 6'.

Studies of the occurrence of runs in random sequences have led to the development of *runs tests. In particular, some sophisticated tests based on the properties of runs are available to check computer generated pseudo-random numbers (*see* random numbers) for randomness.

runs test A type of *nonparametric test based on *runs associated with the sample data. A simple form tests a sequence of observations of a *dichotomous variable for randomness, e.g. whether a sequence of computer generated coin tosses H T T H T ... is consistent with the *null hypothesis that the outcomes H and T occur independently and the order is random. Suppose there are n observations in all, of which n_1 are of one kind (e.g. H) and $n_2 = n - n_1$ of the other (e.g. T). The test statistic r is the total number of runs of identical symbols. The hypothesis of randomness is rejected if r is too small (e.g. as it is for a sequence mostly containing large blocks of H and/or T) or too large (e.g. as it is for a sequence in which H and T almost always alternate).

As an illustration, suppose that an observer notes that the gender of individuals in a long queue at a railway booking office is

M F F M F M F M F M F M M M M
F M F M M F F F F,

and wishes to test whether males and females queue in a random order. Here $n = 24$, $n_1 = 12$ and $n_2 = 12$. The test statistic r, the number of runs, is easily seen to be equal to 16.

Statistical software will give a *p-value for r, and tables of critical values of r are

runs test

Observation	8	11	14	17	27	30	38	39	41	49	55	56
Label	*A*	*A*	*B*	*B*	*B*	*B*	*B*	*B*	*B*	*A*	*A*	*A*

also tabulated for a range of small values of n_1 and n_2. For large values of n_1 or n_2 (e.g. over 20), r has an approximately *normal distribution under the null hypothesis with mean $1 + (2n_1 n_2 /n)$ and variance

$$\frac{2n_1 n_2 (2n_1 n_2 - n)}{n^2(n-1)},$$

and, with an appropriate *continuity correction, a p-value for r can be calculated.

In our example, tables indicate that r needs to be less than or equal to 7 or greater than or equal to 19 for significance at the 5% level. Our value, $r = 16$ does not fall in either range (its p-value is 0.30), so the hypothesis that the genders were randomly ordered in the queue is retained.

This test is sometimes called the *single sample runs test* or *one-sample runs test*. A modified form of it can be used to test a sequence of numerical observations for departures from independence, as when an oral examiner who tests students in succession wonders whether candidates tested towards the end have an advantage over those tested at the beginning. By giving a label *A* or *B* to each exam mark above or below the *median, the sequence of marks is converted into a sequence of symbols to which the runs test can be applied.

The *Wald–Wolfowitz runs test* is a test of the hypothesis that two independent samples are from the same or identical populations as opposed to two that differ in any way, e.g. in *location or *dispersion. It is sometimes called the *two-samples runs test*. Suppose that two samples *A* and *B* contain n_1 and n_2 observations, respectively. The first stage is to combine the observations, arrange them in ascending order, and label those from the first sample *A* and those from the second *B*. This produces a sequence of $n = n_1 + n_2$ symbols *A* and *B*. The test statistic, r, is the total number of runs of identical symbols. Significantly low values of r indicate that the populations differ.

As an illustration, suppose the observations in the two samples were as follows:

$$A: \ 11, 49, 56, 55, 8$$
$$B: \ 30, 14, 41, 39, 17, 38, 27$$

The observations are arranged in ascending order and labelled, as in the table. Here $n_1 = 5$ and $n_2 = 7$, and r, the number of runs, is 3. Tables or software indicate that values of r less than or equal to 3 are significant at the 5% level. So $r = 3$ is significant (its p-value is 0.02), and there is evidence to support the alternative hypothesis that the samples are from populations that differ.

St Petersburg paradox A historical paradox about a gambling game involving two players. Player A tosses a fair coin until it turns up heads, at which point the game ends. If the coin turns up heads on the first toss, he pays player B £2. If it turns up on the second toss he pays £4, if on the third toss £8, if on the fourth toss £16, and so on. Find B's *expectation.

The probabilities of the game ending with the first, second, third, ... toss are the probabilities of the coin turning up 'heads', 'tails, heads', 'tails, tails, heads', ... and these are $\frac{1}{2}, (\frac{1}{2})^2, (\frac{1}{2})^3, \ldots$. Thus B's winnings and their probabilities are as follows:

Amount won (£)	2	4	8	16	...
Probability	1/2	1/4	1/8	1/16	...

The average amount B can expect to win, the expectation, is

$$2 \times \tfrac{1}{2} + 4 \times \tfrac{1}{4} + 8 \times \tfrac{1}{8} + 16 \times \tfrac{1}{16} + \cdots,$$

and this is equal to $1 + 1 + 1 + 1 + \cdots$. Now, this is a series without a finite sum (a *divergent series). So, if the coin can be tossed indefinitely, player B expects to win (and A expects to lose) an unlimited amount. In a *fair game*, B pays a sum equal to his expectation to A before play starts. Here B's expectation is unlimited and a fair game is impossible.

Proposed by Nicholas Bernoulli (1687–1759) in a letter to de Montmort in 1713, the problem was investigated and published by his cousin Daniel Bernoulli (1700–1782).

Note that if the payments are reduced from 2, 2^2, 2^3, ... to, say, 1.98, 1.98^2, $1.98^3, \ldots$, it can be shown that B's expectation is a *convergent series with sum £99. So a fair game becomes possible.

sample A finite *subset of a *population or other set of items. A sample containing n items is often referred to as a *sample of size n*. See cluster sample; convenience sample; multistage sampling; quota sample; random sample; representative sample; stratified sample; systematic sample.

sample estimate The value of an estimate obtained from a *sample. See estimation; sampling error; standard deviation; unbiased estimator; variance.

sample mean The *mean of the numerical values in a *sample.

sample moment See moment.

sample proportion See proportion.

sample reliability See reliability.

sample space The *set of all possible outcomes of an experiment. For example, when a coin is tossed the possible outcomes are 'heads' and 'tails', so the sample space is the set {H, T}. Similarly, when a couple plan to have a family of two children, the outcomes, in order of birth, are the set of four possibilities denoted by (B, B), (B, G), (G, B), (G, G). *See also* event.

sample standard deviation The *standard deviation of the numerical values in a *sample. This is sometimes called the *unadjusted standard deviation* of the sample in order to distinguish it from the *adjusted standard deviation*, i.e. the estimate of the standard deviation of the population made from the sample. If the sample contains n observations, then the sample standard deviation is calculated using n as divisor. The estimate of the population standard deviation is calculated using $n - 1$ as divisor.

sample survey A study that uses observations of a *sample from a population to estimate characteristics of that population. *See also* area sampling; census; cluster sample; multistage sampling; quota sample; random sample; representative sample; stratified sample.

sample unit Any one of the items in a *sample. *Compare* sampling unit.

sample variance The *variance of the numerical values in a *sample. This is sometimes called the *unadjusted variance* of the sample in order to distinguish it from the *adjusted variance*, i.e. the *unbiased estimate of the variance of the population made from the sample. If the sample contains n observations, then the sample variance is calculated using n as divisor. The unbiased estimate of the population variance is calculated using $n - 1$ as divisor.

sampling distribution The *distribution of a *statistic. For example, the *mean $\bar{x}$ of a *sample of size n from a *normal population with mean μ and *variance σ^2 is a statistic whose distribution is normal with mean μ and variance σ^2/n.

sampling error The difference between an estimate based on a *sample and the true value. For example, when the *mean $\bar{x}$ of a random sample of size n is used to estimate the mean μ of a *normal population with *variance σ^2, the sampling error is $\bar{x} - \mu$. This is a random variable with mean 0 and variance σ^2/n. Its *standard deviation $\sigma/\sqrt{n}$ is its *standard error*, often called the *standard error of the (sample) mean*. If σ is unknown, the best estimate of the standard error is $s/\sqrt{n}$, where

$$s^2 = \frac{1}{n-1} \sum_1^n (x_i - \bar{x})^2.$$

For example, the heart rates (beats per minute) of a random sample of seven female students were 73, 82, 87, 68, 106, 60 and 97. The sample mean is 81.9, $s = 16.26$, and the estimated standard error of the (sample) mean is $16.26/\sqrt{7} = 6.1$. If the unknown population mean was in fact 77, then sampling error is $81.9 - 77 = 4.9$.

sampling frame *See* frame.

sampling interval *See* systematic sample.

sampling unit Any one of the set of units from which a *sample is to be taken. *See* multistage sampling; *compare* sample unit.

sampling with *or* without replacement *See* random sample.

SAS *Abbreviation for* Statistical Analysis System. *See* statistical software packages.

scalar A number as distinguished from a *vector or *matrix.

scale A range of values used in measuring or recording something. For example, the Beaufort scale records the strength of the wind on a scale running from 0 (calm) to 12 (hurricane). *See* linear scale; logarithmic scale; rating scale; scale of measurement.

scale of measurement A term used for any type of *scale used in measuring or recording some object. Scales of measurement in common use include the following:

(1) *nominal scale*. A set of names or symbols used to simply label or classify an object. For example, (i) the symbols O, A, B, AB for classifying human blood types; (ii) a range such as 'brown, black, blond, white, grey, ginger' for hair colour; and (iii) categories for recording criminal offences: 'robbery, fraud or forgery, sexual offence, etc.'.

The use of such a scale is sometimes called *nominal measurement*, and the outcome is called *nominal data*. Although the data may well consist of counts of numbers in each category, it is arguable that nominal measurement is misnamed since the observations are essentially qualitative and non-numerical.

(2) *ordinal scale*. A scale with an order property, in the sense that it gives an object a measurement which can be compared with that of others. For example, wine experts use a scale A, B, C, D, E to measure the strength of flavour of red wines, a wine graded E being stronger than one graded D, and so on down to A. An ordinal scale conveys only relative magnitude, so in the above example there is no guarantee that wines graded A and B differ in strength by the same amount as those graded B and C.

Further examples of ordinal scales are (i) the rankings 1, 2, 3, 4, 5, 6 given by a judge to finalists in a competition; (ii) socio-economic scales, e.g. A, B, C1, C2, D, E, used in surveys to rate the status of individuals; and (iii) *rating scales such as 'never, occasionally, frequently, always' used to record responses to *multiple-choice questions.

The use of such a scale is called *ordinal measurement*, and the outcome is called *ordinal data*.

(3) *interval scale*. A scale that reflects precisely the differences between the magnitudes being measured but not their ratios. In an interval scale the unit of measurement and the zero point are arbitrary. For example, the Celsius and Fahrenheit temperature scales are both interval scales. A rise from, say, 20 to 25 degrees Celsius represents the same increase in warmth as a rise from 5 to 10 degrees Celsius, and a fall from 60 to 40 degrees Fahrenheit represents the same decrease in warmth as one from 30 to 10 degrees Fahrenheit. However, their zeros are not absolute zeros. As a result, the ratio of two temperatures is meaningless. For instance, $40°C$ is 'twice' $20°C$, but the ratio of their equivalents in Fahrenheit, $104°F$ and $68°F$, is 1.53.

Other examples of interval scales occur in the measurement of aptitude or intelligence. The use of such a scale is sometimes called *interval measurement*.

(4) *ratio scale*. A scale that reflects precisely the differences between the magnitudes being measured and also their ratios. In a ratio scale there is a true, absolute zero. Most scales in the physical sciences are ratio scales, e.g. those for weight, length and speed. So, for example, if the ratio of two speeds in km/hour is 2 : 1, it will also be 2 : 1 if the speeds are measured in m/second. In contrast to the Celsius and Fahrenheit scales, the absolute temperature scale is a ratio scale.

scatter diagram (scattergram, scatter plot)
A graphical representation of data consisting of pairs of values of two variables. Each pair of values is represented by a point with *Cartesian coordinates equal to these values. The diagram can provide some visual indication of a possible relationship between the variables. For example, suppose that the marks obtained in written and oral French by eight students are as given in the table; then the scatter diagram (*see* diagram) consists of eight points with coordinates (72, 64), (37, 48), ..., (40, 29). This illustrates the relationship between the written and oral marks of this group of students. *See also* correlation; line of best fit.

scattergram *See* scatter diagram.

scatter plot *See* scatter diagram.

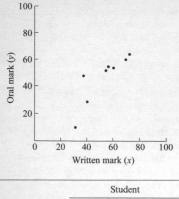

	Student							
	1	2	3	4	5	6	7	8
Written mark (x)	72	37	54	60	31	69	56	40
Oral mark (y)	64	48	52	54	10	60	55	29

scatter diagram

scientific notation *See* exponential notation.

s.d. *Abbreviation for* *standard deviation.

s.e. *Abbreviation for* *standard error.

secondary diagonal *See* matrix.

secondary sampling unit *See* multistage sampling.

sectional bar chart *See* bar chart.

semantic differential scale *See* rating scale.

semi-interquartile range (quartile deviation) A measure of the *dispersion of a set of *data, or of a *random variable, equal to half the difference between the upper and lower quartiles. *See* interquartile range.

semi-logarithmic graph *See* graph.

semi-logarithmic paper *See* logarithmic paper.

sequence A succession of terms formed according to some rule or process. For example, 2, 4, 6, 8, 10 is a sequence of even numbers, 2, 5, 0, 3, 3, 8, 7, 9, 1, 1, 1, 3 is a sequence of *random digits, and $\frac{1}{2}, \frac{1}{4}, \frac{1}{8}, \frac{1}{16}, \ldots$ is a sequence of powers of $\frac{1}{2}$.

More formally, a sequence is a succession of terms

$$a_1, a_2, a_3, a_4, \ldots, a_n, \ldots.$$

The nth term (or *general term*) is a_n, and a rule for a sequence will indicate how the general term is to be calculated. Thus the nth term of the first sequence above is $2n$, so that the first term is 2, the second term is 4, and so on. Similarly, the general term of the third sequence is $1/2^n$. A *finite sequence* has a finite (i.e. limited) number of terms, as in the first two examples. An *infinite sequence* has an unlimited number of terms, as in the third example. An infinite sequence can approach a limiting value as the number of terms, n, becomes very large. Such a sequence is called a *convergent sequence* and is said to tend to a limit as n tends to infinity. The third sequence above is convergent and tends to a limit of zero.

See arithmetic progression; geometric progression; series.

series An expression for the sum of the terms of a *sequence. For the sequence

$$1, 3, 5, 7, 9, 11, 13, 15,$$

the corresponding series is

$$1 + 3 + 5 + 7 + 9 + 11 + 13 + 15.$$

The value of the expression is the *sum* of the series; in this example the sum is 64.

A series is said to be *finite* or *infinite* according to whether it is made up of a finite (i.e. limited) or unlimited number of terms.

More formally, for a finite sequence $a_1, a_2, a_3, \ldots, a_N$ the corresponding series is $a_1 + a_2 + a_3 + \cdots + a_N$. With the aid of the *summation sign $\sum$, this can be written as

$$\sum_1^N a_n.$$

The numbers above and below the summation sign indicate the range of values of n in the series; in this case the numbers $1, 2, 3, \ldots, N$. For example,

$$1 + 3 + 5 + 7 + 9 + 11 + 13 + 15$$

$$= \sum_1^8 (2n - 1).$$

For an infinite sequence $a_1, a_2, a_3, \ldots$, the corresponding series is $a_1 + a_2 + a_3 + \cdots$, and this can be written as $\sum_1^\infty a_n$. For example,

$$\frac{1}{2} + \frac{1}{4} + \frac{1}{8} + \frac{1}{16} + \cdots = \sum_1^\infty \frac{1}{2^n}.$$

See convergent series. *See also* arithmetic series; binomial series; expansion; exponential scries; geometric series.

series expansion *See* expansion.

set (class) A collection of objects of any kind. The objects that make up a set are called its *elements* or *members*. The statement 'a is an element of the set A' can be written as $a \in A$, and a set whose only elements are a, b and c can be denoted by $\{a, b, c\}$. Also allowed as a set is the *empty* or *null set*, denoted by $\varnothing$, which is the set that has no clements. Two sets are said to be equal if they have the same elements.

A set can be specified by stating all its elements, e.g. the set of all English vowels is $\{a, e, i, o, u\}$. Alternatively, a set can be specified by a condition for membership, e.g. $\{x : x \text{ is even}\}$ specifies the set of all even numbers. A *finite set* has a finite number of elements; an *infinite set* has an infinite number of elements. For example, the population of the UK is a finite set, and the set of all prime numbers is infinite.

See also event; sample space; complement; intersection; subset; union; Venn diagram.

s.f. *Abbreviation for* *significant figures.

Sheppard's correction *See* grouped data.

sigma 1. The Greek capital letter Σ used to denote a sum. *See* summation sign.
2. The Greek letter σ used to denote the *standard deviation of a population, with σ^2 denoting the population *variance.

sigma notation *See* summation sign.

slgmoid curve A type of curve resembling a flattened S (*see* diagram). More precisely, it is a form of curve lying between two horizontal *asymptotes, having one *point of inflection and for which the value of y increases as x increases. The cumulative *distribution curve for *unimodal distributions, e.g. the *normal distribution, is of this form. It also arises in *models of growth when variables such as population size are plotted against time. In this context, the *logistic curve*

$$y = \frac{k}{1 + \exp(a - bx)},$$

where k, a and b are constants, and both k and b are positive, is widely used.

significance level In a *hypothesis test, the *p-value of a calculated test statistic is the probability, under the null hypothesis, of the statistic taking a value as extreme as, or more extreme than, the one calculated. The decision to reject the null hypothesis in

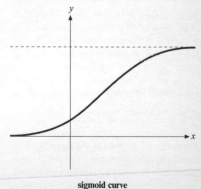

sigmoid curve

favour of the alternative hypothesis is taken if this probability is less than or equal to some low probability α. The value of the test statistic is then said to be *significant* at *significance level* α. Traditional values of α are 0.05, 0.01 and 0.001, often referred to as the 5%, 1% and 0.1% significance levels. A related form of terminology is to describe a result which is significant at the 5% level but not at the 1% level as *significant*, a result significant at the 1% level but not at the 0.1% level as *highly significant*, and one significant at the 0.1% level as *very highly significant*.

Statistical tables of the principal distributions associated with test statistics provide values which correspond to these and other traditional levels of significance. Depending on the context, these are called *critical values*, *percentage points* or *upper percentage points*. For example, if the test statistic z has a standard *normal distribution and the test is two-sided, then the critical value of $|z|$ for significance at the 5% level is 1.9600.

significance testing *See* hypothesis testing.

significant *See* significance level; hypothesis testing.

significant figures (s.f.) The run of figures (or digits) in a number that is relevant to its precision, as distinct from any additional zero digits needed to indicate its magnitude. For example, the height of Mount Everest is 8800 metres to the nearest 100 metres. This has a run of two significant figures, 88, and is said to be 'correct to two significant figures'. The zeros in the tens and units positions are not significant figures but are essential in recording the magnitude of the height.

In general, reading from left to right, the first non-zero digit of a number after *rounding is the start of the run of significant figures. For instance, rounded to three significant figures, the numbers 5856 and 0.05 856 are 5860 and 0.0586 respectively.

sign test A *nonparametric test based on the *signs* of deviations associated with data rather than the actual deviations.

A simple form, the single sample form, tests whether a random *sample comes from a population with a specified *median M. Each observation above or below M is replaced by a plus or minus sign (any observation equal to M is dropped from the sample). The test statistic, r, is the number of plus signs. If the *null hypothesis is true, then plus and minus signs occur with equal probability, and r has a *binomial distribution with parameters equal to n and 0.5, where n is the total number of signed observations. Significantly high or low values of r lead to rejection of the null hypothesis.

For example, suppose that a sample of ten readings of percentage water content at random locations in a field is used to test the null hypothesis that the median content is 9% against the alternative hypothesis that the median content is not 9%. The readings and the signs of their deviations from 9 are as given in the table; here $n = 10$, and the test statistic is $r = 2$. Direct calculation, tables or statistical software will give the probability of a value of 2 or less to be 0.0547. The two-tail probability of getting a value as extreme as 2, i.e. 2 or less or 8 or more, is thus 0.1094. The result is not significant, and the hypothesis $M = 9$ is retained.

The above method can also be applied to a random sample of *matched pairs of values (x, y) to test whether the x- and y-values are samples from populations with equal medians. Each pair of values is replaced by a plus or minus sign according to whether the difference $x - y$ is positive or negative (pairs with a zero difference are dropped from the sample). The test statistic, r, is the number of plus signs. If the hypothesis is true, then plus and minus signs occur

sign test

Reading	5.5	9.1	6.0	8.0	6.7	8.2	7.7	15.1	7.6	7.1
Sign of deviation	−	+	−	−	−	−	−	+	−	−

with equal probability, and r has a binomial distribution with parameters equal to n and 0.5, where n is the number of signed differences. Significantly high or low values of r lead to rejection of the null hypothesis.

simple hypothesis A *null hypothesis is *simple* if it specifies the distribution of a population random variable completely, otherwise it is a *composite hypothesis*. Thus the hypothesis 'X is normally distributed with mean 100 and variance 15' is simple, and the hypothesis 'X is normally distributed with mean 100 and unknown variance' is composite.

simple random sample *See* random sample.

Simpson's paradox A paradox in connection with *contingency tables whereby an association that is significant in each of two tables can disappear or even be reversed if the two tables are combined.

Suppose, for example, that the effectiveness of a new drug is being compared with that of a standard drug. Patients living in urban and rural areas are given one of the drugs and the results (cure/no effect) together with the percentage cure rates are as follows:

	Urban		Rural	
	Standard	New	Standard	New
Cure	100	350	350	180
No effect	500	1050	350	120
Percentage cured	16.7	25	50	60

In each case, a *chi-squared test indicates that there is a significant difference in the effects of the drugs, with the new drug giving a higher proportion of cures in each area.

Combined into a single table, the results for all 3000 patients are shown below.

In this case, a chi-squared test again shows there to be a significant difference

	Standard	New
Cure	450	530
No effect	850	1170
Percentage cured	34.6	31.2

in the effects of the drugs, but this time the standard drug is giving the better cure rate.

The paradox arises because the overall table combines two sets of data in which (i) the proportions of patients receiving each treatment are different, e.g. relatively few received the standard treatment in the urban areas; and (ii) the cure rates for the rural patients are different from those of the urban patients. The paradox exposes the dangers of combining inhomogeneous data.

simulation In general, the study of a physical system in which there is a dynamic and/ or probabilistic element by observing the behaviour of a *model of the system. Simulations are usually run on computers, using *random number generators to provide values for any *random variables. For example, town planners can study the likely effects of changes to the road layout and signalling regime by running simulations of a model of the system. Similarly, simulation can assist a manager to assess the effect on queuing of adding or closing service points at a supermarket checkout (*see* queuing theory).

single-blind *See* blinding.

single log paper *See* logarithmic paper.

skewness The lack of symmetry of a *distribution. A *symmetrical distribution has zero skewness, one with a long tail of higher values to the right (*see* diagram) has *positive skewness*, and one with a long tail of lower values to the left has *negative skewness*. A distribution with positive skewness is also said to be *positively skewed* (or *skew*), and one with negative skewness is said to be *negatively skewed* (or *skew*).

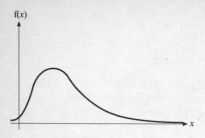

f(x)

skewness The frequency function of a distribution with positive skewness.

More formally, the *coefficient of skewness* is $\gamma_1 = \mu_3/\mu_2^{3/2}$, where μ_i is the ith *moment about the mean. It is zero for a symmetric distribution. If the coefficient is positive (or negative), then the skewness is called positive (or negative). Other measures of skewness include

$$\frac{\text{mean} - \text{mode}}{\text{standard deviation}} \quad \text{and} \quad \frac{Q_3 - 2M + Q_1}{Q_3 - Q_1},$$

where M is the *median, and Q_1 and Q_3 are the first and third *quartiles.

See also g-statistics; *compare* kurtosis.

slippage test A test of whether two or more independent random samples are from identical populations, the alternative being that the populations are identical in form but that one or more of the populations has 'slipped' relative to the others. An example is *Tukey's quick test.

Smirnov test An alternative name for the *Kolmogorov–Smirnov two-sample test.

smoothing The removal of fluctuations in a *time series by using a *moving average or fitting a *trend line.

Snedecor's F-distribution An alternative name for the *F-distribution.

Spearman–Brown formula A general formula for estimating a *reliability coefficient of a test from that of a similar but smaller test. If the smaller test has reliability coefficient r, then the coefficient for a test con-taining similar items and n times as large is given by the formula

$$\frac{nr}{1 + (n - 1)r}.$$

It is not essential for n to be an integer.

When the *split-half method is used to estimate reliability, $n = 2$ since the full test is twice the size of the halves used to calculate r. In this case the formula becomes

$$\frac{2r}{1 + r}.$$

Spearman's rank correlation coefficient (Spearman's rho (ρ)) *See* correlation coefficient.

split-half method (split-test method) A method used mainly in psychological and educational testing to estimate the *reliability of a test. The test is divided into two parts and the *correlation coefficient between the scores on the two parts is calculated. The two halves can be produced in a variety of ways, but it is desirable that they are similar. If there is a gradient of difficulty in the test, a common procedure is to place the odd-numbered *items in one half and the even-numbered items in the other half (the *odd–even method*). Other procedures include alternating small blocks of items and assigning items randomly to the two halves. *See* reliability coefficient; Spearman–Brown formula.

split-half reliability *See* reliability.

S-PLUS *See* statistical software packages.

SPSS *Abbreviation for* Statistical Package for the Social Sciences. *See* statistical software packages.

square matrix *See* matrix.

stability, coefficient of *See* reliability coefficient.

stage sampling A sampling method in which the *sample is obtained in stages. *See* multistage sampling.

standard Cauchy distribution *See* Cauchy distribution.

standard deviation (s.d.) **1.** (of data) The four numbers 1, 10, 11 and 14 have a *mean of 9. Their deviations from the mean are -8, $+1$, $+2$ and $+5$, respectively, and the squares of these deviations are 64, 1, 4 and 25. The average of these squares is $\frac{1}{4}(64+1+4+25)=23.5$. This is the *variance* of the numbers. Its positive square root, $\sqrt{23.5}=4.85$, is their *standard deviation*. It is the positive square root of the average of the squares of the deviations from the mean, and is a measure of the *dispersion or spread of the numbers.

In general, for a set of n numbers $x_1, x_2, \ldots, x_n$, the standard deviation s_x is given by

$$s_x = \sqrt{\frac{1}{n}\sum_1^n (x_i - \bar{x})^2}, \quad \text{where } \bar{x} = \frac{1}{n}\sum_1^n x_i$$

An alternative formula, more useful for manual or calculator computation, is

$$s_x = \sqrt{\frac{1}{n}\sum_1^n (x_i^2) - \left(\frac{1}{n}\sum_1^n x_i\right)^2}.$$

If the n numbers are a *random sample from a population, then s_x is the *sample standard deviation*.

The standard deviation of the population is estimated by s, where

$$s^2 = \frac{n}{n-1}s_x^2.$$

This *sample estimate* can be calculated directly from the formula

$$s = \sqrt{\frac{1}{n-1}\sum_1^n (x_i - \bar{x})^2},$$

or alternatively

$$s = \sqrt{\frac{1}{n-1}\sum_1^n x_i^2 - \frac{1}{n(n-1)}\left(\sum_1^n x_i\right)^2}.$$

When data are recorded in a *frequency table in which each observation x_i has frequency f_i, then the standard deviation of the observations is given by

$$s_x = \sqrt{\frac{\sum_i f_i(x_i - \bar{x})^2}{\sum_i f_i}}, \quad \text{where } \bar{x} = \frac{\sum_i f_i x_i}{\sum_i f_i}.$$

An alternative formula is

$$s_x = \sqrt{\frac{\sum_i f_i x_i^2}{\sum_i f_i} - \left(\frac{\sum_i f_i x_i}{\sum_i f_i}\right)^2}.$$

The sample estimate of the population standard deviation is given by

$$s = \sqrt{\frac{1}{n-1}\sum_i f_i(x_i - \bar{x})^2},$$

$$\text{where } n = \sum_i f_i$$

or, equivalently,

$$s = \sqrt{\frac{1}{n-1}\sum_i f_i x_i^2 - \frac{1}{n(n-1)}\left(\sum_i f_i x_i\right)^2}.$$

Statistical software and most calculators have routines which accept data and offer s_x and s, usually described as 'with divisor n' and 'with divisor $n-1$', or 'σ_n' and 'σ_{n-1}' respectively.

See also grouped data.

2. (of a random variable) For a *random variable X, the positive square root of the variance, i.e. $\sqrt{\text{Var}(X)}$. It is often denoted by σ, the Greek letter sigma, especially when X has a *normal distribution. *See* variance.

standard error (s.e.) The *standard deviation of the *sampling distribution of a *statistic. For example, the *mean $\bar{x}$ of a *sample of size n taken from a *normal distribution with mean μ and *variance σ^2

has a normal distribution with mean μ and variance σ^2/n. Thus its standard error is $\sigma/\sqrt{n}$. This is called the *standard error of the (sample) mean*. When the population variance σ^2 is unknown and is estimated from the sample to be s^2, where

$$s^2 = \frac{1}{n-1}\left(\sum_1^n (x_i - \bar{x})^2\right),$$

then the standard error is estimated to be $s/\sqrt{n}$. *See* sampling error.

standard form *See* exponential notation.

standardization **1.** (of sample values) Expressing the deviations of sample values from their *mean in terms of their *standard deviation. For a sample with mean $\bar{x}$ and standard deviation s_x, a value x is transformed to $z = (x - \bar{x})/s_x$, and z is called the *standardized score*, *standard score* or *z-score* for x. The z-scores of the sample values are a set of values with zero mean and unit standard deviation.

For instance, if a set of examination marks has mean 64 and standard deviation 10, then the standardized scores for marks of 76, 51 and 64, are $\frac{1}{10}(76 - 64) = 1.2$, $\frac{1}{10}(51 - 64) = -1.3$ and 0, respectively.
2. (of a random variable) Expressing the deviation of a variable from its mean in terms of its standard deviation. A random variable X with mean μ and standard deviation σ is thus transformed into $Z = (X - \mu)/\sigma$, and Z is called a *standardized variable* (or a variable in *standard measure*). It has zero mean and unit standard deviation. Values of Z are called *standardized scores*, *standard scores* or *Z-scores*. When X is a *normal variable, Z is the *standard normal variable* $N(0, 1)$. *See also* T-score.

standardized score *See* standardization; normal distribution.

standardized variable *See* standardization.

standard measure *See* standardization.

standard normal curve *See* normal distribution.

standard normal distribution *See* normal distribution.

standard normal variable *See* normal distribution.

standard score *See* standardization; normal distribution.

statistic A term commonly used to describe any item derived from a set of data (*statistics). For example, the largest value, the *mean and the *median of the data are all statistics in this sense.

In formal statistical theory, a statistic is any *function of the data in a *sample. For example, the mean of a sample is a statistic in this sense, and so also is the product moment *correlation coefficient of a sample of pairs of values of two variables.

statistical inference The process of drawing conclusions about a *population or of making predictions about a *model from observational, sample or experimental data where there is a *random element. The random element may be a characteristic of the data (e.g. random errors) or it may reflect the way the data have been obtained (e.g. by random sampling). The validity of any inferences depends on correct assumptions being made about the relevant random elements, populations or models. *See* Bayesian inference; confidence interval; estimation; hypothesis testing.

statistical software packages Software packages are available which can be used to process, analyse and summarize data, and to apply a wide range of statistical methods and tests to the data. The situation is fluid, with new general and specialized products appearing regularly. Some well-known packages currently available include

GenStat, MINITAB, SAS, S-PLUS and SPSS.

statistical significance *See* hypothesis testing; significance level.

statistics 1. A collection of numerical and/or *categorical data; for example, official statistics on crime or on education, the responses to a questionnaire, or daily meteorological records at a weather station. 2. The science of collecting, studying and analysing data. The subject divides broadly into two branches. *Descriptive statistics* is concerned mainly with collecting, summarizing and interpreting data. *Inferential statistics* is concerned with methods for obtaining and analysing data to make inferences applicable in a wider context (e.g. from sample to population). It is also concerned with the precision and reliability of such inferences in so far as this involves probabilistic considerations (e.g. when stating confidence intervals). In this context statistics can be regarded as the branch of applied mathematics based on probability theory. 3. *Plural of* *statistic.

stem-and-leaf diagram An arrangement of a set of data in graphical form. For example, for the data set

67, 49, 72, 43, 54, 22, 45, 59, 68, 58, 65, 50, 74

the tens digits may be taken as *stems* and the units digits as *leaves* and the data displayed as follows:

Stem	Leaf
2	2
3	
4	3 5 9
5	0 4 8 9
6	5 7 8
7	2 4

The diagram is similar in shape to a *histogram turned on its side. However, it also provides a complete ordering of the data and shows the effect of grouping in classes with an interval of width 10. Often the leaf is the last significant digit in the data items.

Stirling's formula The approximation

$$n! \approx \sqrt{(2\pi n)}(n/e)^n$$

for large values of n, where $n!$ is *factorial n.

stochastic Denoting the presence of *random elements or variation. Thus a *stochastic variable* is a *random variable. A *stochastic model* is a *model that is composed entirely of random elements and processes, as opposed to one that is entirely deterministic, or deterministic apart from random error or disturbance. Thus a model of the behaviour of a queuing system with random intervals between customer arrivals and random service times is stochastic. *See* stochastic process.

stochastic matrix A square *matrix of non-negative elements in which either the sum of the elements in each row is equal to 1, in which case it is *row-stochastic*, or the sum of the elements in each column is equal to 1, in which case it is *column-stochastic*. A matrix which is both row- and column-stochastic is said to be *doubly stochastic*. The matrix of transition probabilities associated with a *Markov chain is always a stochastic matrix.

stochastic model *See* stochastic.

stochastic process Suppose that balls are withdrawn one at a time from a bag containing a large number of green and yellow balls. The outcome of each draw will be a green ball (G) or a yellow ball (Y). Let $X_1, X_2, \ldots, X_n$ represent the outcomes of the first, second, ..., nth draws. Each outcome is a *random variable which can take one of two values, G or Y, called its *states*.

This collection of random variables is an example of a *stochastic process*.

More generally, a stochastic process is a family of random variables $\{X_t\}$, where t takes values in some range and is discrete or continuous. Usually X_t is an observation at time t or at some stage t. The possible values of X_t are called its *states*. Examples of stochastic processes are *Markov chains, *Poisson processes and *random walks.

See queuing theory.

stochastic variable A *random variable.

stratified sample A type of *sample taken when the *population is not homogeneous but can be divided into subgroups or strata which are expected to show some uniformity with respect to the characteristic being measured. Division might be made on the basis of gender, age group or socio-economic status. The stratified sample is composed of *random samples taken from each of the strata.

It is common practice to make the size of each random sample proportional to the size of the corresponding stratum. For example, a survey of opinions on adult health-care provision in a small town which used two strata containing 2000 men and 3000 women, would form a stratified sample of 100 with 40 randomly selected men and 60 randomly selected women. In general, a stratified sample gives more representative results than a simple random sample of the same size.

Compare quota sample.

strict inequality *See* inequality.

Student's *t*-distribution *See* *t*-distribution.

subject *See* experimental design.

subjective probability *See* probability.

subset If all the members of a *set A are also members of a set B, then A is a *subset* of B. This can be written as $A \subseteq B$. If A is not equal to B, then A is a *proper subset* of B,

and this is written as $A \subset B$. For example, if $A = \{1, 2, 3\}$, $B = \{1, 2, 3, 4\}$ and $C = \{1, 2, 3\}$, then A is a subset of both B and C, but only a proper subset of B.

sum *See* union.

summation sign The sign Σ (Greek capital sigma) used to denote the summation of a *sequence of terms. The sign is followed by an expression giving the general term of the sequence, often in terms of a variable such as r, i or n. The upper and lower limits of the range of values of r over which the summation is to be made are given above and below (or to the right of) the sign. This form of notation is called *sigma notation*.

For example,

$$\sum_{r=1}^{4} r^2$$

indicates the sum of the values of r^2 when $r = 1, 2, 3, 4$, i.e.

$$\sum_{r=1}^{4} r^2 = 1^2 + 2^2 + 3^2 + 4^2.$$

This is sometimes shortened to

$$\sum_{1}^{4} r^2.$$

More generally, if the rth term of a sequence is a_r, then the sum of the terms from a_M up to a_N is denoted by

$$\sum_{r=M}^{N} a_r \quad \text{or} \quad \sum_{M}^{N} a_r.$$

Thus, for a set of n observations $x_1, x_2, \ldots, x_n$, the sum of the observations can be written as

$$\sum_{1}^{n} x_r,$$

and their *mean is

$$\frac{1}{n} \sum_{1}^{n} x_r.$$

When, as here, the limits of the summation are clear, the sum of the observations is often given in a shorter form, such as

$$\sum_r x_r, \sum_r x_r \text{ or simply } \sum x_r.$$

See series.

symmetrical distribution A *distribution such that values of the variable equally distant from a central value have equal frequency or frequency density. More formally, a symmetrical distribution has a frequency function f and a central value c such that $f(c + x) = f(c - x)$ for all x. For example, every *normal distribution and *binomial distribution $B(n, p)$ with $p = 0.5$ is symmetrical. *See also* skewness.

symmetric matrix *See* matrix.

systematic sample A *sample obtained by selecting units from the population in a systematic rather than a random way, i.e. sampling based on a systematic rule such as 'every fifth individual' or 'every other person'. For example, if from a population of 2000 a sample of 100 is required, then, having chosen a starting point at random, every twentieth person in a list of the population could be selected (returning to the start of the list when the end is reached). The interval between selected units, in the above example 20, is called the *sampling interval*. To obtain a systematic sample of size n from a population of known size N, the sampling interval should be the integer closest to N/n.

A potential danger of systematic sampling is the presence of periodicity in the population being sampled. For example, in a housing survey on a large estate where every tenth house is a corner house and larger than the others, a systematic sample selecting every tenth house would either contain no corner houses or contain nothing but corner houses.

T

target line *see* control chart.

t-distribution Suppose that random samples of n observations $x_1, x_2, \ldots, x_n$ are taken from a *normal population with *mean μ. Let the mean of each sample be denoted by $\bar{x}$, and each sample estimate of the population standard deviation be denoted by s, where

$$\frac{1}{n-1} \sum_{1}^{n} (x_i - \bar{x}^2)$$

Then the distribution of the statistic t, where

$$t = \frac{\bar{x} - \mu}{s/\sqrt{n}},$$

is the t-distribution with $v = n - 1$ *degrees of freedom. The form of the distribution is dependent only on the value of v and not on the particular population, provided it is normal. For each value of $v \geqslant 1$ the distribution is a *symmetrical distribution with zero mean. For $v > 2$ the *variance is $v/(v-2)$. As v becomes large, the distribution approaches the standard normal distribution $N(0, 1)$ (*see* diagram).

This distribution is sometimes referred to as *Student's t-distribution* since its discoverer, W.S. Gosset, was required by his employers, a well-known firm of brewers in Dublin, to publish research anonymously, and he chose the pseudonym 'Student' for his 1908 paper on the distribution.

Sampling from populations which are assumed to be normal, or approximately so, is a common occurrence and the t-distribution enables inferences to be made from samples of any size. Important uses of the t-distribution include establishing a *confidence interval for a population mean and carrying out a *t-test.

Tables such as Table 4 in the Appendix give upper *percentage points of the t-distribution for small values of v. These are values of t exceeded by some percentage of the distribution. For example, for $v = 8$ and $v = 30$ such tables typically give the information presented in the table below.

Degrees of freedom	Percentage				
	5	2.5	1	0.5	0.1
8	1.860	2.306	2.896	3.355	4.501
30	1.697	2.042	2.457	2.750	3.385

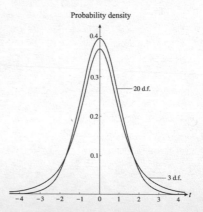

t-distribution The t-distributions with 3 and 20 degrees of freedom.

Thus, when $v = 8$, $2\frac{1}{2}\%$ of the distribution exceeds 2.306. As v becomes very large, the upper $2\frac{1}{2}\%$ point approaches that of the standard normal distribution, i.e. 1.960.

Statistical packages will give the *p-value of a value of t for any relevant v.

The t-distribution is closely related to an *F-distribution. If a random variable X has the t-distribution with v degrees of freedom, then the distribution of X^2 is identical to $F(1, v)$, i.e to the F-distribution with $v_1 = 1$ and $v_2 = v$. Also, the t-distribution with one degree of freedom is identical to the standard *Cauchy distribution.

ternary sampling unit *See* multistage sampling.

test Most generally, any procedure for measuring a factor or assessing some ability. Included in this broad sense of the term are intelligence tests, which give IQ measures, aptitude tests which measure ability or potential in some area, personality tests which assess attitudes or beliefs, and statistical *hypothesis tests which determine the significance of experimental results.

Where a test is composed of a number of questions, individual questions are commonly referred to as *test items*. If all the questions in such a test are *multiple-choice questions*, then it is called a *multiple-choice test*.

See item analysis; reliability.

test of homogeneity Any statistical *test for the equality of *means, *variances, etc. applied to samples taken from different populations. *See* Bartlett's test; Hartley's test; Levene's test; F-test; t-test.

tetrachoric correlation coefficient *See* correlation coefficient.

tied ranks *See* rank.

time series A sequence of observations of a variable, over time, often at regular intervals. Examples are the monthly sales of mobile phones over a five-year period, and records of the daily rainfall at a weather station. Time series are widely used in economics to detect and predict trends in sales, output, prices, etc. When graphing time series it is customary to join successive points with lines. This is simply to aid the eye and does not imply that changes between the points are linear. *See* moving average.

transition matrix *See* Markov chain.

transition probability *See* Markov chain.

transposition A rearrangement of a *set that merely interchanges two elements. The notation (ab) indicates that the elements a and b are interchanged. Thus, for example, the transposition (35) applied to the set $\{1, 2, 3, 4, 5\}$ produces $\{1, 2, 5, 4, 3\}$.

treatment *See* experimental design.

treatment variable *See* regression.

tree A connected *graph without a circuit, i.e. without a route from a vertex back to itself in which no edge is used more than once (*see* diagram (a)). A *binary tree* is one in which one vertex, its *root*, has degree 2 and all others have degree 1 or 3 (*see* diagram (b)). Diagrams designed to help people to make decisions are often based on a binary tree with yes/no questions at the nodes of degree 2 and 3. *See* tree diagram.

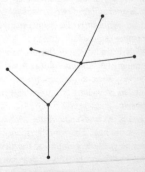

tree (a) A tree with 7 vertices.

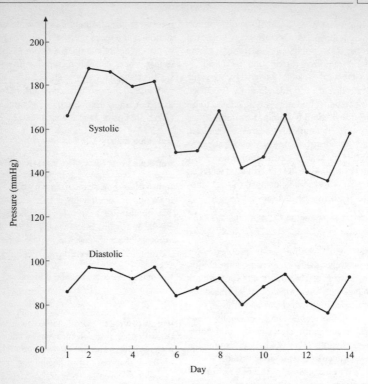

time series Readings of the systolic and diastolic blood pressure of a patient each evening for 14 days.

tree diagram A diagram in the form of a *tree, which is useful in solving problems in probability which involve a sequence of *trials, e.g. tossing a coin several times or drawing playing cards successively from a pack. For example, if two balls are chosen at random (without replacement) from a bag containing five red balls and five white balls, we may want to know the probability of obtaining one of each colour. All possible outcomes can be shown, and the probability calculated by means of a tree diagram (*see* diagram).

The root vertex A shows the original contents of the bag. The edges leading from it show the possible colours of the first ball drawn and the probability of drawing a ball of that colour. The contents of the bag after

the first draw are shown at vertices B and C. The second draw originates at either B or C, and the edges leading from them show the possible colours of the second ball drawn and the probability of drawing a ball of that colour. The final contents of the bag are shown at vertices D, E, F and G.

The probability of reaching any one of these vertices is shown next to it and equals the product of the probabilities on the edges leading to it from the original vertex A. For example, the probability of reaching vertex D (by drawing a red ball and then another red ball) is $\frac{1}{2} \times \frac{4}{9} = \frac{4}{18} = \frac{2}{9}$. Drawing one ball of each colour corresponds to a path from A to either E or F. The probability of this outcome is the sum of the probabilities at vertices E and F, i.e. $\frac{5}{18} + \frac{5}{18} = \frac{5}{9}$. The prob-

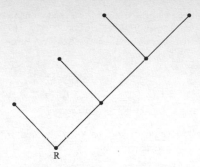

tree (b) A binary tree with its root at the vertex labelled R.

Treize problem *See* problem of coincidences.

trend *See* trend test.

trend line (trend curve) A general term for a line or curve that attempts to indicate the overall pattern of a relation between variables apart from *random variation. Examples are a curve fitted by eye to a set of points, a curve fitted to a *time series by using a *moving average, and a least-squares *regression line fitted to bivariate data. *See also* line of best fit.

trend test A *hypothesis test involving three or more samples in which the alternative hypothesis is that at least two population means (or medians) differ and that the means (or medians) are in a certain specific order, i.e. that there is a *trend* in the means (or medians).

More formally, if the population means are $\mu_1, \mu_2, \mu_3, \ldots$, a trend test involves the

abilities of the other possible outcomes, two red balls and two white balls, are both equal to $\frac{2}{9}$. The sum of the probabilities at vertices D, E, F and G is the sum of the probabilities of all possible outcomes and is equal to 1.

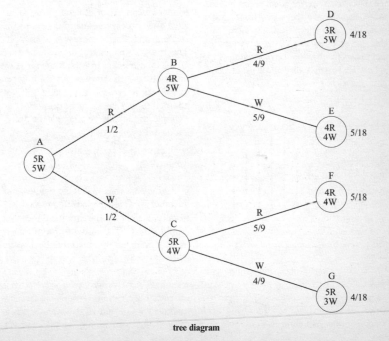

tree diagram

null hypothesis $H_0 : \mu_1 = \mu_2 = \mu_3 = \cdots$, and an *ordered alternative hypothesis* such as $H_1 : \mu_1 \geqslant \mu_2 \geqslant \mu_3 \geqslant \cdots$, where at least one of the inequalities is a *strict inequality.

For example, a trend test would be appropriate in a trial of three varieties of tomato, A, B and C, when the experimenter is predicting that variety B crops more heavily than C, and C more heavily than A.

See Jonckheere–Terpstra test; Page test.

trial A single experiment with an uncertain outcome, e.g. casting a fair die once. A trial with only two possible outcomes is a *Bernoulli trial, e.g. tossing a coin. The term *experiment* is sometimes reserved for a sequence of trials, for example, tossing a coin 60 times to estimate the relative *frequency of heads in repeated tosses of the coin. *See also* event.

triangular distribution The *distribution of the sum of two *independent *random variables, each having the same *uniform distribution. The graph of the frequency function is triangular in shape. A familiar example is the distribution of the sum of the scores on two fair dice thrown independently, as shown in diagram (a).

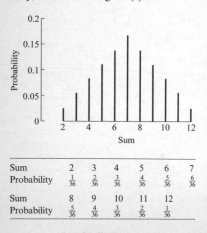

Sum	2	3	4	5	6	7
Probability	$\frac{1}{36}$	$\frac{2}{36}$	$\frac{3}{36}$	$\frac{4}{36}$	$\frac{5}{36}$	$\frac{6}{36}$

Sum	8	9	10	11	12
Probability	$\frac{5}{36}$	$\frac{4}{36}$	$\frac{3}{36}$	$\frac{2}{36}$	$\frac{1}{36}$

triangular distribution (a)

Similarly, the sum of two random numbers chosen from the interval $(0, 1)$ has the triangular distribution with frequency function f(x), where

$$f(x) = \begin{cases} x & \text{for} \quad 0 < x \leqslant 1 \\ 2 - x & \text{for} \quad 1 \leqslant x < 2 \\ 0 & \text{otherwise} \end{cases}$$

The graph of the frequency function is shown in diagram (b).

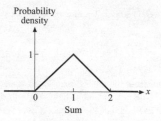

triangular distribution (b)

trimmed mean An arithmetic *mean calculated after dropping equal numbers of the smallest and largest values in a *sample. The aim is to reduce the influence of *outliers, especially in samples from skew distributions (*see* skewness). If the number of outliers is not too extreme, a total of about 10% of values can be dropped. For example, in the following sample the observation 197 is an outlier:

4   9   11   12   12   13   15   18   24   25
30   37   46   48   51   60   73   89   94   197

The sample mean is 43.4. If the smallest and largest observations, 4 and 197, are removed from the sample, the trimmed mean is $667/18 = 37.1$. The use of the trimmed mean eliminates the effect of the outlier. *See also* winsorization.

trimming A procedure for removing extreme observations (*outliers) from a *sample with the aim of reducing the sensitivity of the calculation of sample statistics such as the *mean or *standard deviation to such values. *See* trimmed mean; convex hull trimming. *See also* winsorization.

truncated distribution A *distribution formed from some given distribution by removing and ignoring either the part to the left of some value of the random variable or the part to the right of some value, or both. A *truncated sample* is defined similarly. For example, suppose that the heights of adult males have an approximately *normal distribution. The distribution of the heights of adult males who are taller than 2 metres will be a truncated normal distribution. *See also* censored data.

truncated sample *See* truncated distribution.

T-score Conversion to T-scores is a method of standardizing scores so that they have a *mean of 50 and a *standard deviation of 10. Commonly applied to educational data such as test results or examination marks.

More formally, for a sample of scores with mean $\bar{x}$ and standard deviation s_x, a score of x has a T-score of

$$50 + 10(x - \bar{x})/s_x.$$

For example, if a set of examination results has mean 61 and standard deviation 8, then the T-score of a mark of 69 is $50 + 10(69 - 61)/8 = 60$. Similarly, scores of 61 and 49 have T-scores of 50 and 35.

If X is a *random variable with mean μ and standard deviation σ, then its T-score is given by

$$T = 50 + 10(X - \mu)/\sigma.$$

In particular, if Z is a standardized variable (with mean 0 and standard deviation 1), then its T-scores are given by

$$T = 50 + 10Z$$

(*see* standardization).

t-test A statistical *test involving the *t-distribution.

(1) The *one-sample* test. A test of whether a *random sample of size n and *mean $\bar{x}$ has come from a *normal population with a specified mean μ_0 and unknown variance. The test statistic is given by

$$t = \frac{\bar{x} - \mu_0}{s/\sqrt{n}},$$

where

$$s^2 = \frac{1}{n-1} \sum_{1}^{n} (x_i - \bar{x})^2$$

is the sample estimate of the population *variance. If the *null hypothesis $\mu = \mu_0$ is true, then t has the t-distribution with $n - 1$ degrees of freedom. For either a one-tail or a two-tail test, the significance level of t can be assessed by using statistical software or tables, and the null hypothesis accepted or rejected accordingly.

As an illustration, suppose that a random sample of 1 kg packets of a brand of sugar has the weights (in kg)

1.08 1.04 1.01 0.98 1.00 1.05 0.99
1.05 1.04 1.06

and we wish to know if it has come from a normal distribution with mean $\mu = 1$, the alternative hypothesis being that $\mu \neq 1$. Here, $n = 10$, $\bar{x} = 1.03$ and $s = 0.033$, so the value of t is given by

$$t = \frac{1.03 - 1}{0.033/\sqrt{10}} = 2.87,$$

and the number of degrees of freedom is $10 - 1 = 9$. This is a two-tail test, and the minimum value of $|t|$ for significance at the 5% level is 2.262. Our value of 2.87 is greater than this (its *p-value is 0.018), so the null hypothesis is rejected.

(2) The *paired-samples* test. A test of whether a random sample of n *matched pairs (x, y) is from two identical unknown populations, i.e. the x- and y-values are

t-test

	Patient									
	1	2	3	4	5	6	7	8	9	10
Hours of sleep after (x)	7.2	5.9	6.1	6.2	4.1	4.5	4.7	7.0	2.1	4.5
Hours of sleep before (y)	6.0	6.1	6.1	3.0	2.7	1.3	4.1	7.1	1.7	2.6
Gain $d = x - y$	1.2	−0.2	0.0	2.8	1.4	3.2	0.6	−0.1	0.4	1.9

from populations having equal means μ_x and μ_y, and equal variances. The test is a one-sample test based on the n values of the difference $d = x - y$ between matched pairs of values. The n values of d are assumed to be a random sample from a normal distribution and, since $\mu_d = \mu_x - \mu_y$, the null hypothesis is that $\mu_d = 0$. The test statistic is given by

$$t = \frac{\bar{d}}{s/\sqrt{n}},$$

where $\bar{d}$ is the sample mean and s is the sample estimate of population variance. Under the null hypothesis, t has the t-distribution with $n - 1$ degrees of freedom.

For example, the data in the table above are the hours of sleep the night before (x) and after (y) each of 10 patients have taken a sleeping pill. To investigate whether the pill is effective, the gain $d = x - y$ in hours of sleep is calculated for each patient, and a t-test carried out with null hypothesis $\mu_d = 0$. Since the pill is designed to increase the hours of sleep, the alternative hypothesis $\mu_d > 0$ is appropriate and the test is one-tailed.

From the data, $n = 10$, $\bar{d} = 1.12$ and $s = 1.207$. The value of t is given by

$$t = \frac{1.12}{1.207/\sqrt{10}} = 2.93,$$

and the number of degrees of freedom is $10 - 1 = 9$. The minimum value for significance at the 1% level is 2.821, and our value of 2.93 exceeds this (it has a *p*-value of 0.0083). So the alternative hypothesis that the drug has a significant positive effect is accepted.

(3) The test for *two independent samples*. This tests whether two independent random samples are from normal populations with equal means and variances (or from the same normal population). Suppose that the two samples consist of m observations with *mean $\bar{x}$ and n observations with mean $\bar{y}$. The test statistic is given by

$$t = \frac{\bar{x} - \bar{y}}{\sqrt{s^2\left(\frac{1}{m} + \frac{1}{n}\right)}},$$

where

$$s^2 = \frac{1}{m+n+2}\left(\sum_1^m (x_i - \bar{x})^2 + \sum_1^n (y_j - \bar{y})^2\right)$$

Under the null hypothesis, $\mu_x = \mu_y$, the test statistic t has the t-distribution with $m + n - 2$ degrees of freedom. The quantity s^2 is the *pooled estimate* of the common population variance.

As an illustration, suppose that the scores on a reasoning test of samples of 4 male and 6 female students are as follows:

Male score (x_i)	13	17	14	14		
Female score (y_j)	18	13	16	17	17	15

We test the null hypothesis, $\mu_x = \mu_y$, that these are samples from identical populations with equal means and variances, i.e. that there is no difference due to gender in the scores. The alternative hypothesis is that the means differ ($\mu_x \neq \mu_y$).

Here $m = 4$, $\bar{x} = 14.5$ and

$$\sum (x_i - \bar{x})^2 = 9.$$

Similarly, $n = 6$, $\bar{y} = 16$ and

$$\sum(y_j - \bar{y})^2 = 16.$$

The pooled estimate of variance

$$s^2 = (9 + 16)/(4 + 6 - 2) = 3.125.$$

The value of t is given by

$$t = \frac{14.5 - 16}{\sqrt{3.125\left(\frac{1}{4} + \frac{1}{6}\right)}} = -1.31,$$

and the number of degrees of freedom is $4 + 6 - 2 = 8$. This is a two-tail test, and the minimum value of $|t|$ for significance at the 5% level with 8 degrees of freedom is 2.306. Since $|-1.31| = 1.31 < 2.306$, our value of -1.31 is not significant (its p-value is 0.11), so the null hypothesis is retained.

See also confidence interval; robustness.

Tukey's pocket test *See* Tukey's quick test.

Tukey's quick test. A simple test of whether two independent random samples have been drawn from identical populations, the alternative being that the populations are identical in form but they have 'slipped' apart. For this reason it is called a *slippage test*. The test statistic T is based on the overlap of the sample values.

Call the sample with the largest sample value sample 1. If sample 1 also contains the smallest sample value, then $T = 0$. If not, let T_1 be the number of values in sample 1 which are greater than the largest value in sample 2, and T_2 be the number of values in sample 2 which are less than the smallest value in sample 1. Then, provided both T_1 and T_2 are non-zero, $T = T_1 + T_2$; otherwise $T = 0$. (Tied values, i.e. a value in sample 1 equalling the largest value in sample 2, or a value in sample 2 equalling the smallest

value in sample 1, contribute a count of $\frac{1}{2}$ to T_1 or T_2.) Significantly high values of T lead to rejection of the *null hypothesis that the populations have equal means (or medians).

If the size of each sample is small, e.g. 20 or less, and they are not very different in size, then, for a two-tail test, the critical values of T for significance at the 5%, 1% and 0.1% levels of are 7, 10 and 13, respectively. For a one-tail test these are the critical values for significance at the 2.5%, 0.5% and 0.05% levels. Since the method and the critical values are easy to remember, the test is sometimes called *Tukey's pocket test*.

As an illustration, suppose that random samples of times in hours for an industrial operation to be completed are taken at two different times in order to check whether there has been a change in the speed of the operation. Labelling the sample with the largest observation sample 1, the readings are as given in the table. Here, three values in sample 1 are greater than 25.1, the largest value in sample 2, so $T_1 = 3$. Similarly, five values in sample 2 are less than 18.4, the smallest value in sample 1, so $T_2 = 5$. Thus $T = 3 + 5 = 8$. This exceeds 7, and the test is a two-tail test. So the result is significant at the 5% level, and the null hypothesis that the samples are from identical populations with equal mean speeds is rejected.

two-sided alternative *See* hypothesis testing.

two-tail test (two-tailed test) *See* hypothesis testing.

two-way classification *See* analysis of variance.

two-way table *See* contingency table.

Tukey's quick test

Sample 1	18.4	18.5	20.2	21.9	22.7	23.1	25.7	27.2	27.6
Sample 2	16.1	16.2	16.7	17.4	18.0	21.2	23.4	24.0	25.1

Type I error (error of the first kind) Rejecting the null hypothesis on the basis of a test when in fact the null hypothesis is true (*see* hypothesis testing).

Type II error (error of the second kind) Accepting the null hypothesis on the basis of a test when in fact the null hypothesis is false (*see* hypothesis testing).

U

U-shaped distribution A *frequency distribution which is approximately the same shape as the letter U, with the greatest frequencies occurring at the ends of the range of the variable. The distribution of the proportion of the sky that is cloud covered at 9 a.m. each day is U-shaped in parts of the world where on most days the sky tends to be either cloudless or completely clouded, and is only occasionally partially clouded. The *beta distribution with parameters $m = n = 0.5$ is U-shaped.

unadjusted standard deviation *See* sample standard deviation.

unadjusted variance *See* sample variance.

unbiased estimate *See* unbiased estimator.

unbiased estimator An *estimator T of a population parameter θ is an *unbiased estimator* if the *expectation of T is equal to θ, i.e. if $E(T) = \theta$. For example, the sample mean $\bar{x}$ is an unbiased estimator of the population mean. A particular value of an unbiased estimator is an *unbiased estimate*.

An estimator that is not unbiased is a *biased estimator*. If $E(T) - \theta = b$, where $b \neq 0$, then b is called the *bias* in the estimator T. For example, the sample *variance s_x^2 is a biased estimator of the population variance σ^2. For if the sample size is n, the expectation of s_x^2 is equal to

$$\frac{(n-1)}{n}\sigma^2,$$

so s_x^2 tends to underestimate σ^2. In fact, the bias in s_x^2 is equal to

$$\frac{(n-1)}{n}\sigma^2 - \sigma^2 = -\frac{\sigma^2}{n}.$$

Multiplying s_x^2 by $n/(n-1)$ gives the statistic

$$\frac{n}{(n-1)}s_x^2,$$

and this is an unbiased estimator of the population variance, usually denoted by s^2 or $\hat{\sigma}^2$. The use of $n/(n-1)$ as multiplier is occasionally called *Bessel's correction*.

For example, the lengths to the nearest millimetre of a random sample of a variety of broad-bean seeds were 18, 22, 21, 22, 26, 23, 20, 24, 23 and 23. Here $n = 10$, and the sample mean and sample variance are found to be $\bar{x} = 22.2$ and $s_x^2 = 4.36$, respectively. Using the multiplier 10/9,

$$s^2 = \frac{10}{9} \times 4.36 = 4.84.$$

Thus, based on this sample, unbiased estimates of the population mean μ and variance σ^2 are $\bar{x} = 22.2$ and $s^2 = 4.84$.

uncorrected moment *See* moment.

uniform distribution **1.** A discrete *distribution in which each possible value of the random variable has the same probability. For example, the score when a fair die is thrown is a variable with a uniform distribution, each possible score having the same probability, $\frac{1}{6}$ (*see* diagram (a)). Similarly, a *random number chosen from 0, 1, 2, ..., 9 is a variable with a uniform distribution since each possible number has the same probability, $\frac{1}{10}$.

Probability

uniform distribution (a)

2. (rectangular distribution) A continuous distribution in which each possible value of the random variable has the same *probability density. For example, if X is a number chosen at random from the *interval $0 < x < 1$, then X has a uniform distribution with frequency function $f(x) = 1$ (*see* diagram (b)).

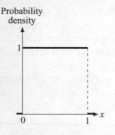

uniform distribution (b)

More generally, if X is chosen at random from the interval $a < x < b$, then X has the uniform distribution on (a, b) with frequency function $f(x) = 1/(b - a)$. The frequency curve is rectangular in shape. The mean is $\frac{1}{2}(a + b)$ and the variance is $\frac{1}{12}(b - a)^2$.

An important example is the distribution of the *rounding errors incurred when values are rounded to some prescribed degree of accuracy. For example, if values are

rounded to the nearest whole number, rounding errors will be between -0.5 and 0.5 and can be assumed to have the uniform distribution on $(-0.5, 0.5)$. The mean of this distribution is 0 and the variance is $\frac{1}{12}$.

unimodal Having only one *mode.

union (join, sum) The union of two *sets A and B, denoted by $A \cup B$, consists of those elements that belong either to A or to B. For example, if $A = \{2, 4, 6, 8\}$ and $B = \{4, 5, 6\}$, then $A \cup B = \{2, 4, 5, 6, 8\}$. Elements that belong to both A and B are included in the union.

The number of elements in a union of two sets is related to the number in their *intersection. Denoting the number of elements in a set A by $n(A)$, the relation for two sets A and B is

$$n(A \cup B) = n(A) + n(B) - n(A \cap B).$$

In our example, $A \cap B = \{4, 6\}$. The numbers of elements in $A \cup B$, A, B and $A \cap B$ are 5, 4, 3 and 2, respectively, and, since

$$5 = 4 + 3 - 2,$$

the relation is satisfied.

If A and B are *mutually exclusive sets, their intersection is empty and the general relation reduces to

$$n(A \cup B) = n(A) + n(B).$$

union The union $E \cup F$ is shaded.

The union of two *events E and F is the event 'E or F occurs'. It is represented by the union of the subsets of the *sample space corresponding to the events E and F. Thus $E \cup F$ represents the event 'E or F occurs'. For example, suppose that a number is selected from the numbers 1, 2, 3, ..., 10, the event E is 'the number is even' and event F is 'the number is divisible by 3' (*see* diagram). The union $E \cup F$ is the event 'the number is even or divisible by 3' i.e. 'the number is 2, 3, 4, 6, 8, 9 or 10'.

Compare intersection; *see* probability.

unit *See* experimental design.

unit matrix *See* matrix.

universal set Relative to a particular domain, the universal set is the set of all objects in that domain. It is usually denoted by $\mathscr{E}$ or I. In statistics, when considering the outcomes of an experiment, the universal set is the set of all possible outcomes of the experiment, i.e. the *sample space. *Compare* null set.

unrelated design *See* experimental design.

upper percentage point *See* percentage point; significance level.

upper quartile *See* quartile.

up run *See* run.

V

Var *See* variance.

variable A quantity or characteristic that can take different values. If the variable can take only discrete, isolated values, then it is a *discrete variable*. If the variable can take any value in a given range, then it is a *continuous variable*. *See* categorical variable; distribution; function; random variable; regression.

variance 1. (of data) The five numbers 1, 8, 10, 12 and 14 have a *mean of 9. Their deviations from the mean are -8, -1, $+1$, $+3$ and $+5$, respectively, and the squares of these deviations are 64, 1, 1, 9 and 25. The average of these squares is

$$\frac{1}{5}(64 + 1 + 1 + 9 + 25) = 100/5 = 20.$$

This is the *variance* of the numbers. It is the average of the squares of the deviations from the mean, and a measure of the *dispersion or spread of the numbers.

In general, for a set of n numbers $x_1, x_2, \ldots, x_n$ with mean $\bar{x}$, the variance s_x^2 is given by

$$s_x^2 = \frac{1}{n} \sum_1^n (x_i - \bar{x})^2, \quad \text{where } \bar{x} = \frac{1}{n} \sum_1^n x_i.$$

An alternative formula, more useful for manual or calculator calculation, is

$$s_x^2 = \frac{1}{n} \sum_1^n x_i^2 - \left(\frac{1}{n} \sum_1^n x_i\right)^2.$$

If the n numbers are a *random sample from a population, then s_x^2 is the *sample variance*. The *unbiased estimate of the population variance is s^2, where

$$s^2 = \frac{n}{n-1} s_x^2.$$

This *sample estimate* can be calculated directly from the formula

$$s^2 = \frac{1}{n-1} \sum_1^n (x_i - \bar{x})^2,$$

or alternatively

$$s^2 = \frac{1}{n-1} \left(\sum_1^n x_i^2 - \frac{1}{n}\left(\sum_1^n x_i\right)^2\right).$$

When data are recorded in a *frequency table in which each observation x_i has frequency f_i, then the variance of the observations is given by

$$s_x^2 = \frac{\sum_i f_i (x_i - \bar{x})^2}{\sum_i f_i}, \quad \text{where } \bar{x} = \frac{\sum_i f_i x_i}{\sum_i f_i}.$$

An alternative formula is

$$s_x^2 = \frac{\sum_i f_i x_i^2}{\sum_i f_i} - \left(\frac{\sum_i f_i x_i}{\sum_i f_i}\right)^2.$$

The sample estimate of the population

variance is given by

$$s^2 = \frac{1}{n-1} \sum_i f_i(x_i - \bar{x})^2,$$

$$\text{where } n = \sum_i f_i,$$

or alternatively

$$s^2 = \frac{1}{n-1} \left(\sum_i f_i x_i^2 - \frac{1}{n} \left(\sum_i f_i x_i \right)^2 \right).$$

Statistical software and most calculators have routines which accept data and give s_x^2 and/or s^2, sometimes described as 'with divisor n' and 'with divisor $n-1$' respectively.

When random samples of size n are taken from a normal population with variance σ^2, the statistic $(n-1)s^2/\sigma^2$ has the *chi-squared distribution with $n-1$ degrees of freedom. This provides the basis for (i) the construction from a sample estimate s^2 of a *confidence interval for the unknown population variance σ^2, and (ii) a significance test (see hypothesis testing) of whether a sample of size n with a sample estimate s^2 comes from a population with known variance σ^2.

See also grouped data.

2. (of a random variable) The variance of a *random variable X is the *expectation of the square of the deviation of X from the mean $\mu = \text{E}(X)$. It is denoted by $\text{Var}(X)$ or σ^2 and equals $\text{E}((X-\mu)^2)$. This is equivalent to $\text{E}(X^2) - (\text{E}(X))^2$.

If X is a *discrete random variable* taking values $x_1, x_2, x_3, \ldots$ with probabilities $p_1, p_2, p_3, \ldots$, then the variance of X is given by

$$\text{Var}(X) = \sum_i (p_i x_i^2) - (\text{E}(X))^2,$$

$$\text{where } \text{E}(X) = \sum_i p_i x_i.$$

For instance, suppose that X is the points obtained when a team plays a match, and X equals 0, 1 or 3 with probabilities $\frac{1}{4}, \frac{1}{2}$ and $\frac{1}{4}$,

respectively. Then

$$\text{E}(X) = \tfrac{1}{4} \times 0 + \tfrac{1}{2} \times 1 + \tfrac{1}{4} \times 3 = 1\tfrac{1}{4},$$

and

$$\text{Var}(X) = \tfrac{1}{4} \times 0 + \tfrac{1}{2} \times 1^2 + \tfrac{1}{4} \times 3^2 - \left(1\tfrac{1}{4}\right)^2$$
$$= \tfrac{3}{16}.$$

If X is a *continuous random variable* with *frequency function $\text{f}(x)$, then the variance of X is given by

$$\text{Var}(X) = \int_{-\infty}^{\infty} x^2 \, \text{f}(x) \, \text{d}x - (\text{E}(X))^2,$$

$$\text{where } \text{E}(X) = \int_{-\infty}^{\infty} x\text{f}(x) \, \text{d}x.$$

If X and Y are independent random variables (see independence), and a and b are constants, then:
(i) $\text{Var}(aX + b) = a^2 \text{Var}(X)$;
(ii) $\text{Var}(X + Y) = \text{Var}(X) + \text{Var}(Y)$;
(iii) $\text{Var}(X - Y) = \text{Var}(X) + \text{Var}(Y)$;
(iv) $\text{Var}(aX + bY) = a^2 \text{Var}(X) + b^2 \text{Var}(Y)$.
In general,

$$\text{Var}(X \pm Y) = \text{Var}(X) + \text{Var}(Y) \pm \text{Cov}(X, Y),$$

where $\text{Cov}(X, Y)$ is the *covariance of X and Y.

variance, analysis of See analysis of variance.

variance ratio The ratio of two sample estimates of *variance with v_1 and v_2 *degrees of freedom. If they are random samples from the same *normal distribution or normal distributions having equal variances (but not necessarily the same *mean), then the ratio has the *F-distribution with v_1 and v_2 degrees of freedom. Under these conditions the variance ratio has important applications in the *analysis of variance and in the *variance ratio test.

variance ratio distribution An alternative name for the *F-distribution.

variance ratio test (F-test) Name given to a *test of whether two random samples are from *normal populations with equal *variances (but not necessarily the same *mean). Its most important application is in the *analysis of variance. If the samples contain n_1 and n_2 observations, and the sample estimates of variance are s_1^2 and s_2^2, respectively, then the test statistic is the *variance ratio F, where

$$F = s_1^2/s_2^2.$$

Under the *null hypothesis that the samples are from populations with equal variances, i.e. $\sigma_1^2 = \sigma_2^2$, F has the *F-distribution with $v_1 = n_1 - 1$ and $v_2 = n_2 - 1$ degrees of freedom. For either a two-tail or a one-tail test the value of F can be assessed with the aid of statistical software or tables. It is convenient, but not essential, to label the samples so that the first has the greater variance.

As an illustration, suppose that from a sample of $n_1 = 10$ observations the estimate of population variance s_1^2 is 36.5, and that from a second sample of $n_2 = 15$ observations the estimate of variance s_2^2 is 14.9. We test the null hypothesis that these are samples from populations with the same variance.

Here $F = 36.5/14.9 = 2.45$, $v_1 = 10 - 1 = 9$ and $v_2 = 15 - 1 = 14$. If the alternative hypothesis is that the population variances are unequal, i.e. that $\sigma_1^2 \neq \sigma_2^2$, then the test is two-tailed. For 9 and 14 degrees of freedom, the upper $2\frac{1}{2}\%$ point of the F-distribution is 3.21 (the lower $2\frac{1}{2}\%$ point being $1/3.21 = 0.312$). Our value of 2.45 is less than 3.21 and is thus not significant at the 5% level (its two-tail *p-value is 0.129). So the null hypothesis is retained.

When the *t-test is used to test whether the means of two independent samples differ significantly, a *pooled estimate* of vari-ance is made on the assumption that the samples are from populations with the same variance. The variance ratio test can be used to verify this assumption.

variate See random variable.

variation If the ratio of two variables x and y is always constant, then y is said to *vary directly* as x, or to be *directly proportional* to x. This is written as

$$y \propto x \quad \text{or} \quad y = kx,$$

where k is the *constant of proportionality*. The shorter forms 'y varies as x' and 'y is proportional to x' are also used.

If y is proportional to the reciprocal of x (i.e. to $1/x$), then y is said to *vary inversely as* x, or to be *inversely proportional to* x. This is written as

$$y \propto \frac{1}{x} \quad \text{or} \quad y = \frac{k}{x},$$

where again k is a constant.

variation, coefficient of The ratio of the *standard deviation to the *mean. It is usually given as a percentage and is a measure of *dispersion relative to the mean.

vary directly See variation.

vary inversely See variation.

vector 1. A *matrix consisting of a single row or column of elements. For example, a student's grades in four tests can be given as a row vector, $(A\ B\ A\ C)$.
2. A physical entity having magnitude and direction, for example, the velocity of a ship travelling at 30 km per hour north-west.

vectorial angle See polar coordinate system.

Venn diagram A diagram used to illustrate *sets and relationships between sets. Usually, a rectangle is used to represent the *universal set, and a circle within it represents a given set (members of the given set can be represented by points inside the circle). A *subset is represented by a circle within a circle, and the *union and *intersection of sets are shown by means of overlapping circles. Such a diagram can be a helpful representation of experiments in probability, the rectangle being the *sample space, the circles corresponding to events, and points corresponding to individual outcomes. *See* event.

vital statistics *See* demography.

W

Wald–Wolfowitz runs test *See* runs test.

waiting time (wait time) *See* exponential distribution; geometric distribution; Poisson process.

wash-out period *See* cross-over design.

Weibull distribution The *distribution of a continuous random variable X with frequency function

$$f(x) = cx^{c-1} \exp(-x^c),$$

where the *parameter c is a positive constant and $x > 0$. The distribution is heavily skewed to the right (*see* skewness) when $c \leqslant 1$, and is identical to the *exponential distribution when $c = 1$. It has proved useful in studies of lifetime distributions of machine components. It is one of three types of *extreme value distribution often used in the study of problems where the interest centres on the distribution of the maximum *order statistic $x_{(n)}$ as $n \rightarrow \infty$. In this context it can provide information useful in, for example, predicting future extreme weather patterns such as maximum gale forces or flood levels on the basis of historical records of these phenomena.

weight *See* mean.

weighted average *See* mean.

weighted aggregate index An *index number that compares estimates of the overall aggregate cost or value of a set of items in one year with that in a base year. For example, a weighted aggregate price index for a set of commodities compares the total expenditure on them in the current year with that in the base year.

More formally, if the prices of a set of k items are $p_{01}, p_{02}, \ldots, p_{0k}$ in the base year and $p_{n1}, p_{n2}, \ldots, p_{nk}$ in the nth year after the base year (year n), and if the quantities of items bought are $q_1, q_2, \ldots, q_k$, respectively, then the weighted aggregate price index for the items in year n is

$$\frac{p_{n1}q_1 + p_{n2}q_2 + \cdots + p_{nk}q_k}{p_{01}q_1 + p_{02}q_2 + \cdots + p_{0k}q_k} \times 100,$$

or

$$\left(\sum_i p_{ni}q_i \bigg/ \sum_i p_{0i}q_i \right) \times 100.$$

For example, suppose that the prices of three household items were 10, 15 and 40 in the base year and 13, 16 and 50 in the current year, and that households typically buy 12, 6 and 4 of each in a year. Using the formula, the weighted aggregate price index for the items in the current year is

$$\frac{13 \times 12 + 16 \times 6 + 50 \times 4}{10 \times 12 + 15 \times 6 + 40 \times 4} \times 100 = 122.2.$$

The price indices of the three items stand at 130, 106.7 and 125, respectively, and the aggregate index falls between them.

weighted index number An *index number for a set of items that is calculated from weights given to the component items according to their relative importance. *See* weighted aggregate index; weighted relatives index; Laspcyres index; Paasche index.

weighted mean *See* mean.

weighted relatives index An index number for a set of items that is a weighted *mean of their index numbers (relatives). In particular, a weighted relatives price index for a set of commodities is a weighted mean of their separate price indices, with the quantities purchased of each commodity as weights.

More formally, if the price indices of n commodities are $I_1, I_2, \ldots, I_n$, and the quantities being purchased are $q_1, q_2, \ldots, q_n$, respectively, then the weighted relatives price index of the commodities is

$$\frac{I_1q_1 + I_2q_2 + \cdots + I_nq_n}{q_1 + q_2 + \cdots + q_n},$$

or

$$\sum_i I_iq_i \Big/ \sum_i q_i.$$

For instance, fuel for a two-stroke engine is commonly made up of 25 units of petrol for each unit of oil. At a time when the price indices of petrol and oil are 110 and 150 respectively, a price index for two-stroke fuel can be calculated using $I_1 = 110$, $I_2 = 150$, $q_1 = 25$ and $q_2 = 1$. The formula gives

$$\frac{110 \times 25 + 150 \times 1}{25 + 1} = 111.5.$$

Since petrol is given a much larger weight than oil in this calculation, the two-stroke price index that results is much closer to the index for petrol than to the index for oil.

See also weighted aggregate index.

Wilcoxon rank sum test A *distribution-free test using *ranks of the *null hypothesis that two independent random samples are from identical populations (or from the same population), the alternative hypoth-

esis being that they are from populations that have different *medians (or *means).

Suppose the two samples A and B contain m and n observations, respectively, where $m \leqslant n$. The first stage is to combine the samples and rank the $m+n$ values in ascending order. Then let R_m be the sum of the ranks given to the values in sample A. The usual test statistic W is the smaller of R_m and $m(m+n+1) - R_m$, i.e.

$$W = \min(R_m, m(m+n+1) - R_m).$$

Significantly low values of W lead to rejection of the null hypothesis. Statistical tables give critical values of W for small values of m and n. These are the greatest values of W for significance at certain levels. Some statistical packages give the *p-value associated with a value of W (or of R_m). For larger values, R_m has an approximately *normal distribution with *mean

$$m(m + n + 1)/2$$

and *variance

$$mn(m + n + 1)/12.$$

As an illustration, suppose that valuations, in thousands of £, of random samples of houses in two areas A and B of a town are made, and we wish to test whether there is a difference between the average price of houses in the two areas. The values and their rankings in the combined sample are as follows:

Sample A	125	158	195	249	
Overall rank	3	5	8	9	
Sample B	97	105	145	163	189
Overall rank	1	2	4	6	7

Here $m = 4$, $n = 5$ and $R_m = 25$, so

$$m(m+n+1) - R_m = 4(4 + 5 + 1) - 25$$
$$= 15.$$

The test statistic W is the smaller of 25 and 15, so $W = 15$. The test is two-tailed, and with $m = 4$ and $n = 5$ the greatest value of W

Wilcoxon signed rank test (a)

Observation	6.3	7.0	7.9	5.6	14.3	8.1	9.4	8.0	8.4	6.5
Deviation from 9	−2.7	−2.0	−1.1	−3.4	+5.3	−0.9	+0.4	−1.0	−0.6	−2.5
Rank	8	6	5	9	10	3	1	4	2	7
Signed rank	−8	−6	−5	−9	+10	−3	+1	−4	−2	−7

for significance at the 5% level is 12. Our value of 15 exceeds this, so the null hypothesis of no difference in average house price is retained.

The *Mann–Whitney test* is equivalent to this test in the sense that, given the same data, both tests come to identical conclusions. For each observation in sample A, the number of observations in sample B which exceed it is found. The sum of these numbers may be denoted by U_{AB}. In the above example the numbers are 3, 2, 0 and 0, so $U_{AB} = 5$. Similarly, for each observation in sample B the number of observations in sample A which exceed it is found, and the sum of these numbers is U_{BA}. In the above example the numbers are 4, 4, 3, 2 and 2, so $U_{BA} = 15$. The usual test statistic U is the smaller of U_{AB} and U_{BA}, i.e. $U = \min(U_{AB}, U_{BA})$. In our example U is the smaller of 5 and 15, so $U = 5$. Significantly low values of U lead to rejection of the null hypothesis. Statistical tables give critical values of U at certain levels for small values of m and n, and some statistical packages give the p-value associated with a value of U (or of U_{AB}). For larger values of m and n, U_{AB} has an approximately *normal distribution with mean $mn/2$ and variance $mn(m + n + 1)/12$.

Wilcoxon signed rank test A *distribution-free test based on the *ranks of deviations associated with data rather than the actual deviations.

(1) The *one-sample test*. A test of whether a *random sample comes from a *symmetrical distribution with a specified *median (or *mean) M. Deviations of sample values from M are calculated and, ignoring signs, ranked in ascending order of

magnitude (any observation equal to M is dropped from the sample). Each rank is then given a sign to indicate whether the corresponding deviation is positive or negative, and thus becomes a *signed rank*.

For example, in a test of whether a sample of readings of percentage water content at random locations in a field are from a symmetrical distribution with a median of 9%, the signed ranks are derived as given in table (a). Next, the sums of the ranks with positive signs and of the ranks with negative signs are found; these may be denoted by R_+ and R_-, respectively. The usual test statistic T is the smaller of the two sums, i.e. $T = \min(R_+, R_-)$. In our example, $R_+ = 11$ and $R_- = 44$, so $T = 11$.

A significantly low value of T leads to rejection of the *null hypothesis that the median is M. Statistical tables give critical values of T for small values of n, where n is the number of observations ranked. These are the greatest values of T for significance at certain levels. Some statistical software packages give the *p-value associated with a value of T (or of R_+). For large n, e.g. over 25, R_+ has an approximately *normal distribution with *mean $n(n + 1)/4$ and *variance $n(n + 1)(2n + 1)/24$. In our example the test is two-tailed, with alternative hypothesis $M \neq 9$, and $n = 10$. The greatest value of T for significance at the 5% level is 8. Our value of 11 exceeds this, so the null hypothesis, that $M = 9$, is retained.
(2) The *paired-samples test*. A test of whether a random sample of n *matched pairs of values (x, y) is from two identical populations having equal medians M_x and M_y (or equal means). It is often called the *matched pairs signed rank test*. The test is a one-sample test based on the difference

Wilcoxon signed rank test (b)

First sentence length (f)	5	26	26	4	6	2	19	23	10	17
Last sentence length (l)	41	38	15	18	18	26	10	35	27	20

Wilcoxon signed rank test (c)

Difference $d = l - f$	36	12	−11	14	12	24	−9	12	17	3
Signed rank	+10	+5	−3	+7	+5	+9	−2	+5	+8	+1

$d = x - y$ between matched pairs of values (pairs with $d = 0$ are dropped from the sample). This sample of values of d is assumed to be from a symmetric distribution, and since $M_d = M_x - M_y$, the null hypothesis is that $M_d = 0$.

To illustrate the procedure, the data in table (b) give the number of words in the first and last sentences of a small random sample of paragraphs from *Animal Farm* by George Orwell. To investigate whether first and last sentences have different median lengths, we form the differences $d = l - f$ and, allowing for *ties, give them signed ranks. The results are as in table (c).

The rank sums R_+ and R_- are 50 and 5, respectively. The test statistic $T = 5$, the test is two-tailed and $n = 10$. The greatest value of T for significance at the 5% level is 8. Our value of 5 does not exceed this so, on the basis of this small sample, there is evidence to support the alternative hypothesis that first and last sentences differ in average length.

winsorization A procedure for reducing the sensitivity of the calculation of sample statistics such as the *mean to extreme observations (*outliers). Equal numbers of the smallest and largest values are replaced by the smallest and largest values in the rest of the sample. Assuming that the number of outliers is not too great, a total of about 10% of values are replaced. The mean of the new set of values is the *winsorized mean* of the sample. For example, in the following sample the observation 197 is an outlier:

4 9 11 12 12 13 15 18 24 25
30 37 46 48 51 60 73 89 94 197.

The sample mean is $868/20 = 43.4$. If the smallest and largest observations, 4 and 197, are replaced by 9 and 94 respectively, the winsorized mean is $770/20 = 38.5$. The use of winsorization reduces the effect of the outlier. *See also* trimmed mean.

winsorized mean *See* winsorization.

with *or* **without replacement** *See* random sample.

within-groups design *See* experimental design; randomized blocks.

within-subjects design *See* randomized blocks.

working mean *See* assumed mean.

x-axis *See* Cartesian coordinate system.

x-coordinate *See* Cartesian coordinate system.

x-intercept *See* intercept.

Yates's correction *See* chi-squared test.

***y*-axis** *See* Cartesian coordinate system.

***y*-coordinate** *See* Cartesian coordinate system.

***y*-intercept** *See* intercept.

Youden square A rectangular *experimental design which is an incomplete *Latin square, since it contains some but not all the rows of a Latin square. An example of a 3×4 design with treatments *A*, *B*, *C* and *D* is shown below:

$$
\begin{array}{cccc}
A & B & C & D \\
B & D & A & C \\
C & A & D & B
\end{array}
$$

The rows can be regarded as a set of *randomized blocks. The columns form a set of *balanced incomplete blocks since each treatment is tested an equal number of times (3), and each pair of treatments, such as *AB*, occurs an equal number of times (2) in the columns.

The design is useful because it avoids the restriction imposed by Latin squares that the number of rows and the number of columns must be equal to the number of treatments. So the above design could be used when testing four fungicides, *A*, *B*, *C* and *D*, on three types of conifer, *I*, *II* and *III*, in plantations at four different altitudes, 1, 2, 3 and 4 as, follows:

Conifer type	Altitude			
	1	2	3	4
I	*A*	*B*	*C*	*D*
II	*B*	*D*	*A*	*C*
III	*C*	*A*	*D*	*B*

See also Graeco-Latin square.

Z

z-score *See* standardization; normal distribution.

Z-score *See* standardization.

z-transformation *See* Fisher's z-transformation.

Table 1. The standard normal distribution function $\Phi(z)$. The tabulated value $\Phi(z)$ is the probability that a random variable, normally distributed with zero mean and unit variance, will be less than or equal to z. For negative values of z, use $\Phi(-z) = 1 - \Phi(z)$.

z	0.00	0.01	0.02	0.03	0.04	0.05	0.06	0.07	0.08	0.09
0.0	0.5000	0.5040	0.5080	0.5120	0.5160	0.5199	0.5239	0.5279	0.5319	0.5359
0.1	0.5398	0.5438	0.5478	0.5517	0.5557	0.5596	0.5636	0.5675	0.5714	0.5753
0.2	0.5793	0.5832	0.5871	0.5910	0.5948	0.5987	0.6026	0.6064	0.6103	0.6141
0.3	0.6179	0.6217	0.6255	0.6293	0.6331	0.6368	0.6406	0.6443	0.6480	0.6517
0.4	0.6554	0.6591	0.6628	0.6664	0.6700	0.6736	0.6772	0.6808	0.6844	0.6879
0.5	0.6915	0.6950	0.6985	0.7019	0.7054	0.7088	0.7123	0.7157	0.7190	0.7224
0.6	0.7257	0.7291	0.7324	0.7357	0.7389	0.7422	0.7454	0.7486	0.7517	0.7549
0.7	0.7580	0.7611	0.7642	0.7673	0.7704	0.7734	0.7764	0.7794	0.7823	0.7852
0.8	0.7881	0.7910	0.7939	0.7967	0.7995	0.8023	0.8051	0.8078	0.8106	0.8133
0.9	0.8159	0.8186	0.8212	0.8238	0.8264	0.8289	0.8315	0.8340	0.8365	0.8389
1.0	0.8413	0.8438	0.8461	0.8485	0.8508	0.8531	0.8554	0.8577	0.8599	0.8621
1.1	0.8643	0.8665	0.8686	0.8708	0.8729	0.8749	0.8770	0.8790	0.8810	0.8830
1.2	0.8849	0.8869	0.8888	0.8906	0.8925	0.8944	0.8962	0.8980	0.8997	0.9015
1.3	0.9032	0.9049	0.9066	0.9082	0.9099	0.9115	0.9131	0.9147	0.9162	0.9177
1.4	0.9192	0.9207	0.9222	0.9236	0.9251	0.9265	0.9279	0.9292	0.9306	0.9319
1.5	0.9332	0.9345	0.9357	0.9370	0.9382	0.9394	0.9406	0.9418	0.9429	0.9441
1.6	0.9452	0.9463	0.9474	0.9484	0.9495	0.9505	0.9515	0.9525	0.9535	0.9545
1.7	0.9554	0.9564	0.9573	0.9582	0.9591	0.9599	0.9608	0.9616	0.9625	0.9633
1.8	0.9641	0.9649	0.9656	0.9664	0.9671	0.9678	0.9686	0.9693	0.9699	0.9706
1.9	0.9713	0.9719	0.9726	0.9732	0.9738	0.9744	0.9750	0.9756	0.9761	0.9767
2.0	0.9772	0.9778	0.9783	0.9788	0.9793	0.9798	0.9803	0.9808	0.9812	0.9817
2.1	0.9821	0.9826	0.9830	0.9834	0.9838	0.9842	0.9846	0.9850	0.9854	0.9857
2.2	0.9861	0.9864	0.9868	0.9871	0.9875	0.9878	0.9881	0.9884	0.9887	0.9890
2.3	0.9893	0.9896	0.9898	0.9901	0.9904	0.9906	0.9909	0.9911	0.9913	0.9916
2.4	0.9918	0.9920	0.9922	0.9925	0.9927	0.9929	0.9931	0.9932	0.9934	0.9936
2.5	0.9938	0.9940	0.9941	0.9943	0.9945	0.9946	0.9948	0.9949	0.9951	0.9952
2.6	0.9953	0.9955	0.9956	0.9957	0.9959	0.9960	0.9961	0.9962	0.9963	0.9964
2.7	0.9965	0.9966	0.9967	0.9968	0.9969	0.9970	0.9971	0.9972	0.9973	0.9974
2.8	0.9974	0.9975	0.9976	0.9977	0.9977	0.9978	0.9979	0.9979	0.9980	0.9981
2.9	0.9981	0.9982	0.9982	0.9983	0.9984	0.9984	0.9985	0.9985	0.9986	0.9986
3.0	0.9987	0.9987	0.9987	0.9988	0.9988	0.9989	0.9989	0.9989	0.9990	0.9990
3.1	0.9990	0.9991	0.9991	0.9991	0.9992	0.9992	0.9992	0.9992	0.9993	0.9993
3.2	0.9993	0.9993	0.9994	0.9994	0.9994	0.9994	0.9994	0.9995	0.9995	0.9995
3.3	0.9995	0.9995	0.9995	0.9996	0.9996	0.9996	0.9996	0.9996	0.9996	0.9997
3.4	0.9997	0.9997	0.9997	0.9997	0.9997	0.9997	0.9997	0.9997	0.9997	0.9998
3.5	0.9998	0.9998	0.9998	0.9998	0.9998	0.9998	0.9998	0.9998	0.9998	0.9998
3.6	0.9998	0.9998	0.9998	0.9999	0.9999	0.9999	0.9999	0.9999	0.9999	0.9999

Table 2. Upper percentage points of the standard normal distribution. The tabulated value z_p is such that, if the random variable Z is normally distributed with zero mean and unit variance, the probability that $Z > z_p$ is p.

p	0.05	0.025	0.01	0.005	0.001	0.0005
z_p	1.6449	1.9600	2.3263	2.5758	3.0902	3.2905

Table 3. Critical values of r, the product moment correlation coefficient. If r is calculated from a sample of n pairs of values, the number of degrees of freedom, v, is equal to $n - 2$. The tabulated value r_p is such that, if there is no correlation in the parent population, the probability that $r > r_p$ is p.

v	p			
	0.05	0.025	0.01	0.005
1	0.9877	0.9969	0.9995	0.9999
2	0.9000	0.9500	0.9800	0.9900
3	0.8054	0.8783	0.9343	0.9587
4	0.7293	0.8114	0.8822	0.9172
5	0.6694	0.7545	0.8329	0.8745
6	0.6215	0.7067	0.7887	0.8343
7	0.5822	0.6664	0.7498	0.7977
8	0.5494	0.6319	0.7155	0.7646
9	0.5214	0.6021	0.6851	0.7348
10	0.4973	0.5760	0.6581	0.7079
11	0.4762	0.5529	0.6339	0.6835
12	0.4575	0.5324	0.6120	0.6614
13	0.4409	0.5139	0.5923	0.6411
14	0.4259	0.4973	0.5742	0.6226
15	0.4124	0.4821	0.5577	0.6055
16	0.4000	0.4683	0.5425	0.5897
17	0.3887	0.4555	0.5285	0.5751
18	0.3783	0.4438	0.5155	0.5614
19	0.3687	0.4329	0.5034	0.5487
20	0.3598	0.4227	0.4921	0.5368
25	0.3233	0.3809	0.4451	0.4869
30	0.2960	0.3494	0.4093	0.4487
35	0.2746	0.3246	0.3810	0.4182
40	0.2573	0.3044	0.3578	0.3932
45	0.2428	0.2875	0.3384	0.3721
50	0.2306	0.2732	0.3218	0.3541
60	0.2108	0.2500	0.2948	0.3248
70	0.1954	0.2319	0.2737	0.3017
80	0.1829	0.2172	0.2565	0.2830
90	0.1726	0.2050	0.2422	0.2673
100	0.1638	0.1946	0.2301	0.2540

Table 4. Upper percentage points of the t-distribution. The tabulated value t_p is such that, if the random variable X has the t-distribution with v degrees of freedom, the probability that $X > t_p$ is p.

v	p					
	0.10	0.05	0.025	0.01	0.005	0.001
1	3.078	6.314	12.706	31.821	63.657	318.310
2	1.886	2.920	4.303	6.965	9.925	22.327
3	1.638	2.353	3.182	4.541	5.841	10.213
4	1.533	2.132	2.776	3.747	4.604	7.173
5	1.476	2.015	2.571	3.365	4.032	5.893
6	1.440	1.943	2.447	3.143	3.707	5.208
7	1.415	1.895	2.365	2.998	3.499	4.785
8	1.397	1.860	2.306	2.896	3.355	4.501
9	1.383	1.833	2.262	2.821	3.250	4.297
10	1.372	1.812	2.228	2.764	3.169	4.144
11	1.363	1.796	2.201	2.718	3.106	4.025
12	1.356	1.782	2.179	2.681	3.055	3.930
13	1.350	1.771	2.160	2.650	3.012	3.852
14	1.345	1.761	2.145	2.624	2.977	3.787
15	1.341	1.753	2.131	2.602	2.947	3.733
16	1.337	1.746	2.120	2.583	2.921	3.686
17	1.333	1.740	2.110	2.567	2.898	3.646
18	1.330	1.734	2.101	2.552	2.878	3.610
19	1.328	1.729	2.093	2.539	2.861	3.579
20	1.325	1.725	2.086	2.528	2.845	3.552
21	1.323	1.721	2.080	2.518	2.831	3.527
22	1.321	1.717	2.074	2.508	2.819	3.505
23	1.319	1.714	2.069	2.500	2.807	3.485
24	1.318	1.711	2.064	2.492	2.797	3.467
25	1.316	1.708	2.060	2.485	2.787	3.450
26	1.315	1.706	2.056	2.479	2.779	3.435
27	1.314	1.703	2.052	2.473	2.771	3.421
28	1.313	1.701	2.048	2.467	2.763	3.408
29	1.311	1.699	2.045	2.462	2.756	3.396
30	1.310	1.697	2.042	2.457	2.750	3.385
40	1.303	1.684	2.021	2.423	2.704	3.307
60	1.296	1.671	2.000	2.390	2.660	3.232
120	1.289	1.658	1.980	2.358	2.617	3.160
∞	1.282	1.645	1.960	2.326	2.576	3.090

Appendix

Table 5. Upper percentage points of the chi-squared distribution. The tabulated value χ_p^2 is such that, if the random variable X has the chi-squared distribution with v degrees of freedom, the probability that $X > \chi_p^2$ is p.

v	p							
	0.99	0.95	0.50	0.20	0.10	0.05	0.025	0.01
1	0.0002	0.0039	0.45	1.64	2.71	3.84	5.02	6.63
2	0.020	0.103	1.39	3.22	4.61	5.99	7.38	9.21
3	0.115	0.352	2.37	4.64	6.25	7.81	9.35	11.34
4	0.30	0.71	3.36	5.99	7.78	9.49	11.14	13.28
5	0.55	1.15	4.35	7.29	9.24	11.07	12.83	15.09
6	0.87	1.64	5.35	8.56	10.64	12.59	14.45	16.81
7	1.24	2.17	6.35	9.80	12.02	14.07	16.01	18.48
8	1.65	2.73	7.34	11.03	13.36	15.51	17.53	20.09
9	2.09	3.33	8.34	12.24	14.68	16.92	19.02	21.67
10	2.56	3.94	9.34	13.44	15.99	18.31	20.48	23.21
11	3.05	4.57	10.34	14.63	17.28	19.68	21.92	24.72
12	3.57	5.23	11.34	15.81	18.55	21.03	23.34	26.22
13	4.11	5.89	12.34	16.98	19.81	22.36	24.74	27.69
14	4.66	6.57	13.34	18.15	21.06	23.68	26.12	29.14
15	5.23	7.26	14.34	19.31	22.31	25.00	27.49	30.58
16	5.81	7.96	15.34	20.47	23.54	26.30	28.85	32.00
17	6.41	8.67	16.34	21.61	24.77	27.59	30.19	33.41
18	7.02	9.39	17.34	22.76	25.99	28.87	31.53	34.81
19	7.63	10.12	18.34	23.90	27.20	30.14	32.85	36.19
20	8.26	10.85	19.34	25.04	28.41	31.41	34.17	37.57
21	8.90	11.59	20.34	26.17	29.62	32.67	35.48	38.93
22	9.54	12.34	21.34	27.30	30.81	33.92	36.78	40.29
23	10.20	13.09	22.34	28.43	32.01	35.17	38.08	41.64
24	10.86	13.85	23.34	29.55	33.20	36.42	39.36	42.98
25	11.52	14.61	24.34	30.68	34.38	37.65	40.65	44.31
26	12.20	15.38	25.34	31.79	35.56	38.89	41.92	45.64
27	12.88	16.15	26.34	32.91	36.74	40.11	43.19	46.96
28	13.57	16.93	27.34	34.03	37.92	41.34	44.46	48.28
29	14.26	17.71	28.34	35.14	39.09	42.56	45.72	49.59
30	14.95	18.49	29.34	36.25	40.26	43.77	46.98	50.89
40	22.16	26.51	39.34	47.27	51.81	55.76	59.34	63.69
50	29.71	34.76	49.33	58.16	63.17	67.50	71.42	76.15
60	37.48	43.19	59.33	68.97	74.40	79.08	83.30	88.38
70	45.44	51.74	69.33	79.71	85.53	90.53	95.02	100.43
80	53.54	60.39	79.33	90.41	96.58	101.88	106.63	112.33
90	61.75	69.13	89.33	101.05	107.57	113.15	118.14	124.12
100	70.06	77.93	99.33	111.67	118.50	124.34	129.56	135.81

Table 6(a). Upper 5% points of the F-distribution. The tabulated value is F_p with $p = 0.05$. If the random variable X has the F-distribution with v_1 and v_2 degrees of freedom, the probability that $X > F_p$ is p.

v_2	v_1 1	2	3	4	5	6	7	8	9	10	12	15	20	24	30	∞
1	161.4	199.5	215.7	224.6	230.2	234.0	236.8	238.9	240.5	241.9	243.9	245.9	248.0	249.1	250.1	254.3
2	18.51	19.00	19.16	19.25	19.30	19.33	19.35	19.37	19.38	19.40	19.41	19.43	19.45	19.45	19.46	19.50
3	10.13	9.55	9.28	9.12	9.01	8.94	8.89	8.85	8.81	8.79	8.74	8.70	8.66	8.64	8.62	8.53
4	7.71	6.94	6.59	6.39	6.26	6.16	6.09	6.04	6.00	5.96	5.91	5.86	5.80	5.77	5.75	5.63
5	6.61	5.79	5.41	5.19	5.05	4.95	4.88	4.82	4.77	4.74	4.68	4.62	4.56	4.53	4.50	4.36
6	5.99	5.14	4.76	4.53	4.39	4.28	4.21	4.15	4.10	4.06	4.00	3.94	3.87	3.84	3.81	3.67
7	5.59	4.74	4.35	4.12	3.97	3.87	3.79	3.73	3.68	3.64	3.57	3.51	3.44	3.41	3.38	3.23
8	5.32	4.46	4.07	3.84	3.69	3.58	3.50	3.44	3.39	3.35	3.28	3.22	3.15	3.12	3.08	2.93
9	5.12	4.26	3.86	3.63	3.48	3.37	3.29	3.23	3.18	3.14	3.07	3.01	2.94	2.90	2.86	2.71
10	4.96	4.10	3.71	3.48	3.33	3.22	3.14	3.07	3.02	2.98	2.91	2.85	2.77	2.74	2.70	2.54
11	4.84	3.98	3.59	3.36	3.20	3.09	3.01	2.95	2.90	2.85	2.79	2.72	2.65	2.61	2.57	2.40
12	4.75	3.89	3.49	3.26	3.11	3.00	2.91	2.85	2.80	2.75	2.69	2.62	2.54	2.51	2.47	2.30
13	4.67	3.81	3.41	3.18	3.03	2.92	2.83	2.77	2.71	2.67	2.60	2.53	2.46	2.42	2.38	2.21
14	4.60	3.74	3.34	3.11	2.96	2.85	2.76	2.70	2.65	2.60	2.53	2.46	2.39	2.35	2.31	2.13
15	4.54	3.68	3.29	3.06	2.90	2.79	2.71	2.64	2.59	2.54	2.48	2.40	2.33	2.29	2.25	2.07
16	4.49	3.63	3.24	3.01	2.85	2.74	2.66	2.59	2.54	2.49	2.42	2.35	2.28	2.24	2.19	2.01
17	4.45	3.59	3.20	2.96	2.81	2.70	2.61	2.55	2.49	2.45	2.38	2.31	2.23	2.19	2.15	1.96
18	4.41	3.55	3.16	2.93	2.77	2.66	2.58	2.51	2.46	2.41	2.34	2.27	2.19	2.15	2.11	1.92
19	4.38	3.52	3.13	2.90	2.74	2.63	2.54	2.48	2.42	2.38	2.31	2.23	2.16	2.11	2.07	1.88
20	4.35	3.49	3.10	2.87	2.71	2.60	2.51	2.45	2.39	2.35	2.28	2.20	2.12	2.08	2.04	1.84
21	4.32	3.47	3.07	2.84	2.68	2.57	2.49	2.42	2.37	2.32	2.25	2.18	2.10	2.05	2.01	1.81
22	4.30	3.44	3.05	2.82	2.66	2.55	2.46	2.40	2.34	2.30	2.23	2.15	2.07	2.03	1.98	1.78
23	4.28	3.42	3.03	2.80	2.64	2.53	2.44	2.37	2.32	2.27	2.20	2.13	2.05	2.01	1.96	1.76
24	4.26	3.40	3.01	2.78	2.62	2.51	2.42	2.36	2.30	2.25	2.18	2.11	2.03	1.98	1.94	1.73
25	4.24	3.39	2.99	2.76	2.60	2.49	2.40	2.34	2.28	2.24	2.16	2.09	2.01	1.96	1.92	1.71
26	4.23	3.37	2.98	2.74	2.59	2.47	2.39	2.32	2.27	2.22	2.15	2.07	1.99	1.95	1.90	1.69
27	4.21	3.35	2.96	2.73	2.57	2.46	2.37	2.31	2.25	2.20	2.13	2.06	1.97	1.93	1.88	1.67
28	4.20	3.34	2.95	2.71	2.56	2.45	2.36	2.29	2.24	2.19	2.12	2.04	1.96	1.91	1.87	1.65
29	4.18	3.33	2.93	2.70	2.55	2.43	2.35	2.28	2.22	2.18	2.10	2.03	1.94	1.90	1.85	1.64
30	4.17	3.32	2.92	2.69	2.53	2.42	2.33	2.27	2.21	2.16	2.09	2.01	1.93	1.89	1.84	1.62
40	4.08	3.23	2.84	2.61	2.45	2.34	2.25	2.18	2.12	2.08	2.00	1.92	1.84	1.79	1.74	1.51
60	4.00	3.15	2.76	2.53	2.37	2.25	2.17	2.10	2.04	1.99	1.92	1.84	1.75	1.70	1.65	1.39
120	3.92	3.07	2.68	2.45	2.29	2.18	2.09	2.02	1.96	1.91	1.83	1.75	1.66	1.61	1.55	1.25
∞	3.84	3.00	2.60	2.37	2.21	2.10	2.01	1.94	1.88	1.83	1.75	1.67	1.57	1.52	1.46	1.00

Table 6(b). Upper $2\frac{1}{2}\%$ points of the F-distribution. The tabulated value is F_p with $p = 0.025$. If the random variable X has the F-distribution with v_1 and v_2 degrees of freedom, the probability that $X > F_p$ is p.

v_2	1	2	3	4	5	6	7	8	9	10	12	15	20	24	30	∞
1	647.8	799.5	864.2	899.6	921.8	937.1	948.2	956.7	963.3	968.6	976.7	984.9	993.1	997.2	1001	1018
2	38.51	39.00	39.17	39.25	39.30	39.33	39.36	39.37	39.39	39.40	39.41	39.43	39.45	39.46	39.46	39.50
3	17.44	16.04	15.44	15.10	14.88	14.73	14.62	14.54	14.47	14.42	14.34	14.25	14.17	14.12	14.08	13.90
4	12.22	10.65	9.98	9.60	9.36	9.20	9.07	8.98	8.90	8.84	8.75	8.66	8.56	8.51	8.46	8.26
5	10.01	8.43	7.76	7.39	7.15	6.98	6.85	6.76	6.68	6.62	6.52	6.43	6.33	6.28	6.23	6.02
6	8.81	7.26	6.60	6.23	5.99	5.82	5.70	5.60	5.52	5.46	5.37	5.27	5.17	5.12	5.07	4.85
7	8.07	6.54	5.89	5.52	5.29	5.12	4.99	4.90	4.82	4.76	4.67	4.57	4.47	4.41	4.36	4.14
8	7.57	6.06	5.42	5.05	4.82	4.65	4.53	4.43	4.36	4.30	4.20	4.10	4.00	3.95	3.89	3.67
9	7.21	5.71	5.08	4.72	4.48	4.32	4.20	4.10	4.03	3.96	3.87	3.77	3.67	3.61	3.56	3.33
10	6.94	5.46	4.83	4.47	4.24	4.07	3.95	3.85	3.78	3.72	3.62	3.52	3.42	3.37	3.31	3.08
11	6.72	5.26	4.63	4.28	4.04	3.88	3.76	3.66	3.59	3.53	3.43	3.33	3.23	3.17	3.12	2.88
12	6.55	5.10	4.47	4.12	3.89	3.73	3.61	3.51	3.44	3.37	3.28	3.18	3.07	3.02	2.96	2.72
13	6.41	4.97	4.35	4.00	3.77	3.60	3.48	3.39	3.31	3.25	3.15	3.05	2.95	2.89	2.84	2.60
14	6.30	4.86	4.24	3.89	3.66	3.50	3.38	3.29	3.21	3.15	3.05	2.95	2.84	2.79	2.73	2.49
15	6.20	4.77	4.15	3.80	3.58	3.41	3.29	3.20	3.12	3.06	2.96	2.86	2.76	2.70	2.64	2.40
16	6.12	4.69	4.08	3.73	3.50	3.34	3.22	3.12	3.05	2.99	2.89	2.79	2.68	2.63	2.57	2.32
17	6.04	4.62	4.01	3.66	3.44	3.28	3.16	3.06	2.98	2.92	2.82	2.72	2.62	2.56	2.50	2.25
18	5.98	4.56	3.95	3.61	3.38	3.22	3.10	3.01	2.93	2.87	2.77	2.67	2.56	2.50	2.44	2.19
19	5.92	4.51	3.90	3.56	3.33	3.17	3.05	2.96	2.88	2.82	2.72	2.62	2.51	2.45	2.39	2.13
20	5.87	4.46	3.86	3.51	3.29	3.13	3.01	2.91	2.84	2.77	2.68	2.57	2.46	2.41	2.35	2.09
21	5.83	4.42	3.82	3.48	3.25	3.09	2.97	2.87	2.80	2.73	2.64	2.53	2.42	2.37	2.31	2.04
22	5.79	4.38	3.78	3.44	3.22	3.05	2.93	2.84	2.76	2.70	2.60	2.50	2.39	2.33	2.27	2.00
23	5.75	4.35	3.75	3.41	3.18	3.02	2.90	2.81	2.73	2.67	2.57	2.47	2.36	2.30	2.24	1.97
24	5.72	4.32	3.72	3.38	3.15	2.99	2.87	2.78	2.70	2.64	2.54	2.44	2.33	2.27	2.21	1.94
25	5.69	4.29	3.69	3.35	3.13	2.97	2.85	2.75	2.68	2.61	2.51	2.41	2.30	2.24	2.18	1.91
26	5.66	4.27	3.67	3.33	3.10	2.94	2.82	2.73	2.65	2.59	2.49	2.39	2.28	2.22	2.16	1.88
27	5.63	4.24	3.65	3.31	3.08	2.92	2.80	2.71	2.63	2.57	2.47	2.36	2.25	2.19	2.13	1.85
28	5.61	4.22	3.63	3.29	3.06	2.90	2.78	2.69	2.61	2.55	2.45	2.34	2.23	2.17	2.11	1.83
29	5.59	4.20	3.61	3.27	3.04	2.88	2.76	2.67	2.59	2.53	2.43	2.32	2.21	2.15	2.09	1.81
30	5.57	4.18	3.59	3.25	3.03	2.87	2.75	2.65	2.57	2.51	2.41	2.31	2.20	2.14	2.07	1.79
40	5.42	4.05	3.46	3.13	2.90	2.74	2.62	2.53	2.45	2.39	2.29	2.18	2.07	2.01	1.94	1.64
60	5.29	3.93	3.34	3.01	2.79	2.63	2.51	2.41	2.33	2.27	2.17	2.06	1.94	1.88	1.82	1.48
120	5.15	3.80	3.23	2.89	2.67	2.52	2.39	2.30	2.22	2.16	2.05	1.94	1.82	1.76	1.69	1.31
∞	5.02	3.69	3.12	2.79	2.57	2.41	2.29	2.19	2.11	2.05	1.94	1.83	1.71	1.64	1.57	1.00

Table 6(c). Upper 1% points of the F-distribution. The tabulated value is F_p with $p = 0.01$. If the random variable X has the F-distribution with v_1 and v_2 degrees of freedom, the probability that $X > F_p$ is p.

v_2	v_1															
	1	2	3	4	5	6	7	8	9	10	12	15	20	24	30	∞
1	4052	4999.5	5403	5625	5764	5859	5928	5981	6022	6056	6106	6157	6209	6235	6261	6366
2	98.50	99.00	99.17	99.25	99.30	99.33	99.36	99.37	99.39	99.40	99.42	99.43	99.45	99.46	99.47	99.50
3	34.12	30.82	29.46	28.71	28.24	27.91	27.67	27.49	27.35	27.23	27.05	26.87	26.69	26.60	26.50	26.13
4	21.20	18.00	16.69	15.98	15.52	15.21	14.98	14.80	14.66	14.55	14.37	14.20	14.02	13.93	13.84	13.46
5	16.26	13.27	12.06	11.39	10.97	10.67	10.46	10.29	10.16	10.05	9.89	9.72	9.55	9.47	9.38	9.02
6	13.75	10.92	9.78	9.15	8.75	8.47	8.26	8.10	7.98	7.87	7.72	7.56	7.40	7.31	7.23	6.88
7	12.25	9.55	8.45	7.85	7.46	7.19	6.99	6.84	6.72	6.62	6.47	6.31	6.16	6.07	5.99	5.65
8	11.26	8.65	7.59	7.01	6.63	6.37	6.18	6.03	5.91	5.81	5.67	5.52	5.36	5.28	5.20	4.86
9	10.56	8.02	6.99	6.42	6.06	5.80	5.61	5.47	5.35	5.26	5.11	4.96	4.81	4.73	4.65	4.31
10	10.04	7.56	6.55	5.99	5.64	5.39	5.20	5.06	4.94	4.85	4.71	4.56	4.41	4.33	4.25	3.91
11	9.65	7.21	6.22	5.67	5.32	5.07	4.89	4.74	4.63	4.54	4.40	4.25	4.10	4.02	3.94	3.60
12	9.33	6.93	5.95	5.41	5.06	4.82	4.64	4.50	4.39	4.30	4.16	4.01	3.86	3.78	3.70	3.36
13	9.07	6.70	5.74	5.21	4.86	4.62	4.44	4.30	4.19	4.10	3.96	3.82	3.66	3.59	3.51	3.17
14	8.86	6.51	5.56	5.04	4.69	4.46	4.28	4.14	4.03	3.94	3.80	3.66	3.51	3.43	3.35	3.00
15	8.68	6.36	5.42	4.89	4.56	4.32	4.14	4.00	3.89	3.80	3.67	3.52	3.37	3.29	3.21	2.87
16	8.53	6.23	5.29	4.77	4.44	4.20	4.03	3.89	3.78	3.69	3.55	3.41	3.26	3.18	3.10	2.75
17	8.40	6.11	5.18	4.67	4.34	4.10	3.93	3.79	3.68	3.59	3.46	3.31	3.16	3.08	3.00	2.65
18	8.29	6.01	5.09	4.58	4.25	4.01	3.84	3.71	3.60	3.51	3.37	3.23	3.08	3.00	2.92	2.57
19	8.18	5.93	5.01	4.50	4.17	3.94	3.77	3.63	3.52	3.43	3.30	3.15	3.00	2.92	2.84	2.49
20	8.10	5.85	4.94	4.43	4.10	3.87	3.70	3.56	3.46	3.37	3.23	3.09	2.94	2.86	2.78	2.42
21	8.02	5.78	4.87	4.37	4.04	3.81	3.64	3.51	3.40	3.31	3.17	3.03	2.88	2.80	2.72	2.36
22	7.95	5.72	4.82	4.31	3.99	3.76	3.59	3.45	3.35	3.26	3.12	2.98	2.83	2.75	2.67	2.31
23	7.88	5.66	4.76	4.26	3.94	3.71	3.54	3.41	3.30	3.21	3.07	2.93	2.78	2.70	2.62	2.26
24	7.82	5.61	4.72	4.22	3.90	3.67	3.50	3.36	3.26	3.17	3.03	2.89	2.74	2.66	2.58	2.21
25	7.77	5.57	4.68	4.18	3.85	3.63	3.46	3.32	3.22	3.13	2.99	2.85	2.70	2.62	2.54	2.17
26	7.72	5.53	4.64	4.14	3.82	3.59	3.42	3.29	3.18	3.09	2.96	2.81	2.66	2.58	2.50	2.13
27	7.68	5.49	4.60	4.11	3.78	3.56	3.39	3.26	3.15	3.06	2.93	2.78	2.63	2.55	2.47	2.10
28	7.64	5.45	4.57	4.07	3.75	3.53	3.36	3.23	3.12	3.03	2.90	2.75	2.60	2.52	2.44	2.06
29	7.60	5.42	4.54	4.04	3.73	3.50	3.33	3.20	3.09	3.00	2.87	2.73	2.57	2.49	2.41	2.03
30	7.56	5.39	4.51	4.02	3.70	3.47	3.30	3.17	3.07	2.98	2.84	2.70	2.55	2.47	2.39	2.01
40	7.31	5.18	4.31	3.83	3.51	3.29	3.12	2.99	2.89	2.80	2.66	2.52	2.37	2.29	2.20	1.80
60	7.08	4.98	4.13	3.65	3.34	3.12	2.95	2.82	2.72	2.63	2.50	2.35	2.20	2.12	2.03	1.60
120	6.85	4.79	3.95	3.48	3.17	2.96	2.79	2.66	2.56	2.47	2.34	2.19	2.03	1.95	1.86	1.38
∞	6.63	4.61	3.78	3.32	3.02	2.80	2.64	2.51	2.41	2.32	2.18	2.04	1.88	1.79	1.70	1.00

Table 7. Random numbers.

19	21	17	33	36	80	58	60	86	81	28	01	24	88	81	34	32	14	01	56	03	77	64	51	50
94	52	04	44	51	07	03	23	65	61	41	31	12	84	21	95	90	89	12	80	74	62	78	63	59
70	98	60	38	17	40	25	16	13	10	25	94	09	24	11	34	79	68	54	16	00	99	39	94	87
65	24	97	96	77	03	15	50	92	32	96	78	41	71	26	50	35	08	64	69	41	30	06	27	15
82	10	20	30	98	01	78	50	06	53	39	43	84	36	60	02	40	60	84	04	24	54	08	00	00
91	60	09	46	35	35	39	28	17	37	01	50	50	49	67	91	09	70	20	11	26	64	23	85	40
20	55	98	53	61	20	09	34	60	00	83	30	49	66	24	62	54	14	17	22	79	67	69	89	70
53	30	57	95	44	99	93	78	77	27	32	21	01	94	38	58	25	07	72	65	02	99	80	29	73
57	10	88	64	98	14	15	86	06	97	41	67	31	80	87	46	08	81	12	38	82	13	57	90	35
08	27	01	19	29	92	04	03	73	90	71	19	05	89	52	98	70	24	16	38	95	72	52	27	98
90	11	92	32	06	75	63	46	00	53	90	72	42	90	80	69	42	36	68	15	11	89	61	86	07
45	12	46	96	07	17	07	86	17	47	15	89	16	99	04	79	58	96	81	37	19	00	61	90	45
83	08	40	25	89	37	66	06	38	82	99	02	53	48	31	92	04	82	36	71	68	89	57	37	95
04	68	53	10	35	93	82	81	61	59	05	01	55	48	00	76	53	42	29	74	13	58	90	18	01
61	34	90	45	38	89	31	82	76	93	02	67	43	43	68	24	72	04	06	82	20	94	03	73	92
14	08	26	50	20	49	95	60	13	36	41	68	50	17	58	49	24	25	21	22	01	03	06	03	78
82	61	55	34	77	58	01	46	22	29	72	64	03	20	42	73	52	11	41	66	45	85	00	23	72
50	94	27	86	33	16	58	81	92	75	62	25	82	07	73	67	60	19	30	65	69	00	20	39	85
76	38	17	74	55	81	21	80	25	20	22	90	08	01	30	61	55	49	89	01	26	93	97	87	32
05	64	53	50	63	85	93	22	24	10	31	35	47	90	39	70	79	43	48	11	96	98	97	55
76	59	18	37	50	46	13	77	49	89	39	93	13	30	68	35	15	54	94	86	28	15	60	45	56
31	94	58	79	60	04	85	24	14	11	63	10	54	41	16	95	25	00	40	46	59	21	16	72	70
08	64	88	98	22	04	17	03	83	65	23	84	26	19	17	57	45	30	34	95	61	43	02	01	54
32	51	10	79	99	18	92	07	70	45	44	29	98	50	57	51	39	51	74	57	24	20	70	27	30
79	34	85	61	94	58	14	58	86	45	84	86	74	15	94	28	14	88	49	85	89	94	92	66	89
61	97	30	36	60	32	98	87	06	89	17	79	46	13	40	58	31	13	25	69	23	94	98	56	26
92	03	26	01	27	34	06	62	81	49	22	35	21	29	07	53	78	88	66	48	57	64	90	78	87
74	60	97	10	72	63	95	85	83	36	67	81	44	05	98	12	62	63	07	54	75	89	54	21	94
98	66	87	60	74	25	63	45	69	13	88	25	44	16	47	05	39	86	94	63	49	77	83	13	82
65	24	87	20	78	58	63	48	86	78	21	76	46	79	40	45	66	68	46	64	35	71	44	30	81
82	00	29	69	16	94	13	87	47	39	99	12	20	39	04	46	05	29	72	77	60	24	33	74	24
79	10	05	59	38	23	21	11	01	11	17	11	59	05	77	94	20	20	10	63	85	52	26	43	78
30	92	37	17	10	70	25	70	55	96	42	31	00	24	49	31	21	15	00	25	99	74	47	80	84
90	51	35	09	66	78	98	17	03	91	45	93	21	35	35	21	68	16	65	89	94	91	50	88	55
94	47	47	93	56	16	09	89	58	06	79	25	21	41	90	88	72	23	98	87	15	55	35	83	86
65	23	66	29	48	19	96	82	20	71	49	89	89	61	40	80	26	45	75	80	56	77	56	31	38
80	50	20	41	92	84	28	73	25	89	50	66	46	38	46	71	59	06	72	20	71	50	32	79	42
01	31	50	46	32	50	20	28	91	48	41	55	61	15	84	35	91	61	39	79	25	01	63	25	11
81	52	57	66	70	88	71	42	86	81	56	54	08	49	63	85	54	36	97	15	86	19	27	93	73
19	50	04	17	20	79	21	42	00	79	42	05	32	98	44	02	29	41	13	06	78	53	76	50	98
25	81	27	70	90	45	19	89	81	62	13	78	26	05	96	99	09	25	01	88	65	40	56	32	27
80	85	99	42	20	92	30	90	19	98	45	09	02	48	15	13	41	58	69	89	01	67	73	90	92
41	10	73	35	61	04	37	64	00	72	78	90	96	10	42	04	09	87	33	04	21	89	26	31	12
00	46	50	08	58	22	77	48	07	30	07	09	88	05	15	09	97	04	04	76	10	31	42	47	92
58	13	70	24	54	15	65	72	49	57	48	40	10	29	40	92	82	82	63	72	31	07	15	81	92
32	01	39	71	47	69	72	57	88	67	73	32	97	49	35	69	27	64	60	01	04	18	13	88	38
17	04	88	47	88	12	53	10	17	73	43	55	13	45	86	61	23	98	79	27	03	23	23	13	12
33	93	50	79	44	98	45	61	19	22	96	17	42	41	00	00	30	78	56	97	06	52	73	43	81
47	63	34	93	94	38	67	32	22	81	68	09	67	65	99	38	46	21	66	62	81	95	90	33	58
82	16	19	25	21	10	71	25	88	39	18	54	63	29	20	89	22	09	04	93	73	72	52	23	27

Table 8. Derivatives.

y	$\dfrac{\mathrm{d}y}{\mathrm{d}x}$
x^n	nx^{n-1}
$u+v$	$\dfrac{\mathrm{d}u}{\mathrm{d}x}+\dfrac{\mathrm{d}v}{\mathrm{d}x}$
uv	$u\dfrac{\mathrm{d}v}{\mathrm{d}x}+v\dfrac{\mathrm{d}u}{\mathrm{d}x}$
$\dfrac{u}{v}$	$\dfrac{1}{v^2}\left(v\dfrac{\mathrm{d}u}{\mathrm{d}x}-u\dfrac{\mathrm{d}v}{\mathrm{d}x}\right)$
ax	a
e^x	e^x
e^{ax}	$a\,e^{ax}$
a^x	$a^x \times \ln a$
$\ln x$	$\dfrac{1}{x}$

Table 9. Integrals.

y	$\int y\,\mathrm{d}x$
x^n	$\dfrac{x^{n+1}}{n+1}$ for $n \neq -1$
a	ax
$u\dfrac{\mathrm{d}v}{\mathrm{d}x}$	$uv - \int v\dfrac{\mathrm{d}u}{\mathrm{d}x}\,\mathrm{d}x$
$\dfrac{1}{x}$	$\ln|x|$
$\dfrac{f'(x)}{f(x)}$	$\ln|f(x)|$
e^x	e^x
e^{ax}	$\dfrac{1}{a}e^{ax}$
a^x	$\dfrac{a^x}{\ln a}$
$\ln x$	$x\ln x - x$

Note that the constant of integration has been omitted.

Table 10. The Greek alphabet.

Capital	Lower-case		Capital	Lower-case	
A	α	alpha	N	ν	nu
B	β	beta	Ξ	ξ	xi
Γ	γ	gamma	O	o	omicron
Δ	δ	delta	Π	π	pi
E	ε	epsilon	P	ρ	rho
Z	ζ	zeta	Σ	σ	sigma
H	η	eta	T	τ	tau
Θ	θ	theta	Y	υ	upsilon
I	ι	iota	Φ	ϕ	phi
K	κ	kappa	X	χ	chi
Λ	λ	lambda	Ψ	ψ	psi
M	μ	mu	Ω	ω	omega